AFTER READING THIS BOOK, YOU'LL HAVE ALL THE ANSWERS

What is the difference between *imply* and *infer*?

What is the connection between *monk* and *monopoly*?

What are the mythic roots of *hymeneal*?

Where is the key to understanding *circumambient*?

How can you take words apart to see how they work and what they mean?

Why is a dictionary often unnecessary even with the most unfamiliar words?

> "The authors are convinced (and we join them in their conviction) that there are . . . memory aids, or better yet, systems, whereby one may familiarize himself with entire sets of words at once . . . analyze and penetrate their meaning even when they have never been seen before . . . Highly rewarding."
>
> —Mario Pei
>   author, scholar, and Professor of Romance Languages at Columbia University

OUTSTANDING REFERENCE BOOKS

Webster's New World Dictionary of the American Language

A Dictionary of Synonyms and Antonyms

Webster's New World Thesaurus

A New Guide to Better Writing

How to Build a Better Vocabulary

Speed Reading Made Easy

Harper's English Grammar

Webster's Red Seal Crossword Dictionary

Better English Made Easy

Available from
WARNER BOOKS

HOW TO BUILD A BETTER VOCABULARY

Completely revised and up-dated

MAXWELL NURNBERG
and
MORRIS ROSENBLUM

With an Introduction by Mario Pei

WARNER BOOKS

A Time Warner Company

WARNER BOOKS EDITION

Copyright © 1949 by Prentice-Hall, Inc.
Copyright © 1961 by Maxwell Nurnberg and Morris Rosenblum
Copyright © renewed 1977 by Maxwell Nurnberg and Morris Rosenblum.
All rights reserved.

This Warner Books Edition is published by arrangement with Prentice-Hall, Inc., Englewood Cliffs, New Jersey 07632

Warner Books, Inc.
1271 Avenue of the Americas
New York, N.Y. 10020

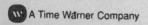 A Time Warner Company

Printed in the United States of America

First Warner Books Printing: July, 1983

Reissued: August, 1989

20   19   18   17

"In Basic English, Miss Jones—I love you." *

Acknowledgments

WE SHOULD LIKE to express our indebtedness to Rose Nurnberg and Dora J. Rosenblum for their patient and helpful counsel; to Jason Wingreen and Leo Dressler for helpful suggestions.

* Drawing reproduced courtesy New York *Times Book Review.*

For permission to use original drawings, and cartoons and textual matter published elsewhere, acknowledgment is made to the following individuals, newspaper, magazine, and book publishers:

Dwight Chapman, Jon Cornin, Tom Courtos, Chon Day, Alan Dunn, John Hersey, A. John Kaunus, Reamer Keller, Harry Lazarus, Lou Lilly, David McCord, James S. MacDonald, Hal McIntosh, Mendelsohn, Joseph Mirachi, Garry Moore, Christopher Morley, Ralph Newman, Ed Nofziger, Virgil Partch, Hesketh Pearson, Gardner Rea, Salo Roth, Charles D. Saxon, Burr Shafer, Charles Strauss, Martino Weiler, Anne Whitney.

The New York Herald Tribune, The New York Times.

Atlantic Monthly, Collier's, Coronet, Cue, Harper's Magazine, Life, Look, New Republic, Pageant, Redbook, The New Yorker, The Reader's Digest, The Saturday Evening Post, The Saturday Review, This Week Magazine, Variety.

"IV!"

"*IV!*" *

Authors' Preface

WHY another book on vocabulary?

For two reasons.

First, because most books on the subject are solemn affairs. As if improving and enriching your knowledge of words were a grim business! We don't believe it. We believe that learning more words and more about words can and *must* be a pleasurable activity. In fact, when it comes to learning of any kind, we're all for the old childhood rhyme:

> What's learned with pleasure
> Is learned full measure.

---

* Drawing reproduced from *This Week*. Copyright 1947 by the United Newspapers Magazine Corporation.

That's where this book comes in. We have designed it for your enjoyment. We have tried to make it chatty and informal, readable, and entertaining. We have not hesitated to include anecdotes, puns, rhymes, cartoons, and even fillers wherever they belong and whenever they can help.

Second, because we want to give you a method of building a bigger and better vocabulary solidly and securely. Our chief purpose, therefore, has been to help you acquire a *permanent* interest in words. We think this is a better way than the hit-and-run method of memorizing lists of unconnected words. We ask you to stay with the words and make them permanently yours.

That's our purpose. Now, what's yours? You are reading this because you want to improve and enrich your vocabulary. You may consider the effective use of words a business and social asset. You may desire to improve your reading, writing, and speaking vocabulary. You may want to keep up with your friends who know more words than you do. You may have a scholarly interest in words as a branch of knowledge worth cultivating. For these reasons, you may also find it extremely necessary to take note of the changing meanings of old words and keep up with the formation of the new words that are becoming a part of our language in great numbers at a rapid pace. Finally, you may have the more practical purpose of wanting to get a high rating on civil service, scholarship, College Board, professional, or any other examinations in which a knowledge of vocabulary has become increasingly important.

Whatever your purpose, we think you will find what you want in this book. We can show you how to acquire the words; the rest is up to you.

And—oh, yes—if, after reading this book, you should happen to marry the boss's daughter, it won't be because of your increased vocabulary. The only words you'll need for that are: "I love you." They still do the trick.

Contents

"That is the letter 'A,' as in arson, accolade, amphibian, and acrimonious."

Introduction

IT IS AN astounding fact that the average cultured speaker of English knows no more than one out of ten words in his own language. Very roughly speaking, the total number of English words is about one million. Rare indeed is the man who is acquainted with more than 100,000 of that total number.

It is perfectly true that the grand total of one million is attained by summing up not only the words in general use, but also thousands upon thousands of "special" words—obscure slang and cant, dialectal and local forms, words described as archaic, obsolete and obsolesecnt, and above all, the numerous specialized jargons of the various trades, businesses, occupations, professions and sciences. There is no reason why the engineer or industrial manufacturer should be expected to know the thousands of medical, physiological and anatomical terms that aré a must to the physician, or those other thousands of words contained in U.S. Pharmacopeia that the druggist or chemist must be familiar with. Conversely, there is no reason for expecting the physician to know the complicated terminology of the automotive engineer, or of the atomic scientist, or of the linguistic scholar.

Still, when all is said and done, there remains a large residue of words in common use—words which have a way of showing up in the columns of a newspaper editorial, or in the pages of a review of general culture, or even of a popular magazine.

The average man, whose practical vocabulary embraces perhaps 30,000 words, is often enough faced with many thousands of additional words which he must admit he does not know, if he is willing to be honest with himself. There are two things he can do about them: look them up on the spot in his handy dictionary, or bypass them and rely on the general meaning of the context in which he finds them.

The first method is time-consuming and not always feasible (he may, for example, encounter an unfamiliar word as he scans his morning paper on the subway or bus on his way to work). At any rate, even if he looks up the word, his chances of retaining it so that he will recognize it the next time he meets it are slim, human memory being the fallible tool it is. Relying on the context is frustrating at best; at worst, it may lead to an altogether incorrect interpretation of that context.

Are there memory aids, or better yet, systems, whereby one may familiarize himself with entire sets of words at once, break them up into their component parts, analyze and penetrate their meaning even when they have never been seen before? The authors are convinced (and we join them in their conviction) that there are such devices. We can call them short cuts to word understanding, or aids to building a wider personal vocabulary, or word-histories and word-etymologies pure and simple. But they exist, and are available.

The authors, men of long experience in this field, have selected and gathered together in this volume a number of such short cuts or aids. These are now offered to the intellectually curious, who want to know how language is built up; to the practically minded, who recognize the dollars-and-cents value of a wider range of vocabulary as an instrument of self-expression and a tool in human relations; to those who want to broaden their enjoyment of life, so often expressed in terms of language.

Such rules and devices are not always easy to apply and follow; but in this book they are expressed in the clearest, simplest fashion in which it is possible to express them. Their application will be found highly rewarding, in terms of expansion of word-power, increased enjoyment and understanding of what one reads, control of others through that most effective of public-relations devices, language.

But even if your goal is not a serious one; even if you pick up a book not in order to learn, but in order to amuse yourself; even if you seek pure relaxation and fun, this book will suit your purpose, for the authors have prepared their pills of learning in such a way that you will find it pleasurable to swallow them.

So—enjoy while you learn, and learn while you enjoy.

MARIO PEI
Professor of
Romance Languages
Columbia University

I. WAYS AND MEANS

"Don't you think it's high time we bought him an abridged edition?" *

---

1. Anyday Words for Everyday Use

THE CONVERSATION had been somewhat desultory—the weather, golf, *his* law practice, John F. Kennedy. Then our visitor brightened up.

"I've just finished reading *The Nine Young Men*."

"Oh, the book about the Supreme Court."

He brushed aside the interruption. "Have you ever read any of Justice Frankfurter's decisions?"

We hadn't.

"You should. You'd be interested in the words he uses. For instance, there's one word he uses a lot—*nexus*."

A slight pause—then: "By the way, what does the word *nexus* mean?"

"Nexus? Why, it means—a connection. The English spell connection—c-o-n-n-e-x-i-o-n. It means a link, something to tie two things together."

"Yeah?"

"Yeah."

EVEN AS YOU AND I

There you have it—the conversation just as it took place one summer on an Adirondack porch. Our visitor had run true to form as a member in good standing of the human race. Here was a curiosity—still warm—about a word he had read. Would he look it up in a dictionary? No. Would you?

Well, we're all a little bit like that. It seems more fun to ask someone than to look a word up in the dictionary. It isn't really laziness. Anyone who has a curiosity about words isn't lazy. He just hasn't discovered how exciting an experience thumbing a ride through a dictionary can be.

FOR WHOM THIS BOOK

So this book is written for our visitor and all others like him—who haven't yet learned how much fun there is hunting a word down the columns of a dictionary, who would still rather buttonhole a friend and ask, "Hey, Buddy, what's a nexus?"

It is written for the kind of person who would like to know more words, and know more about those he knows, but who somehow never has gotten around to doing anything about it. It is written for the kind of person who always has a word on the tip of his tongue—precariously perched—instead of safely filed away in his mind. It is written for the kind of person who would like to feel greater security with those words with which he now has a reading, listening, and speaking acquaintance. It is written for you.

PURPOSE OF THIS BOOK

It is our purpose not only to help you add new words to our vocabulary but to bring into sharp and permanent focus those words that are now on the blurred fringe of your mind.

It is our purpose to help you to use all words with maximum effectiveness—so that they become precision tools for the shaping of your thoughts.

Finally, it is our purpose to make the dictionary something that you will use not only with ease but with pleasure.

WHAT ARE ANYDAY WORDS?

At this point you may want to interrupt and ask, "All this is very nice, but where did you get the words you think it so important for me to know and feel secure with?"

Well, we didn't go for our words to the morgues of former lists or to that best repository of all, the dictionary. We hunted them down in their natural habitat—the newspapers, magazines, and books that *you* read—and we brought them back alive! In other words, we did the kind of reading you did the last year or two. We covered the same ground you did—from sports news to world affairs, from picture magazines to best sellers. But we did it not only with our eyes. We read with blue pencils, scissors, paste, and index cards. We read with an eye to selecting and collecting those words that occurred frequently enough to make them standard equipment for the educated man or woman. In this way we assembled the several thousand words that appear in this book. These are not everyday words; these are *anyday* words—words you may encounter *any day* while listening to others or reading your favorite newspapers, magazines, and books.*

HAS THIS EVER HAPPENED TO YOU?

Now, we'll ask you a question. Has this ever happened to you? You come across a word you don't know and, breaking precedent, you consult a dictionary for its meaning. And what happens? Three weeks later you meet the same word. You shake your head in puzzlement. Sure, you remember the word —you remember looking it up—but exactly what does it

---

* Here we do not refer to many of the words in the tests in the last two chapters. These were obviously chosen for their difficulty and are not recommended for daily use.

mean? You throw the dictionary open again. "This time
you say to yourself, "I'll memorize it."

But you'll probably have to look it up again. Learni
something by rote, memorizing it on the surface of yo
mind is not the surest way to remember it. Things you me
orize that way are like floating toy balloons. They'll st
around for a while, but unless you tie them down, they'll blc
away. You have to *associate* something you want to rememb
with something that you know—you have to tie it down
your mind, you have to make a permanent nexus.

THE PERMANENT WAY

In this book we're going to try to tie words down for yo
to fix them *inside* your mind. To do this, we're going to g
inside the word.

Words, like human beings, have a past. Their roots a
deep. Their family trees go back to the dawn of history a
they grow on those trees not singly but in *clusters*. Li
Walter Mitty, words have a secret life. We're going to fi
out the secret of getting at their meanings and we're goi
to find a way of fixing them permanently.

THROUGH CONTEXT

Let's see how it works. Suppose we take the word *desulto
which we used in the first sentence of this chapter. It's a wo
of only moderate difficulty. But does it mean much to y
right here in the open all by itself—DESULTORY? You
tempted to turn back to the opening sentence. All right, le
yield to that temptation. Here's the sentence again: "The co
versation had been somewhat desultory—the weather, go
his law practice, John F. Kennedy." Now, restored to t
other words and ideas with which it was associated, *desulto
means a lot more. But we haven't gotten *inside* the word y
We've just gotten *alongside*.

WORDS HAVE A PAST

We can understand words better if we know somethi
about their past. *Desultory* has a past. It goes back to Rom
times and Roman circuses. The circus rider who, before sho
ing crowds in the arena, performed the feat of changi
horses in mid-scream was called a *desultor*, because he jump

om one horse to another. Now look at that first sentence
gain. The conversation was *desultory,* because it *jumped* from
ne topic to another. We're closing in on the word; we're get-
ng inside.

THEY GROW IN CLUSTERS

Desultory didn't pop out of someone's brain as an isolated
ord. Words belong to family groups. *Desultory* belongs to
ne SULT family. Some of its members spell it SAL, SIL, and
ven SAULT, but no matter how it's spelled, the family name
neans *jump* or *leap.* If you in*sult* someone, you are figura-
vely "jumping on (*in*) him." A re*sil*ient substance is one that
an jump back (*re*) to its original state after being stretched.
f you are in an ex*ult*ant mood, you are "jumping out of (*ex*)
our skin with joy." A *sal*ient feature is one that leaps out at
ou. To do a somer*sault* is to leap or jump while turning the
eels over (*somer,* from *supra,* above) head without touching
ne ground. A de*sult*ory conversation is one that jumps aim-
ssly from (*de*) one topic to another. And now we think we
ave completed our as*sault* (a jumping toward, *as* for *ad*)
n the word de*sult*ory. We have breached the outer defenses.
Ve are *inside* the word.

YOU CAN PRE-FIX THE WORD

Often just knowing the meaning of the prefix (such as *re,*
1, ex,* and *de*) will give us the essential force of the word. A
ery strong prefix that everybody knows is *anti.* You can be
retty sure that a word beginning with *anti* is "agin' some-
ning," even though the rest of the word by itself may mean
ttle to you. *Anti*gonize, *anti*pathy (in contrast with *sym*-
athy), *anti*thesis, *anti*podes, *anti*nym (in contrast with
ynonym) are shot through and through with the idea of
*gainst*ness. A prefix can often be not only the key that un-
ocks the meaning of a word but the key that locks it inside
our mind.

OTHER METHODS

That's the way we're going to handle it. We're going to get
nside the word whenever possible. And around it—in clusters,
ot only of roots but also of synonyms (words related in mean-
ng) or antonyms (words opposite in meaning).

We do not recommend the learning of lists of unconnected isolated words at a fixed rate per day like so many setting-up exercises. We believe that *you learn more words by learning more about words*. Rudyard Kipling once wrote, "What should they know of England who only England know?" It's the same with words: if you really want to know them, you must know more than the mere word. We shall try to indicate for you every possible method of learning about words. We shall indicate every possible method of association. We may even stoop to trickery. BUT WE'LL FIX THAT WORD!

TAKING INVENTORY

The sixty words given below were taken from Regents Scholarship Examinations given in New York State to graduating high school students of superior ability. It follows, therefore, that they are fairly difficult words, but we came across every one of them in our newspaper reading.

If you get 52 or more right, you are in the select scholarship group. If you get 48-51, you are doing extremely well. You are good if you get 42-47 right, and even if you get 37-46, you're doing well. If you get fewer than 35, don't be discouraged. There are 383 more pages in this book, and they were all written for you.

In each line below you will find one italicized word followed by five words or phrases numbered 1 to 5. In each case select the word or phrase that has most nearly the same meaning as the italicized word. Answers will be found on page 361.

1. *abacus*   1 casserole 2 blackboard 3 slide rule
                     4 long spear 5 adding device
2. *acquiescence*   1 advice 2 advocacy 3 compliance
                     4 friendliness 5 opposition
3. *adroit*   1 hostile 2 serene 3 pompous 4 skillful
                     5 allergic
4. *ambulatory*   1 able to walk 2 confined to bed
                     3 injured 4 quarantined 5 suffering
                     from disease
5. *ameliorate*   1 favor 2 improve 3 interfere 4 learn
                     5 straddle
6. *antithesis*   1 contrast 2 conclusion 3 resemblance
                     4 examination 5 dislike
7. *astute*   1 shrewd 2 futile 3 potent 4 provoca-
                     tive 5 ruthless
8. *attrition*   1 annihilation 2 encirclement 3 coun-
                     terattack 4 appeasement 5 wearing
                     down

9. *augment*   1 curtail 2 change 3 restore 4 conceal
                  5 increase

0. *banal*   1 commonplace 2 flippant 3 pathetic
                  4 new 5 unexpected

1. *bizarre*   1 boastful 2 warlike 3 sluggish 4 fan-
                  tastic 5 oriental

12. *boorish*   1 sporting 2 tiresome 3 argumentative
                  4 monotonous 5 rude

13. *coalesce*   1 associate 2 combine 3 contact
                  4 conspire 5 cover

14. *corpulent*   1 dead 2 fat 3 full 4 organized
                  5 similar

15. *decant*   1 bisect 2 speak wildly 3 bequeath
                  4 pour off 5 abuse verbally

16. *deplore*   1 condone 2 forget 3 forgive 4 deny
                  5 regret

17. *dissonance* 1 disapproval 2 disaster 3 discord
                  4 disparity 5 dissimilarity

18. *emolument*   1 capital 2 compensation 3 liabilities
                  4 loss 5 output

19. *enigma*   1 ambition 2 foreigner 3 instrument
                  4 officer 5 riddle

20. *ethnology*   1 causation 2 morals 3 social psychology
                  4 study of races 5 word analysis

21. *expunge*   1 clarify 2 copy 3 delete 4 investigate
                  5 underline

22. *fiasco*   1 disappointment 2 turning point 3 loss
                  4 celebration 5 complete failure

23. *finite*   1 impure 2 firm 3 minute 4 limited
                  5 unbounded

24. *flotsam*   1 dark sand 2 fleet 3 life preserver
                  4 shoreline 5 wreckage

25. *fulminating* 1 throbbing 2 pointed 3 wavelike
                  4 thundering 5 bubbling

26. *glib*   1 cheerful 2 delightful 3 dull 4 fluent
                  5 gloomy

27. *graphic*   1 serious 2 concise 3 short 4 detailed
                  5 vivid

28. *imminent*   1 declining 2 distinguished 3 impend-
                  ing 4 terrifying 5 unlikely

29. *incipient*   1 beginning 2 dangerous 3 hasty
                  4 secret 5 widespread

30. *indubitable* 1 doubtful 2 fraudulent 3 honorable
                  4 safe 5 undeniable

31. *inexorable* 1 unfavorable 2 permanent 3 crude
                  4 relentless 5 incomplete

32. *inveterate* 1 evil 2 habitual 3 inconsiderate

21

4 reformed 5 unintentional

33. *jettison* 1 throw overboard 2 dismantle 3 scuttl
   4 unload cargo 5 camouflage

34. *latent* 1 inherent 2 lazy 3 dormant
   4 crushed 5 anticipated

35. *lesion* 1 injury 2 contortion 3 suffering
   4 convulsion 5 aggravation

36. *litigation* 1 publication 2 argument 3 endeavor
   4 lawsuit 5 ceremony

37. *lucrative* 1 debasing 2 fortunate 3 influential
   4 monetary 5 profitable

38. *macabre* 1 gruesome 2 meager 3 sordid 4 fantastic 5 cringing

39. *malediction* 1 curse 2 mispronunciation 3 grammatical error 4 tactless remark 5 epitaph

40. *nefarious* 1 clever 2 necessary 3 negligent
   4 shortsighted 5 wicked

41. *obsequious* 1 courteous 2 fawning 3 respectful
   4 overbearing 5 inexperienced

42. *paucity* 1 abundance 2 ease 3 hardship 4 lack
   5 stoppage

43. *perusal* 1 approval 2 estimate 3 reading
   4 translation 5 computation

44. *petulant* 1 lazy 2 loving 3 patient 4 peevish
   5 wary

45. *phlegmatic* 1 tolerant 2 careless 3 sensitive
   4 stolid 5 sick

46. *placate* 1 amuse 2 appease 3 embroil 4 pity
   5 reject

47. *plagiarize* 1 annoy 2 borrow 3 steal ideas
   4 imitate poorly 5 impede

48. *proclivity* 1 backwardness 2 edict 3 rainfall
   4 slope 5 tendency

49. *propriety* 1 advancement 2 atonement 3 fitness
   4 sobriety 5 use

50. *protracted* 1 boring 2 condensed 3 prolonged
   4 comprehensive 5 measured

51. *pugnacious* 1 bold 2 combative 3 brawny 4 pug-
   nosed 5 valiant

52. *pulchritude* 1 beauty 2 character 3 generosity
   4 intelligence 5 wickedness

53. *pusillanimous* 1 cowardly 2 extraordinary 3 ailing
   4 evil-intentioned 5 excitable

54. *redundant* 1 necessary 2 plentiful 3 sufficient
   4 diminishing 5 superfluous

55. *relevant* 1 ingenious 2 inspiring 3 obvious
   4 pertinent 5 tentative

56. *seismism* 1 inundation 2 tide 3 volcano 4 earth-
   quake 5 tornado

"This Thesaurus is admirable, advantageous, beneficial, capital, choice, edifying, excellent, faultless, nonpareil, perfect, splendid, superb, unparalleled." *

2. The Company Words Keep

YOU ARE comfortably seated, reading the latest killer-thriller. The suspense has been mounting. Bug-eyed, you read this:

Jim Devers ran toward the reclining figure. Suddenly the lights were switched off, and an eldritch cry transfixed him with gelid fear. . . .

* Drawing reproduced courtesy the *Saturday Review*.

Do you immediately run to the nearest dictionary to look up the words *eldritch* and *gelid*? You do not. Like most people, you continue reading to find out who was responsible for the cry—eldritch or otherwise—that caused Jim Devers to go gelid—whatever that is—with fear.

No matter what you're reading, your primary interst is in the story or the thought that's coming through. The drive of the thought, the momentum of the story will carry you right past such words as *eldritch* and *gelid* without mishap or hesitation. And that is as it should be.

You don't want to read and at the same time stop to think of individual words you will have to look up in a dictionary. You want to do one thing at a time. You want to read one book at a time—the book you're reading. The dictionary can wait—and it does!

Take the case of Yogi Berra, catcher and outfielder of the New York Yankees. One day during a tight game, Bucky Harris, then Yankee manager, was scanning the bench for a pinch hitter. His hand finally came down on Yogi's shoulder. "All right, Yogi," he said, "go in there and hit. Sure, you've been hitting in a slump. But it's because you aren't thinking enough at the plate. Think before you pick out a ball. Make sure it's good before you swing. Think!"*

Yogi went up to the plate and swung—three times, not once getting even a piece of the ball. He stamped angrily back to the bench, muttering away to himself in a corner of the dugout. Curious, Bucky Harris decided to walk past him to find out what Yogi had on his mind. Under his breath Yogi was repeating over and over, "How can a guy hit and think *at the same time?*"

It is admittedly hard to hit and think at the same time. In the same way, it is hard to read with unalloyed pleasure and stop to think of the meaning of individual words.

But if you're really serious about increasing your vocabulary in a big way, you'll find it pays to stop to think of individual words. You'll even want to give up a little of the relaxed enjoyment there is in reading and devote some thoughtful attention to new words that look up at you eagerly and point in the direction of the dictionary.

However, even without the help of a dictionary, you can increase your vocabulary by wide reading. For words, like

---

* Although in his autobiography (*Yogi* by Yogi Berra and Ed Fitzgerald, Doubleday, New York, 1961) Mr. Berra stamps this story as apocryphal, we like it and we'll stick with it.

people, are known by the company they keep, and the context in which you meet an unfamiliar word will frequently reveal its meaning.

You are bound to learn new words in this way because the context often acts as a catalytic agent. And there's one of those words right now—*catalytic.*

Just what is a catalytic agent? A wit recently came up with this definition. "A catalytic agent," he quipped, "is one that doesn't get ten per cent."

And a good definition it is, too. For in the science laboratory a substance whose *mere presence* causes or speeds a reaction, while it itself remains *unchanged*, is called a catalytic agent. In the same way, the context in which a word is embedded may act as a *catalyst.*

Here, for example, are twenty words dug out of their contexts. Look them over carefully. Check those whose meanings you are sure of.

abrogation	detergent	nadir
abstemious	ecumenical	paradox
aficionado	enclave	pyromaniac
apathy	ephemeral	recalcitrant
bucolic	euthanasia	serrated
clandestine	logistics	subterfuge
dearth	mendicancy	

They look pretty difficult, don't they, all by themselves—away from the words that help clothe them with meaning? When you take words by themselves in a list, you're taking only dictionary words—inert, inactive. In a dictionary, words are quick-frozen for easy inspection. They don't thaw out and come to life until you see them used in a sentence.

Some of these words are unusual. They may not look to you like words you've met in newspapers and magazines. But that's where we got them.

And now we're going to make it possible for you to get the meaning of every one of these words right. How? By simply putting the words back into the sentences in which we found them and in which the context acted as a catalytic agent.

You can check your answers on page 362.

WORDS IN THEIR CONTEXTS

Under each newspaper excerpt, we give you four choices. Select the one you think comes closest in meaning to the word under examination.

1. **ABROGATION**

> Termination of Dutch air privileges in India will take the form of the *abrogation* by India of the temporary civil aviation agreement between the Netherlands and India effected at the end of the war.

(a) repeal (b) short extension (c) investigation (d) promulgation

2. **ABSTEMIOUS**

> With the cup filled with champagne, Bucky Harris posed for more pictures, but being privately a rather *abstemious* fellow he sipped it cautiously.

(a) hesitant (b) temperate (c) superstitious (d) careful

3. **AFICIONADO**

> To an *aficionado* this is all to the good, for your true baseball fanatic can get as inflamed over a game played twenty years ago as over one played last night.

(a) an old-timer (b) a second-guesser (c) a Mexican Leaguer (d) an ardent follower of a sport

4. **APATHY**

> Sicilians have shown remarkable *apathy*, distressing the professional politicians. There are several reasons for this lack of interest.

(a) indifference (b) suffering (c) patience (d) curiosity

5. **BUCOLIC**

> It is chockfull of delightful characters, the homely humor of the rural English and the *bucolic* beauty of the countryside.

(a) quiet (b) lush (c) rustic (d) indescribable

6. **CLANDESTINE**

Published Secret Paper

> M. Depreux said the organization published a *clandestine* newspaper.

(a) daily (b) hand-written (c) secret (d) subversive

7. DEARTH

Fear of Dollar Dearth
Stressed in Trade Survey

Growing fears of a world-wide dollar shortage are being examined in a special study of United States foreign trade since the war.

(a) scarcity (b) control (c) depreciation (d) inflation

8. DETERGENT

They [researchers] find that if only half the proper amount of soap or *detergent* is used for a twenty-minute washing period, twice as much work is required to remove the same amount of dirt.

(a) materials (b) antiseptics (c) powder (d) cleansing agent

9. ECUMENICAL

Dr. T. Hooft said that the goal of the council was to achieve "an *ecumenical* fellowship in Christ."
He described an *ecumenical* relationship as one which "includes but also transcends all nationalities and races and which must therefore be independent of all political constellations."

(a) spiritual (b) world-wide (c) unselfish (d) whole-minded

10. ENCLAVE

An *enclave*, such as Porkkala, is a tract enclosed within a foreign country—in this case by the Russians inside Finland.

(a) district enclosed within alien territory (b) fortified area (c) conquered territory (d) free city

11. **EPHEMERAL**

It is our task so to train them that they may, through their reading, learn to distinguish the true from the false, the enduring from the *ephemeral*, the significant from the trivial, the beautiful from the ugly, the good from the evil.

(a) flimsy (b) shoddy (c) short-lived (d) everlasting

12. **EUTHANASIA**

The *Euthanasia* Society of America is now conducting a campaign to legalize euthanasia, or "mercy killings."

(a) pain-killing (b) Europe and Asia (c) painless death (d) aid and charity

13. **LOGISTICS**

It is shortsighted to consider the civil wars around the globe in terms of *logistics*, of supplying with material, weapons and financial helps.

(a) reasoning (b) results (c) diplomacy (d) supplying and quartering troops

14. **MENDICANCY**

That challenge is summarized in the witticism coined in London that under the Marshall Plan Europe would merely substitute organized *mendicancy* for individual beggary.

(a) bartering (b) the habit of begging (c) self-improvement (d) repairing destruction

15. **NADIR**

With Jeeter and his family we reach humanity's *nadir*: below this point, all is sub-human.

(a) zenith (b) the lowest point (c) common level (d) disgrace

16. PARADOX

A Rabbi was the only perfect Christian
in his town—that is the *paradox* achieved
in this witty and warm-hearted book.

(a) moral lesson (b) self-contradictory but true statement (c) climax (d) convincing result

17. PYROMANIAC

Alert armed guards patrolled grounds
and buildings of the sprawling Duke
University Hospital tonight in search of
an elusive *pyromaniac* who has started
eight fires in the institution in three days.

(a) escaped convict (b) mental defective (c) drug
addict (d) persistent incendiary

18. RECALCITRANT

If troops are necessary to seize live-
stock and other items being withheld by
recalcitrant farmers, they may be mo-
bilized for this purpose.

(a) hoarding (b) dairy (c) rebellious (d) remotely
situated

19. SERRATED

Swordfish Fight Rubber Bale

Three swordfish attacked a bale of
rubber in the sea off Capetown recently
and met a tragic fate. This was revealed
when their bodies, minus their *serrated*
weapons, were washed up on the beach.
Nearby was a bale of rubber with the
three swords stuck fast in it.

(a) dull (b) thick (c) gleaming (d) saw-toothed

20. SUBTERFUGE

It should be done openly and by the
deliberate choice of the people, not by
subterfuge and indirection.

(a) evasion (b) compulsion (c) bribery (d) prearrangement

DON'T GO AWAY YET!

You haven't learned these words. Suppose you were to meet these words alone some dark night without their contexts? Could you recognize them? Or would you need the help of a dictionary to identify them?

Context is not enough. You have to tie the words down to your mind. Learn them in context; get alongside. Fix them through association; get inside.

SOMETHING TO REMEMBER THEM BY

ABROGATION

You can approach the meaning of this word and thousands of others through the prefix which begins it. *Ab* has the negative idea *away from*. *Roga*, which you find also in *interrogative* and many other words, means asking, begging, proposing. To *ab*rogate is to *ab*olish, to beg off, to do away with, and *abrogation* is, therefore, an annulment, cancellation, revocation, or repeal. In the context, the word *termination* helped reveal the meaning.

ABSTEMIOUS

Here, too, the prefix *abs*, away, offers a clue. *Abstemious* means staying away from heavy eating or strong drinks (*temetum* is Latin for an intoxicating drink). You can fix the word by remembering *abs*tain, to keep *from*. Incidentally, *abstemious* is an oddity among words, being one of only three English words with five vowels in their alphabetical order. (*Arsenious* and *facetious* are the others.)

AFICIONADO

This is a borrowing from the Spanish. *Aficionado* tells us that the Spaniards have their rabid fans, too, especially among the followers of bullfighting. Actually, *aficionado* means an amateur or lover of a sport. It is derived from the same Latin word which gives us *affection*.

Carl Dreher in a short story in *Good Housekeeping* uses it effectively in this sense in a sentence whose context is revelatory: "He was no longer a professional researcher; he was an *aficionado* of research."

APATHY

The prefix *a* from the Greek says, No. *Path* is the root of *pathos*, a strong feeling or suffering. *Apathy*, therefore, is no feeling one way or another, or as the context tells us "a lack of interest." It should be distinguished from *antipathy* which means a decided feeling *against* or hatred. The opposite of antipathy is *sympathy*, a sharing of feelings with (*sym*) somebody else.

BUCOLIC

In the poetry of the ancients, shepherds and herdsmen led an idyllic existence while tending their flocks. They made pleasant music on the pipes of Pan, and the city dweller sighed for the pastoral existence of the countryside. The word *bucolic* describes this type of living. It comes from the word for herdsman, *bucolicus*, a person who has to do with cows and oxen. From the related Latin root we get *bovine*, cowlike (*bos, bovis*, cow).

CLANDESTINE

It would be perfect if *clandestine* were related to the English word *clam* as used in the expression, "As secretive as a clam." *Clandestine*, meaning secret, comes from another *clam*, the Latin word *clam*, meaning secretly. It is related to the Latin verb *celare*, to hide, from which we get *conceal*. *Clandestine* (accent on the DES) has the sinister meaning of keeping something secret illegally or by trickery.

DEARTH

Dearth is just the word *dear* and the ending *th* as in warm*th*, heal*th*, weal*th*, dep*th*, grow*th* and tru*th*. It once meant dearness but now means scarcity, thereby reminding us that the law of supply and demand is old—what was scarce became dear.

DETERGENT

A radio announcer proclaiming the merits of a cleanser declared that it was not a soap but a *detergent*. He was off the beam there because if soaps clean, they are *detergent*. *Detergent* is formed from the root of a Latin verb *detergere*, to rub or wipe dry. Another name for a detergent is an *abstergent*. From the same root comes *terse* applied to style or manner of speaking. It means wiped dry of unnecessary material, polished, and therefore concise and neatly elegant.

31

ECUMENICAL

The root of this word is found also in *economy* which originally meant the management of the home or domestic economy, from the Greek word *oikos*, a dwelling or house. The *ecumenical* world is the inhabited world, wherever people have homes. *Ecumenical*, therefore, means world-wide and liberal as opposed to *parochial* in its sense of local and provincial, i.e. restricted to a *parish*.

ENCLAVE

The newspaper sentence quoted gives a very good dictionary definition. The key to the meaning of the word is *clavis*, Latin for *key*. An *enclave* is territory locked within a foreign country. There is a growing figurative use of this word to denote areas within the same country differing in customs or culture as in the following:

> The Copper Belt is a tiny *enclave* of
> peace in an expanse of troubled Africa.

A *conclave* is a meeting held in a closed room. A *clavichord* or *clavier*, the predecessor of the piano, is a keyboard instrument. The *clavicle* is the scientific name for the collarbone, perhaps because it resembles a little key, a skeleton key, of course. *Auto*clave, a Greek and Latin mixture, comes to us via French. The word was coined from *auto* and *clavus*, nail, or *clavis*, key, and hence means "self-fastening" or "self-locking." *Autoclave* originally designated a kind of French *marmite* or stewpan with a steamtight lid designed for cooking or roasting in a closed vessel. The word is more frequently used here to denote a type of airtight vessel used for sterilization; it also means a pressure cooker.

EPHEMERAL

This is a lovely word meaning frail and perishable or living but a day, from the Greek *hemera*, a day. The same root is found in the *Decameron*, the title of Boccaccio's collection of stories, which tells of the events of ten (*deca*) days. The May flies, those delicate insects which live only a few hours or days after they are hatched, are called *Ephemerida*.

EUTHANASIA

This word means an easy manner of dying, from the Greek prefix *eu*, well or easily, and *thanatos*, death. In modern times it means the act or practice of putting a hopelessly incurable invalid to death painlessly. *Thanatos* was the Greek personification of death, twin brother of Sleep and the son of Night. William Cullen Bryant's poem *"Thanatopsis"* is a view or contemplation of death.

LOGISTICS

Logistics is a descendant of the French verb *loger*, to billet, or put up for the night. An army has to be fed, transported, supplied, and *lodged*, and logistics is that most important branch of military art and science which attends to these details.

MENDICANCY

Mendicus is a Latin word meaning a poor man or a beggar. The word gave its name to the group of *mendicant* friars or religious brothers who took the vow of poverty, practiced collective ownership of property, and lived by begging alms and charity.

NADIR

The Arabians, who gave us a number of words in astronomy and science, called the point of the celestial sphere directly *under* the observer the *nadir*. It is directly opposite to the highest point or *zenith*. Keats joined the two in "Hyperion" in such a way that the difference between *nadir* and *zenith* is easy to remember:

> Sweet-shaped lightnings· from the nadir deep
> Up to the zenith.

PARADOX

Para means beside, beyond, or contrary to, and *dox* comes from *doxa*, a Greek word meaning opinion. A *paradox* is a statement or belief contrary to accepted belief, or an idea contrary to common sense which nevertheless has truth in it. W. S. Gilbert, music by Sullivan, stressed this aspect of a paradox in *The Pirates of Penzance*:

> How quaint the ways of Paradox!
> At common sense she gaily mocks.

As used so frequently in our newspapers, *paradox* means a contradiction. *Dogma* from the same root means accepted or

authoritative belief. A *dogmatic* person is self-opinionated
one who asserts opinion as fact. *Heterodoxy* (*hetero*—other
different) means a set of beliefs and opinions contrary to
established beliefs. It is a departure from *orthodoxy* (*ortho*—
right), opinions or beliefs held to be true.

PYROMANIAC

A *pyromaniac* is mad about fires: he has an irresistible im
pulse to set something on fire. *Pyr*, the Greek word for fire
is found in this word as it is in *pyre*, a funeral pile on which
the ancients cremated their dead. Where there's *pyr*, *pyri*, or
pyro in a word, there's pretty sure to be fire. *Pyrotechnics* are
fireworks. An *antipyretic* works *against* the "fire" or fever
In ancient times, the highest sphere or heaven was described
as a region of fire or light. Hence we have the word em
pyrean, meaning in the region of fire. Now it is a poetic word
meaning simply the high heaven or "the wild blue yonder."

RECALCITRANT

To be *recalcitrant* means "to kick the heels back" and refuse
to budge, from *re*, back, and *calx*, heel.

A recalcitrant person or animal is obstinate and rebellious
To *inculcate* is literally to stamp or press in with the heel
Schoolteachers no longer hammer in knowledge by physical
pounding but figuratively they do press it in by frequent
repetition when they *inculcate* ideas or learning.

Decalcomania is a specially prepared design or picture that
can be permanently transferred to glass or any smooth sur
face by rubbing or pressing (not necessarily with the heel).

SERRATED

This means toothed and notched like a saw, from the Latin
serra, a saw. The Spanish influence in our continent is seen
in many place names which still bear Spanish names. *Sierra*,
the Spanish form of *serra*, was used as a description of mountains which had a jagged, saw-like outline. When the early
Californians pushed eastward and saw the very high mountains, they called them Sierra Nevada, the snow-capped range.
Later the name was changed to the Californian Mountains
but General Frémont popularized the earlier name, which
has stuck.

SUBTERFUGE

This is an underhanded (*subter*—beneath, under) method

of escaping (*fugere*—to flee or escape). It's applied to the trick whereby one dodges an issue or gets out of doing something. The root of *fugere* has given us many words of escape like *refuge, refugee,* and *fugitive.* The herb known as the *feverfew* is really the *febrifuge,* an agent that, like an antipyretic, causes a fever to flee.

So, if you want to enrich and increase your vocabulary, it's a good idea to read widely, for it's better to meet words in context in the newspapers, magazines, and books that interest you than in lists, where words are isolated and unconnected items. And when you read:

STOP, LOOK, AND LIST THEM

When you come across new or unfamiliar words STOP. Then LOOK around and see whether the context reveals their meaning as the twenty excerpts in this chapter do. If the context doesn't give you first aid, LIST THEM. Sometime, perhaps, you will LOOK them up in a dictionary. If you do, find some way to fix their meaning or your trip to the dictionary will be wasted. It might even be a good idea to LIST THEM after you've looked them up. The list you make of words you've actually met in your reading is worth a great deal more than any list made for you. It's connected with your reading; it's associated with your ideas; it's yours. And it will stick.

Oh, by the way, there's a rather personal question we'd like to ask you. Did you rush off to a dictionary to look up the words *eldritch* and *gelid?* You didn't? Was it because you know what they mean? Well, if you don't and you're panting with curiosity, you'll find a word index at the back of the book with *eldritch* and *gelid* in their correct alphabetical order.

THE WORD LOOKS FAMILIAR

These words look familiar because we have reproduced them in the phrases in which they originally appeared. Can you place them?

Although these words may be just as difficult as or more difficult than the sixty in the previous chapter, we think you will find them easier because of the company they're in. (Answers will be found on page 362.)

1. any benefits *accruing* (a) belonging jointly (b) accumulating (c) deductible (d) accomplished

2. an *admonitory* gesture keeping them back — (a) violent (b) stern (c) warning (d) conciliatory

3. to *allay* suspicions — (a) hold off (b) set at rest (c) confirm (d) destroy

4. blizzards of ticker tape and *adulation* — (a) wild shouting (b) public celebration (c) flattering praise (d) speech making

5. the immigrants being easily *assimilable* — (a) likable (b) understood (c) absorbed (d) disposed of

6. after an hour of *bootless* attempts — (a) barefoot (b) unavailing (c) unceasing (d) frustrating

7. *burnishing* the statuette with affectionate hands — (a) polishing (b) singeing (c) cleaning (d) brushing

8. his long *cadaverous* face — (a) wrinkled (b) haggard (c) sensitive (d) sombre

9. *cajoling* him away from the sandpile — (a) coercing (b) rudely brushing (c) politely asking (d) coaxing

10. the *canons* of respectable behavior — (a) laws (b) details (c) essentials (d) defiance

11. as *capricious* judgment or fancy deemed best — (a) thoughtless (b) whimsical (c) light-hearted (d) soundly motivated

12. *chaotically* tossed — (a) with complete confusion (b) with uncontrollable violence (c) without definite plan (d) with malice

13. characteristically *chimerical* schemes — (a) tentative (b) scientific (c) visionary (d) miraculous

14. an intolerable and *consummate* rascal — (a) complete (b) scheming (c) overbearing (d) grasping

15. listening with *corrugated* brows — (a) anxious (b) narrow (c) lifted (d) furrowed

16. a *craven* abandoning his post — (a) sentinel (b) base villain (c) coward (d) supernumerary

17. judged by artificial *criteria* — (a) distinctions (b) data (c) standards of judgment (d) measures

18. *dexterously* parrying the thrust — (a) rightly (b) adroitly (c) viciously (d) revengefully

19. speaking softly, almost *diffidently* — (a) carelessly (b) indifferently (c) shyly (d) apologetically

20. a huge book, *diffuse* and formless — (a) unusual (b) rambling (c) argumentative (d) incisive

21. intrigue, corruption, and *dissimulation* — (a) ridicule (b) vileness (c) treachery (d) deception

22. a complete *dossier* of his activities — (a) analysis (b) repudiation (c) failure (d) documented file

23. his weak, *emaciated* body
(a) badly scratched (b) paralyzed (c) skinny (d) partly healed

24. sending *emissaries* to Washington
(a) agents (b) missionaries (c) protests (d) delegations

25. *enthralling* and holding him captive
(a) fascinating (b) seizing (c) exciting (d) encompassing

26. a *fastidiously* neat woman
(a) questionably (b) hungrily (c) supposedly (d) over-carefully

27. stressing the *fiscal* issues of sound economy
(a) mechanical (b) financial (c) legal (d) yearly

28. the chill of such *forebodings*
(a) uncertainties (b) threats (c) apprehensions (d) apathy

29. great legal and *forensic* skill
pertaining to: (a) prophecy (b) public debate (c) outdoors (d) mechanics

30. laughing at our incredible *gullibility*
(a) stupidity (b) credulity (c) objective (d) cupidity

31. the *hallowed* halls of old Carnegie
(a) empty (b) welcoming (c) consecrated (d) undecorated

32. hoping for world *hegemony*
(a) regimen (b) vastness (c) dominance (d) popularity

33. accepting their *homage* very modestly
(a) hospitality (b) respect (c) ovation (d) flattery

34. a *homogeneity* of outlook
(a) diversity (b) unspoiled freshness (c) similarity (d) stubbornness

35. safe in his *impregnable* fortress
(a) impressive (b) unmolested (c) lofty (d) unassailable

36. his face, *inarticulate*, dumb
(a) inexpressive (b) disjointed (c) uncultured (d) solemn

37. the *infallibly* graceful cats
(a) sure-footedly (b) unbelievably (c) solidly (d) unfailingly

38. *inferring* much from the look on her face
(a) concluding (b) assuming (c) not understanding (d) interrogating

39. *intangible* impurities of the water
(a) inconsequential (b) incredible (c) imperceptible (d) deluding

40. propaganda *inundating* the people
(a) misleading (b) deluging (c) influencing (d) not reaching

41. *inviolable* rights of free people
(a) sacred (b) inherited (c) intangible (d) permanent

42. ruining his prospects *irretrievably*
(a) temporarily (b) unnecessarily (c) irresponsibly (d) irrevocably

43. "Reckon," he replied *laconically*.
(a) tersely (b) insultingly (c) mysteriously (d) incredibly

44. driving along the North Sea *littoral*
(a) peninsula (b) coastal region (c) highway (d) surface

45. a mechanical and *meretricious* melodrama
(a) well-planned (b) tawdry (c) worthy (d) stupid

46. a *morass* of mathematical symbols
(a) abundance (b) quagmire (c) conglomeration (d) arrangement

47. falling in great *oscillating* circles
(a) swinging (b) dizzying (c) tangential (d) descending

48. ashamed of his brother's *parsimony*
(a) stinginess (b) piety (c) wickedness (d) strangeness

49. *percolates* down to the ordinary man
(a) bubbles (b) filters (c) reflects (d) ascends

50. *poignant* memories of a sad youth
(a) keenly distressing (b) nostalgic (c) sensitive (d) almost forgotten

51. the weakest *poltroon* alive
(a) sentimentalist (b) uniformed soldier (c) dastard (d) performer

52. the *polyglot* tumult of New York's East Side
(a) foreign (b) overwhelming (c) many-languaged (d) multitudinous

53. *precluding* any other conclusion
(a) foretelling (b) disregarding (c) prefacing (d) preventing

54. usually a *precursor* of heavy snows
(a) prevention (b) condemnation (c) forerunner (d) promise

55. *profligate* county politicians
(a) recklessly wasteful (b) hypocritical (c) falsely promising (d) patriotic

56. the *proliferation* of atomic-weapon stockpiles throughout the world
(a) gradual reduction (b) explosion (c) rapid growth (d) favorable discussion

57. sneering at such *prosaic* statements
(a) unesthetic (b) commonplace (c) favorable (d) feeble

58. within the *purview* of the committee
(a) sight (b) authority (c) approval (d) supervision

59. a woman's voice droning *querulously*
(a) insistently (b) complainingly (c) questioningly (d) quietly

60. the *recondite* pursuits of the far-out branch of modern theater
(a) questionable (b) repetitious (c) abstruse (d) calculated

61. the grass bending *resiliently* under one's feet
(a) forever (b) backwards (c) elastically (d) unchangingly

62. denouncing her in *scurrilous* terms
(a) contemptuous (b) vague (c) sly (d) abusive

63. the *secular* interests of the common man
(a) spiritual (b) worldly (c) selfish (d) secret

64. the *strident* sound breaking the silence — (a) amplified (b) long-drawn-out (c) shrill (d) unesthetic

65. advertisers experimenting with *subliminal* appeals — (a) under-the-skin (b) exalted (c) underhanded (d) unconscious

66. open to suspicion of *subornation* — (a) treason (b) bribery (c) underhandedness (d) forgery

67. his face *suffused* with joy — (a) transfixed (b) atremble (c) overspread (d) delirious

68. *surreptitiously* pocketing the fragments of food — (a) shamelessly (b) speedily (c) stealthily (d) nervously

69. under rigid, restricted *surveillance* — (a) imprisonment (b) legal search (c) appraisal (d) close watch

70. *taciturn*, icy, aloof — (a) silent (b) nervous (c) indifferent (d) touchy

71. a misunderstanding of basic *terminology* of diplomacy — (a) agreement (b) vocabulary (c) objectives (d) finality

72. *undulating* hills — (a) overwhelming (b) wavelike (c) unimpressive (d) sentinel-like

73. experiencing it *vicariously* — (a) with enthusiasm (b) religiously (c) intimately (d) by proxy

74. dangers and *vicissitudes* of life — (a) changing circumstances (b) unavoidable evils (c) substitute joys (d) unexpected thrills

75. a half-consumed *wizened*-looking candle — (a) shriveled (b) waxen (c) bedraggled (d) bright

We know that some of the words given in the definitions are more difficult than the words to be defined. But that's just another way of increasing your stock of words (if you looked them up in a dictionary).

"Philatelic appurtenances?"*

3. Divide and Conquer

YOU WANT to know something? There are no long words. They only seem that way. When you look a long word squarely in the eyes, you find that it is only a lot of little fellows huddled together. The words you consider long are combinations of short words or parts of words written together. The trick is to be able to divide the long word into recognizable short units.

That's not too hard. Imagine what reading a book or a newspaper would be like if allthewordswereruntogetherlike

---

* Drawing reproduced courtesy the *Saturday Review*.

thisandyouhadtoseparatetheindividualwordsinordertoknowwh▪ tasentencemeant. Believe it or not, that's how words use▪ to be jammed together in the handwritten books before th▪ invention of printing.

To understand what we wrote above as one continuou▪ word, you had to separate it into its word units. You divide▪ it in order to conquer its meaning. In the same way—b▪ separating a word into its recognizable units—you can ofte▪ tame the toughest and longest words in the English language▪

WHAT IS THE LONGEST WORD?

When we went to high school, *antidisestablishmentarianism* was generally regarded as the longest word in the language▪ But there's nothing long or formidable about it, if we divid▪ it into its parts. If we use a verbal scalpel on it, if we cu▪ away the prefixes fore and the suffixes aft we're left wit▪ the word *establish.*

Establish can be further cut down to the root STA, whic▪ comes from the Latin verb *stare,* to stand. And so this 28▪ letter word becomes a three-letter basic root, S-T-A, surrounde▪ by a choice collection of prefixes and suffixes. All these part▪ add up to a word that means an *ism,* or doctrine, of the op▪ position (*anti*) to the separation (*dis*) of an establishe▪ church from the state.

As a long word *antidisestablishmentarianism* belongs to th▪ past, and we wouldn't even think of entering it in a longest▪ word contest today. Back in 1939, in reply to a query, th▪ editors wrote that the longest word in Webster's *New Inter*▪ *national Dictionary* was:

PNEUMONOULTRAMICROSCOPICSILICOVOLCANOKONIOSIS.

Forty-five letters long! But we said there were no lon▪ words and now we're going to prove it by breaking this gian▪ into very fine particles. Here goes:

pneumono:	pertaining to the lungs, as in *pneumonia*
ultra:	beyond, as in *ultra*violet rays
micro:	small, as in *micro*scope
scopic:	from the root of Greek verb *skopein,* to view o▪ look at
silico:	from the element *silicon,* found in quartz, flint, an▪ sand

volcano: the meaning of this is obvious
KONI: the principal root, from a Greek word for dust
osis: a suffix indicating illness, as trichin*osis*

Now, putting the parts together again, we deduce that *pneumonoultramicroscopicsilicovolcanokoniosis* is a disease of the lungs caused by extremely small particles of volcanic ash and dust.

In John Hersey's novel *The Child Buyer*, Barry Rudd, a ten-year-old genius, who loved to swap long words as other boys swap stamps, found these two long words "old hat." This is what Miss Perrin in the novel said of him:

> It's uncanny the way Barry can decipher these marathon words. John Sano brought one in the other day and asked Barry what it meant—eccentroöosteochondrodysplasia, and Barry didn't bat an eye. "Let's see," he says. "*Eccentro*- means off center, out of line; -*osteo*-, bone; -*chondro*-, cartilage; -*dys*-, wrong or bad; -*plasia*, connection. Guess that gives you the main idea, John," he says. He's very offhand but not at all superior about it.*

Science indeed has marched on with seven-league boots since 1939 and we have only to glance at our newspapers to know that the length of words for new chemical compounds has kept pace with science. Not to settle any arguments, but just as a curiosity, we throw in the longest word we have come across. It is the name of a new drug announced by the *Journal of the American Veterinary Medical Association*. Here it comes; take a deep breath:

DIISOBUTYLPHENOXYETHOXYETHYLDI-
METHYLBENZYLAMMONIUMCHLORIDE.

BARNUM'S WORD

Yes, if you can divide a word properly you can generally conquer it. You will no longer be afraid of a long word, and you won't be fooled by a short one as some of P. T. Barnum's patrons once were. Before his famous circus days, Barnum ran an equally famous museum in lower Manhattan. People liked the exhibits so much they just kept going around and

---

* From *The Child Buyer* by John Hersey (Alfred A. Knopf, New York, 1960)

around and staying so long that others couldn't get in. Being an astute businessman, Barnum tried to find a way out for himself and for customers who overstayed their welcome. Over the cage of the tigress and her cubs, he placed a large sign reading, "TIGRESS." Then, over a doorway next to the cage, he put up another large sign which read: "TO THE EGRESS." Thinking they were going to see some new curiosity, many of those in the crowded museum trooped through the door—and found themselves in the street!

But those who knew how to divide the word *egress* into its recognizable units weren't fooled. They saw *e*, a prefix meaning *out*, and *gress*, a Latin stem meaning *step*, so that they knew that an *egress* was nothing more than a stepping-out place, an exit. We find *gress* in pro*gress*, to step forward (*pro*), in di*gress*, to step away (*di*) or depart from a topic, in retro*gress*, to step backward (*retro*), and in trans*gress*, to step across (*trans*) the line of righteousness. How much more meaning is attached to a word like *transgression* when you realize that its meaning of sin is connected with the idea of stepping across the line that divides right from wrong!

That's the way to divide many words, long or short, strange or familiar. Let's try our scalpel on one or two other words to see just how it helps. The word *imperturbable* may puzzle you for a moment. But then you quickly recognize that *im*, *per*, and *able* are not the basic units. Cutting them away, you lay bare the root TURB. *Turb* appears in dis*turb*, per*turb*, *turb*ulent, and per*turb*ation, and wherever it occurs it spells *trouble*. *Troub*led waters are *turb*id. An imper*turb*able person is, therefore, one whose spirits cannot be troubled or ruffled, one who is calm and serene.

A headline about one of the trouble spots of the world tells us that in Pakistan

MOSLEMS EXCULPATE ENEMIES
TO AVOID REPRISALS

Here's *exculpate*, a really difficult word. But it's easy to cut away the prefix *ex* and the suffix *ate* and expose the root CULP, which comes from the Latin word *culpa* meaning *fault* or *blame*. To *exculpate* is therefore to free from (*ex*) blame. To *inculpate* is to charge with blame. We can help fix the meaning of the root CULP by associating it with other words in which it occurs. A *culp*rit is the person at fault. *Culp*able means deserving of blame, and *culp*ability is blame or guilt. A culpable person is a culprit whose culpability has been established. If he is not culpable, exculpatory evidence will set him free.

We can see that glazed, faraway look coming into your eyes. We can hear you saying:

"Wait a minute, fellows! I didn't come here to learn Latin and Greek. I want to know more about English words. I never took up Greek and all I remember of my high school Latin is *amo, amas, amat* and that Caesar once said, *'Veni, vidi, vici.'* I can't go through all that again."

Relax! We're not asking you to learn Latin and Greek. We are asking you to learn the English elements that come from Greek and Latin words, not as reminders or remainders of dead languages but as vital parts of the living and growing language you speak and write. Latin and Greek form the basis of about 70 per cent of all English words—with new words from Latin and Greek constantly being added.

So it's not our fault that Latin and Greek are at the roots of so many of our words. It makes us feel like the small boy who was returning a book to the library. The librarian was turning the pages of the book, when she noticed how small the little boy was.

"This is rather technical, isn't it?" she asked, holding the book open before her.

Half defiant, half apologetic, the little boy replied, "It was that way when I got it."

Well, English words were that way when we got them— studded with Latin and Greek roots in a setting of Latin and Greek prefixes and suffixes. That's our defiant apology.

It is because we want you to know more about *English* words that we think it is necessary to acquire a knowledge of the *live* roots of these not-so-dead languages. What's more, this isn't the hard way; it's the interesting and therefore the easy way. It is also the permanent way.

Dividing a word into its recognizable units can accomplish the following:

1. Let light in on a familiar word. It illuminates it. It makes you see it as you have never seen it before.

2. Make a long unfamiliar word seem less formidable. You handle one part at a time and so conquer the whole word.

3. Help you remember the word, because you associate other similarly rooted words with it.

4. Help you spell the word correctly. (See Chapter 15.)

Finally, if you learn to separate a word into its units, you will be able to come away from a long word and say, *"Veni divisi, vici.* I came, I divided, I conquered!"

If you use the method of Divide and Conquer you must of course, learn the meanings of the roots. Be sure to associate a word with its root. We are going to give you ten words on which you can practice. We shall supply the meaning of the roots and stems; you will select the meaning of the words from the list on the right. Answers will be found on page 362.

Example: If NOV means "new" then to *renovate* means to make new again.

1. Indubitably DUBIT—doubt	a. scattering or spreading abroad like seeds
2. Corroboration ROBOR—strength	b. put off
3. Indefatigability FATIG—to weary, to tire	c. unchangeable d. generosity
4. Procrastinate CRAS—tomorrow	e. confirmation f. doubtlessly
5. Presentiment SENT—feel	g. a feeling that something is going to happen
6. Immutable MUT—change	h. transparent i. having keen mental vision
7. Imperviousness VI(A)—road, way	j. quality of not allowing a passage through
8. Perspicacious SPIC—look, see	k. inability to be measured; vastness
9. Dissemination SEMIN—seed	l. inability to be tired
10. Incommensurability MENS—measure	

THE GREEKS HAD A LONG WORD

The longest word in print in any language is the combination concocted by Aristophanes: *lopadotemachoselachoga leokranioleipsanodrimypotrimmatosilphiotyromelitokatakechy menokichlepikossyphophattoperisteralektryonoptekephalliokin gklopeleiolagoosiraiobaphetraganopterygon.* Aristophanes threw into it oysters and fish and sharks and cheese and birds

---

* Found in *Ecclesiazusae,* "Women in Parliament."

and other delicacies so that appropriately the word means nothing more than *hash*.

SHAKESPEARE HAD A LONG WORD

Costard says in Act V of *Love's Labour Lost:* "I marvel thy master hath not eaten thee for a word; for thou are not so long by the head as *honorificabilitudinitatibus*," which is from a medieval nonsense word for "honorableness."

THE ENGLISH SCHOOLBOY'S LONG WORD

From a rule in a Latin grammar used by the boys at Eton was coined the word *floccinaucinihilipilification*, which means nothing more than "the act of estimating as worthless."

A LONG WORD MAY SOMETIMES BE A SHORT CUT

A lot is being said these days against the use of long words and in favor of the short, vigorous, direct word. That's all to the good and we're all for it, but before the movement frightens us out of using any but one-syllable words, we'd like to put in a word for the long word in the right place.

There are times when the long word gets you there faster. It's a little like the story of the applicant who was being interviewed by a prospective employer. "And do you take shorthand?" she was asked. "I do," she replied, "but that way usually takes longer." In the same way, the short words may sometimes be the long way around.

We learn that Congress has authorized an *equestrian* statue of some great American general. How else are you going to describe the statue? You can't say a horsy statue. That doesn't quite get the idea. To get the idea you would have to say something like "a statue in which the figure is mounted on a horse." All that for *equestrian!*

An editorial writer tells us that criticism of Congress "will reach its *quadrennial* peak this fall." You lose something besides brevity and smoothness if you try to substitute a string of short words for the one long word. Somehow a "quadrennial peak" is higher than one "that is reached every four years."

Another such word that has been appearing in print recently

is *eponymous,* a long short cut for "from the book (or whatever) of the same name." In highlighting *Fiorello,* a musical based on the life of former Mayor La Guardia, the *New Yorker* refers to the actor Tom Bosley as "a dead ringer for the *eponymous* floweret." John K. Hutchens, writing in the *Herald Tribune* of February 8, 1961, tells us that E. M. Forster in his book *Alexandria* likes Alexander the Great for "defeating the Persian enemies of the Greeks and bringing Hellenic culture to his *eponymous* city."

Here, *eponymous* means "named after him," or "to which he gave his name." Its dictionary meaning is "giving one's name to a tribe, people, nation, or place."

Knowledge of words spreads its roots like the banyan tree.

Though there are times when the long word is the short cut, that doesn't mean we approve of the pompous, pretentious long word that leads down the road to "gobbledygook." We are in complete sympathy with Maury Maverick, who coined the word *gobbledygook,* and with the order he issued while head of a bureau in Washington. The order read in part, "Be short, and use plain English. A memorandum should be as short as clearness will allow. Stay off gobbledygook language. . . . Anyone using the words *activation* or *implementation* will be shot."

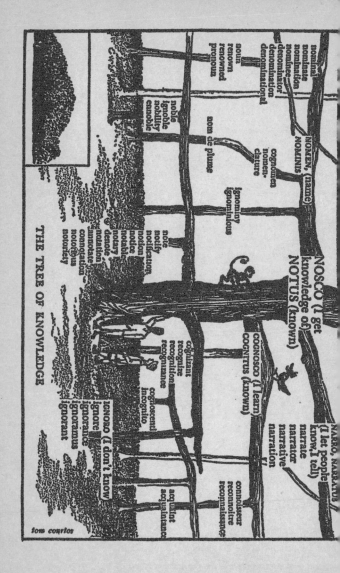

THE TREE OF KNOWLEDGE

NOMEN, (name)
NOMINIS

nomini
nominate
nomination
nominee
denominate
denomination
denominational
noun
renown
renowned
pronoun

noble
ignoble
nobility
ennoble

cognomen
nomen-
clature

nom de plume

ignominy
ignominious

NOSCO (I get
knowledge of)
NOTUS (known)

note
notify
notice
notable
notion
notify
notification
notation
denote
annotate
connotation
notorious
notoriety

COGNOSCO (I learn)
COGNITUS (known)

cognizant
recognize
recognition
recognizance

cognoscenti
incognito

IGNORO (I don't know)
ignore
ignorance
ignoramus
ignorant

NARRO, NARRATUS
(I let people
know, I tell)
narrate
narrator
narrative
narration

connoisseur
reconnoitre
reconnaissance

acquaint
acquaintance

tom corrtos

50

4. Deep Are the Roots

AMONG THE famous sights of India which the tourist is told not to miss is a banyan tree that grows near Calcutta. When you reach the site a few miles from that city, you look for a solitary tree. What you see is a miniature forest, and at first glance, you are disappointed. "I've seen bigger trees in California," you say to yourself, and you wonder why you were bounced over rough roads for this.

But then, like the others, you look around more carefully. You walk into the "forest" and around the trees which seem to form its borders—and you make a discovery. What you thought was a forest is one tree—a remarkable tree that's a hundred trees in one! The branches of the parent tree send down shoots that reach the ground, take root, and develop new trunks. These accessory trunks form a connected cluster or grove. That's why you think you are looking at a forest instead of a single tree.

The banyan tree *is* a remarkable tree but no more remarkable than our tree of knowledge. (See facing page.) For words grow like the banyan tree. The original parent (in this case Nosco) sends out roots which in turn develop clusters of accessory roots and stems found in *cognosco, nomen, ignoro, narro.** Together they form a family of hundreds of related words.

* *Roots* and *stems* are *elements* from which words are built or grow. Although there is a technical difference between a root and a stem, most modern popular books on words use *root* to include *stem*.

51

And yet the tree of knowledge as we have represented i here is only a bird's-eye view. The eye of a camera in a recon naissance plane would reveal another part of the forest where Greek and Anglo-Saxon trunks send out their branches and roots. We would have to add such words as diagnosis, progno sis, agnostic, gnomic, anonymous, homonym, metonymy patronymic, onomatopoeia, paronomasia (Greek), and ken canny, cunning, acknowledgment (Anglo-Saxon).

From this tree of knowledge we're going to pick only a few of the more useful and unusual words for special mention.

Sometimes a word suggests or implies more than its dic tionary meaning—emotions and memories cling to it. This overtone of the word is called its *connotation*—and that con notation may be good or bad. The word *home,* for example, has always had a good connotation; it suggests comfort, warmth, privacy, love. On the other hand the memories of World War II have given the word *collaborator* a bad con notation. Charles Poore in a book review asks, *"Collaborator* —will that word ever lose its traitorous *connotation?"*

The word *misnomer* almost always has a bad connotation. We use it to refer to something that in our opinion doesn't live up to its name.

> [Tourist cabins] called Klean Kamp
> Komfort may turn out to be a hideous
> *misnomer* covering conditions that will
> be something to shudder at for days.

NAME CALLING

Nomenclature is "name calling" in its good sense—refer ring to a system of assigning names to classifications in the animal, vegetable, and mineral world.

Man has always prized his good name. When he loses it, when he is publicly disgraced, he suffers *ignominy*.

Sometimes we can go too far in trying to fit the word *name* into definitions of these words. That's what probably hap pened to a sweet young thing who was filling out an applica tion form. Where it asked for "denominational preference," she wrote, "I like to be called Betty." *Denominational,* as used here, refers, of course, to a religious sect having a com mon faith and a distinctive name.

It was on the sports page that we came across the word

cognoscenti (pronounced "con yoh shen' tee"). The writer was telling about the probable reaction of "the cognoscenti among the 14,060 fans on hand." The *cognoscenti* * are those who "know what the score is," those who know their stuff. Like its French twin, *connoisseurs*, it is used to describe those who are experts in the fine arts (including wine, women, and baseball).

WORD FAMILIES

So much for the specific words that belong to the NOSCO family. You're going to become acquainted with the names of many of our leading word families. As you do so, you will discover that you will be getting a better insight into familiar words and learning a way of remembering new ones. You'll begin to associate words in clusters as we did with the SAL, SIL, SULT, SAULT family in Chapter 1.

And don't be frightened. Not all word families are as large or as varied as those that stem from NOSCO on our tree of knowledge. Many exist only as compact clusters like those gathered around *grex, gregis,* Latin for herd or flock. To con*greg*ate means to flock together (*con*). A pastor is the spiritual shepherd of his flock or con*greg*ation. To se*greg*ate is to keep apart (*se*) or *se*parate from others. An e*greg*ious error stands out (*e*) from the common or ordinary flock of mistakes. An ag*greg*ate is the sum total, the units of the flock added to (*ag* for *ad*) each other. Those who don't like to be alone, who want and seek the company of others are *greg*arious.

There's something very relaxing and comforting about the root GREG. It gives you a feeling of security. It's always spelled G-R-E-G, and it always means *flock*.

DON'T PUT YOUR FOOT IN IT

But some roots fool you. They look like members of the same family but on closer inspection turn out to be impostors! There's the familiar Latin root PED meaning *foot*. It has left its imprint on a great many English words. We easily recognize its footprints in *ped*estrian, *ped*al, *ped*ometer, *ped*estal, quadru*ped*, and centi*ped*e.

There are other words in which we do not so easily see just

---

* *Cognoscenti*, the plural, is generally used, as here. The singular *cognoscente* is hardly ever seen.

how the shoe fits. To im*pede* someone's progress is to plac
something in the way of his feet, thus barring his way o
tripping him up. To ex*pedi*te means to do just the opposit
At a U.N. Security Council meeting, the American delega
was trying to explain the literal meaning of this word. H
was speaking about "expediting" the report of the Atom
Energy Committee. After mentioning that the word *expedi.*
was Latin in origin, he went on to say:

> You know its derivation. I can see a
> very distinguished doctor here, who real-
> izes that this word is derived, has some-
> thing to do with pediatrics, and the use of
> this word is specific, has a specific mean-
> ing, is derived from the past participle of
> the word *expedire*, that is, to let go of the
> foot.

Right here the American delegate put *his* foot in
Though many people share the same confusion, a *pediatricia*
does not specialize in diseases of the feet; he specializes
children's diseases. The PED in his title is an altered spellin
of *pais, paidos*, the Greek word for boy or child. It appears
*ped*agogue, which once meant a slave who led a boy to scho
and took care of him at home. An ortho*ped*ist, like the *pe*
iatrician, is a specialist. He corrects (*ortho*, correct or righ
or prevents body deformities, especially in children.

Of course, our American delegate confused *pediatricia*
with *pod*iatrist. The Greek word for foot is *pous* (also wri
ten as *pus*), *podos*. An arthro*pod* is an animal with jointe
feet like a lobster or a spider. A *pod*ium is a pedestal or pla
form. The anti*pod*es are the lands "down under." It one
meant the people living on the other side of the globe, who
feet were directly opposite (*anti*) ours. The word is also us
without geographical reference in the sense of the exact opp
site. The form *pus* is seen in octo*pus*, which is all feet, eig
of them, and in the distinguished zoological visitor from t
antipodes, the platy*pus*, who is nothing more than a flat-foo

So we can see that we are dealing with at least three kin
of roots:

1. Those like NOSCO that spread like a banyan tree.
2. Those like GREG that form a compact, easily identifiab
cluster.
3. Those like PED that can fool you if you don't watch o

WORDS OF CAUTION

That's why we don't recommend the use of roots as an exclusive method of arriving at the meanings of words. When you aren't sure of the meaning of a word, this method should be used with circumspection.

But we do recommend the "root" method *after* you know the meaning of the word. Then a knowledge of a word's derivation does two important things for you that nothing else can do:

1. It gives you a greater insight into the significance of a familiar word, revealing its inner meaning. Take the word *revealing* just used. It's a familiar word, but its meaning is enriched when you know that it means drawing back (*re*) the *veil*.

2. It gives you a way of permanently fixing a new word. Take *circumspection* which we used a little while ago. It means *caution*, but when you also know that by derivation it means looking (*spect*) around (*circum*) before going ahead, the meaning of the word is not only enriched but it is *fixed* in your memory.

So when you deal with roots, don't put *your* foot in it. Put your thumb—into a good dictionary and pull out the correct derivation. Always check!

A FINAL WARNING

As we have already pointed out, you can go way out on a limb unless you properly identify the root. If you are not careful, you may make the mistake a pupil of ours made when he was confronted by:

AMENABLE: (a) contemptible (b) religious (c) capable of being persuaded (d) stubborn

Relying on *his* idea of the use of the root-suffix method, he checked (b) *religious*. When asked how he had arrived at that answer he triumphantly replied, "Well, the suffix *able,* of course, means 'able,' and *amen* means what is says, 'amen'; so if you're able to say 'amen' you're religious!"

The correct answer, of course, is (c) *capable of being persuaded.* The root of *amenable* is found in the French verbs *mener* and *amener* (*a*, to), meaning "to lead, to bring to, to conduct"; and so the word *amenable* means "easily led, submissive, tractable, responsive, docile." From the root MEN, we get also the words *promenade, mien, demeanor,* and *mis-demeanor.*

And now let's check on your knowledge of roots. Answers to these tests will be found on page 362.

In Exercises *I* and *II* below, each dot represents a letter.

I. What Do You Know?

The Greek root GNO means *know.*

1. The prefix *a* says "No" or "Not." An agnostic is therefore a person who says "I don't . . . ." when asked about the existence of God.

2. *Pro* means *before.* Prognosis is therefore literally fore . . . . and a medical prognosis is the art of . . . . telling the course of a disease.

3. *Dia* means *between* or *apart.* When a doctor discriminates between symptoms of various illnesses to discover what ails a patient, he is making a dia . . . . . .

4. The pointer on a sundial that lets you know the time of day by its shadow is called a . . . mon.

5. The dwarfs who guarded the treasures in mines were called . . . . . . because they were considered wise little fellows.

6. A wise saying is also known as a *gnome.* Writing or speaking that is full of maxims and wise sayings is called . . . mic.

II. Can You Name These?

The Greek *onoma* and *onyma* mean name. They belong on the tree of knowledge for a *name* is something by which a person or thing is *known.*

In the column on the left are eight English words containing a Greek root meaning *name.* On the right are the meanings of the prefixes or other roots in these words. Using all eight words, complete the sentences below the lists.

*an*onymous	not
*ant*onym	against
*homo*nym	same
onomato*poeia*	making
*par*onomasia	beside
*patr*onymic	father
*pseud*onym	false
*syn*onym	together

1. Words like *bare* and *bear* that sound the same but are spelled differently are called . . . . nyms.

2. Words like *black* and *white* that are opposites are called . . . onyms.

3. The *unnamed* author to whom most anecdotes are attributed is . . . .

4. Names like McDonald and Johnson are called . . . .- onymics because they indicate that the sons are named after the *father*.

5. Different words like *sharp* and *keen* that have similar meanings are called . . . onyms.

6. Another name for punning is . . . onomasia.

7. Words like *buzz* and *hiss* made by imitating sounds are examples of . . . .

8. William Sydney Porter is better known by his . . . . .- onym of O. Henry.

III. Take Your Fill

The words on the left are filled with the idea of completeness. From the definitions in the column on the right select the ones that will most closely match each of the words on the left.

1. plenary	a.	superfluous use of words
2. plenipotentiary	b.	overabundance
3. plethora	c.	fullness
4. plenitude	d.	having full powers
5. pleonasm	e.	fully attended
6. plenum	f.	fulfillment
7. deplete	g.	filled with
8. expletive	h.	full meeting
9. replenish	i.	fill again
10. replete	j.	empty
	k.	expression used as a "filler"

IV. One Root's Family

A. GEN is a Latin and Greek root meaning to give birth to. This prolific root has given birth to nearly one hundred English words.

In each of the sentences below, we have substituted an italicized word for the word originally used. The original word contained the root GEN. Can you put the original GEN word back in its proper place by choosing from among these words:

indigenous, progeny, generation, engendered, genesis, degenerated?

1. War's *origin* lies in the despotic lust for power (General MacArthur).

2. Prodded by his wife and his ecstatic *offspring*, he rushed frantically to his agent.

3. The TV network has conceived of "neutral names." What's that? Names that are not *native* to any one group.

4. In the heat of the excitement *created* by the big Chicago bout M'sieu George had forgotten about the 2500-mile bicycle race around France.

B. Match the phrases on the right with the words on the left:

1. gene   a. existing from birth
2. eugenics   b. study of the family tree
3. congenital   c. inheritance by the first born
4. genealogy   d. unit or factor of heredity
5. primogeniture   e. science of improving offspring
6. psychogenic   f. born in or caused by the mind

V. To Tell of Time

A. CHRON is a Greek root meaning time. On the left are six words that deal with time. Match them with the definitions on the right.

1. synchronize   a. story of events in order of time
2. chronology   b. timepiece
3. anachronism   c. lasting a long time
4. chronometer   d. science of measuring time
5. chronic   e. make agree in time
6. chronicle   f. event placed out of its proper time

B. TEMPOR is the Latin root corresponding to CHRON. Using this root or part of it, complete the word fragments to form the words defined. The dots represent the number of additional letters needed. We'll help you in some places with a prefix.

1. *contempor* . . .   happening at the present or same time
2. *tempor* . . .   to act to gain time; to delay
3. *temp* .   relative rate of speed in music; pattern of activity
4. *extempor* . . . . . . said or composed on the spur of the moment; impromptu
5. *tempor* . .   not permanent; secular as opposed to spiritual
6. *tempor* . . .   for the time being

"We learned a new word today, Momma. Try and surmise what it is. I'll give you three surmises." *

5. Brief Encounters

ONE DAY not long ago, red pencil in hand, we read through a copy of the New York *Times* in search of the longest words we could find. We set fifteen letters as the minimum. We found exactly eleven words containing fifteen letters or more. Here

---

* Drawing reproduced courtesy the *Saturday Review*.

they are in the order in which we found them:

nationalization	internationally
ineffectiveness	notwithstanding
constitutionality	superintendency
unprecedentedly	classifications
proportionately	dissatisfaction
disenfranchisement	

Easy, aren't they? These are the longest words we found in one day's newspaper, and yet you would have little trouble in identifying at least ten of them correctly. It's not the length of a word that makes it hard; it's the density. These long words are transparent. You can look right through them at the words *nation, effect, constitution, franchise,* etc. It's easy to divide and conquer.

Now look at these eleven words—*aver, crux, dour, fiat, icon, limn, mine, sate, [sic], tome, tort.* These three-and four-letter words—brief encounters in our newspaper reading—have density. If you can identify ten out of these eleven correctly, you're doing very well indeed. Not that they're so hard. We have harder ones for you later on, but right now how about trying these eleven?

Test your ability by selecting the definition you think closest in meaning:

AVER — assert, turn away, dispute, decline
CRUX — outcome, critical point, candle-holder, weakness
DOUR — insulting, thrifty, stern, stingy
FIAT — failure, decree, success, message
ICON — glass, Russian coin, old book, image
LIMN — draw, threshold, fruit, decide
MIME — machine, mask, actor in a dumb show, pretense
SATE — glut, ridicule, drink, declare
[SIC] — incorrect, thus, always, again
TOME — monument, statute, book, praise
TORT — cake, tightness, vessel, wrongful act

We chose these short words because, with the exception of [sic], they are not dead-end words. They are through streets to a larger and richer vocabulary. Here's how:

AVER

To a*ver* is to assert positively, as if you were sure you posessed the truth, as in the headline:

AVERS REPUBLICANS
CAN SHOW THE WAY

The root VER (VERI) means *true* and gives us a better insight into such familiar words as:

very, verily	truly.
verity	truth, most often used in plural and with *eternal.*
veracity	truthfulness.
veracious	truthful.
verdict	a true saying; therefore a presumably just judgment made on the basis of *veri*fied evidence.

And here is one that may be new to you:

*veri*similitude — likeness to truth or reality.

Can you find the superfluous word in this picture caption that we found in a magazine?

Although Miss [Lana] Turner insists she played softball while in high school, she attained true *verisimilitude* only when she struck out with a grunt.

Pooh-Bah, in W. S. Gilbert's *Mikado*, uses the word in its true sense when he explains the gruesome evidence he has given as, "Merely corroborative detail, intended to give artistic *verisimilitude* to an otherwise bald and unconvincing narrative."

CRUX

CRUX is the Latin word for *cross*. The crux of a matter is the point that needs to be decided or resolved in order to clear up the situation—hence the *crucial* or critical point.

Mr. [Russell] Hill comes to the *crux* of the whole German problem when he writes: "The Allies had to make peace with each other before they could make peace with Germany."

The cross as a religious symbol appears in the words *cruci*fix, *Cru*sade, *cruci*fier, one who carries the cross at the head of a religious procession, and *cruci*ble, originally a hanging lamp. the eternal light hanging before the cross of Christ.

*Cruci*form means shaped like a cross. *Cruise* comes to us via Dutch; its original meaning is to move *cross*wise, or to sail *cross*wise.

Because the Romans used the cross as a form of capital punishment, we get the idea of agony and torture in the word ex*cruci*ating.

DOUR

DOUR, which rhymes with *tour*, means *hard, severe, sour* (in appearance). There's nothing pleasant about the newspaper headline:

EASTER WEATHER FORECAST IS DOUR

DOUR, which is frequently used in Scotland, goes back to *durus*, the Latin word for *hard*. But most of the words that come from it are easy, such as *during*, en*during*, *durable*, *duration*.

An ob*dura*te person is one who is hard to move, unyielding, obstinate. When you do something "under *dur*ess," you are doing it the hard way—under threat or coercion. A morally hardened or callous person is said to be in*dura*ted.

FIAT

FIAT is a complete Latin sentence meaning, "Let it be done." Therefore, the English word *fiat* (rhyming with *riot*) means an authoritative order or decree.

> With wages held down by Government *fiat* while the cost of living soars, the workers are becoming increasingly restive.

FIAT may also be translated as "Let there be made," or "Let there be," as in *Fiat lux*, "Let there be light."

FIAT is a form of the verb *facere*, to do or make, which in its various guises, FAC, FIG, FY, FACT, FECT, etc. has made thousands of English words. We list here only a few—those that are dif*fic*ult or that are hard to recognize as members of the family:

FACTIOUS is the adjective form of *faction* and means "making trouble," causing dissension.

FACTITIOUS means "made up," hence arti*fic*ial, not genuine, spurious.

SURFEIT (via French) means an "overdoing," an excess. If

you are *surfeited* you have "overdone" (*sur*, from *supra*, over) something; you've had more than enough even of a good thing.

FETISH (via Portuguese) originally meant an idol or charm which was believed to possess magical power and was worshiped by the owner. Today we generally use the word figuratively. We say a person makes a *fetish* of some object, idea, or belief if he has a blind or unreasoning af*fection* for it.

FEASIBLE (via French) means "do-able." A *feasible* plan is one that is practicable, workable. Mal*feasance* is "wrongdoing," especially official misconduct. A right that is inde*feasible* is one that cannot be de*feated* or un*done*.

ARTIFACTS are things that man has made, especially relics of simple, primitive art. Describing the expedition of Professor Charles L. Camp in search of traces of man who lived a million years ago, the New York *Times* said:

> While the search will be carried on for complete specimens of this earliest human and for the *artifacts* that will throw light on his manner of living, Professor Camp hopes for the early discovery of a major clue.

ICON

An ICON (also *ikon*) is an image, a statue. An *icon*oclast, literally a smasher of idols, is one who attacks cherished beliefs, who does not respect conventional ideas.

> Shea [former Yankee pitcher] is a comic, a mimic, an *iconoclast* and a practical jokester who is no respecter of age, position, or previous condition of servitude in the big leagues.

LIMN

To LIMN (silent *n*) is to paint or depict. It is the collapsed form of *illuminate,* one of whose meanings is to decorate with colored designs or initial letters, as in medieval manuscripts.

> Here, as in his *Night Cafe* and *Hospital,* he [Van Gogh] not only *limns* the actual scene but accuses a society which forces men into such brutality.

LUMEN and the related Latin root LUC light up so many

English words that we can list only a few:

*lumin*ary	"a shining light."
*lumin*ous	shining.
*luc*id	clear.
e*luc*idate	light up, clarify.
pe*lluc*id	crystal clear, *pel* being the prefix *per, through.*
*luc*ubrate	to burn the midnight oil in laborious studies. Hence the word *lucubrations* is rarely complimentary, since it implies a product that is too studied, "smelling of the lamp."
*luc*ite	a trade name for a translucent plastic (*translucent* letting light but not the image through).

MIME

A MIME (Latin *mimus*, Greek *mimos*) is an actor who *mim*ics or imitates. Other members of this theatrical family are:

*mim*esis	imitation.
*mim*etic	adjective form of *mimesis,* meaning imitating or quick to imitate.
panto*mime*	literally "all imitating;" acting that is unaccompanied by words.
*mim*icry	the art of mimicking (in radio—imitating the crowing of roosters, barking of dogs; in nature—an animal's or plant's ability to imitate its background as a means of self-protection).
*mim*osa	a sensitive tropical plant so called because it puts on an act—curling its leaves when touched.
*mim*eograph	a coined trademark word for a copying machine invented by Thomas A. Edison and much used by theatrical press agents.

SATE

Had enough? Then you are SATED: you're fully *sati*sfied. (Latin *satis*, enough, + *fy*, made.) In fact, you are in a state of *satiety.*

An in*sati*able curiosity is one that cannot be satisfied.

> But oceanography is an *insatiable* science, constantly asking for more facts.

[SIC]

SIC is a Latin word meaning *thus* or *so*. In English it always comes wrapped in parentheses or brackets and is tossed into a quoted passage thus:

> "We have demonstrated that our is
> a united party, with a sound, forward-
> looking program in contrast with the
> divided Democrat [sic] party dominated
> by quarrelsome, radical masters," the
> Senator declared.

The [sic] points an accusing finger at the word immediately before it and says for the writer who has tossed it into the quotation, "This is the way it appeared in the original. Don't hold me responsible for this misspelling or misusage. I know better." When a writer really wants to rub it in, he puts an exclamation mark after *sic*, thus [*sic!*].

Though *sic* doesn't form the basis for any long words, it does appear in two frequently quoted Latin sentences:

Sic semper tyrannis!	Thus always to tyrants!
Sic transit gloria mundi.	So passes away the glory of the world.

TOME

A TOME (from Greek *tomos*, a slice; a piece cut off) was originally a book that formed part of a larger work.

Today we use *tome* in a humorous way for any book, or specifically for a heavy book. When we cut away all the non-essential material of a tome and have only the essence left, we give an epi*tome*, or condensation of it. The word *epitome* is more often used in the sense of an embodiment or dis-tillation of characteristic qualities, as when we say, "She is the *epitome* of grace."

The ending *ectomy* (*ec*, out) is strictly a surgical cutting, from append*ectomy* to tonsill*ectomy*.

An a*tom* was so named because it was thought to be un-cuttable. Modern scientists have nullified the effect of the negative prefix *a*; they have split the unsplittable.

TORT

A TORT is a legal term for a special type of *wrong*ful act. The Latin word *tortus* means twisted or crooked. *Tort* has insinuated its way into a number of English words:

re*tort*	to twist *back* a reply, the perfect retort being one by which your opponent's statement or argument is turned *against* him.
dis*tort*	to twist *out of* shape.

con*tort*	to twist *together* or upon itself; a face can be con torted with pain; a contortionist can do it painlessly with his body.
ex*tort*	to twist *out* by force.
nas*turt*ium	a nose twister, so named because of its pungent odor.
*tort*ure	twisting parts of the body has always been a form of torture.

And so our *tort*uous path has led us through a maze of words and right back to another group of three- and four-letter words which we challenge you to get your wisdom teeth into. They have all appeared in our newspaper reading. How many can you get right? Answers will be found on page 363.

I. SELECTED SHORT SUBJECTS

A score of 25-30 is excellent, 20-25 good, 15-20 fair.

1. ABET (a) wager (b) defeat (c) commit (d) encourage
2. ARID (a) creamy (b) barren (c) refreshing (d) eager
3. AURA (a) coronet (b) perfume (c) atmosphere (d) design
4. BANE (a) ruin (b) detestation (c) wickedness (d) prohibition
5. BOGY (a) golf stick (b) bugbear (c) darkness (d) vehicle
6. BYRE (a) funeral (b) farm (c) barn (d) shrub
7. CODA (a) sad song (b) secret writing (c) poem (d) concluding passage
8. DAIS (a) raised platform (b) district (c) after-dinner speaker (d) easy chair
9. DIRE (a) uncertain (b) dreadful (c) tough (d) showy
10. DIVA (a) dancer (b) sculptress (c) temptress (d) prima donna
11. EKE (a) exclaim (b) thin out (c) supplement (d) live
12. FLUX (a) grouping (b) change (c) failure (d) conclusion
13. GIST (a) explanation (b) essence (c) shadow (d) climax
14. IOTA (a) very small quantity (b) number (c) fine distinction (d) detail
15. KILN (a) large oven (b) small cave (c) pot (d) crate
16. LAVE (a) heat (b) dislike (c) wash (d) depart
17. MIEN (a) anger (b) bearing (c) Chinese vase (d) compromise
18. MOOT (a) frequent (b) debatable (c) important (d) fitting
19. MOTE (a) blind spot (b) distance (c) speck of dust (d) method
20. NUB (a) wheel (b) crux (c) termination (d) solution
21. OLIO (a) oil compound (b) yodel (c) medley (d) butter substitute

22. **ONUS** (a) hardship (b) piece of music (c) burden (d) shame

23. **OPT** (a) hope (b) make a choice (c) look into (d) change

24. **PALL** (a) long stick (b) facial expression (c) gloomy covering (d) casket

25. **PEON** (a) flower (b) plant (c) Mexican laborer (d) song of praise

26. **RIFE** (a) prevalent (b) commonplace (c) boisterous (d) rebellious

27. **SILT** (a) small opening (b) excuse (c) lather (d) sediment

28. **TAUT** (a) relaxed (b) fatigued (c) tense (d) straight

29. **TYRO** (a) cruel person (b) beginner (c) rich man (d) mechanic

30. **WEIR** (a) old man (b) terror (c) dam (d) oddity

II. Cornerstones

Short words are often used as the cornerstones on which larger words are constructed. The italicized words in the excerpts quoted below have come from the short words printed in capitals or from their roots. Using your knowledge of the shorter words, select the correct meaning of the longer words from the four choices given at the end of each excerpt.

1. **LAVE** (Roots LAV, LUV, LOT)

> The great silt-bearing rivers from the northwest and northeast, with other streams and channels meandering across Bengal, have built up a vast *alluvial* plain.

(a) fertile (b) densely populated (c) distant (d) deposited by running water

2. **FIAT** (Roots FECT, FAC, FIC, etc.)

> General Hasal's *defection* is considered to be of major military importance, since he was in the top hierarchy in the Czechoslovak military structure.

(a) allegiance (b) desertion (c) rise (d) loyalty

3. VILE (Roots VIL, VILI)

> It was Blaine's conclusion that no persons in public life had been *vilified* as had been Jefferson, John Quincy Adams, Andrew Jackson and Henry Clay.

(a) honored (b) extolled (c) maligned (d) esteemed

4. ONUS (Root ONER)

> In spite of our Government's sincere belief in the criminality of these organizations, two of them, the S.S. and the general staff, were *exonerated*.

(a) praised (b) reinstated (c) freed from charges (d) pensioned off

5. DOUR (Root DUR)

> We are becoming *indurated* to thinking, without too much of a shudder, of atomizing some city of a million men, women, and children "on the other side of the globe."

(a) encouraged (b) hardened (c) compelled (d) softened

III. Collapsed Forms

On the left are a dozen short words that are the collapsed or related forms of longer words that appear on the right. Can you pair them off correctly?

1. alms   (a) alimony (b) eleemosynary (*charitable*)
2. bedlam   (a) Bethlehem (b) belladonna
3. blame   (a) emblematic (b) blaspheme
4. coy   (a) quiet (b) corny
5. flail   (a) fluctuate (b) flagellate (*whip*)
6. kiln   (a) calumniate (*insult*) (b) culinary
7. limn   (a) illuminate (b) eliminate
8. maim   (a) madam (b) mayhem
9. manure   (a) manufacture (b) maneuver
10. palsy   (a) paralysis (b) pulsation
11. proxy   (a) proximity (b) procuracy (*management for another*)
12. sexton   (a) sacristan (b) secularist

"When you say 'unimpeachable authority,' Mulligan, I presume you mean the bunch that hangs out at Sloppy Mike's?"*

6. Words That Make the Headlines

THE FELLOW who looks up from what he is doing and suddenly asks, "What's a thin six-letter word for allegiance?" is not a crossword-puzzle fan. He's a headline writer who has to squeeze a telling word into the space allotted him. *Allegiance* won't do. He has only eight spaces. He needs a slim

six-letter word, one without *m*'s or *w*'s. Someone mention
fealty. The headline writer's thumb and index finger come
together in a that-does-it-brother gesture, and tomorrow's
headline reads:

Throng Vows Fealty to U.S.
In American Day Ceremony

The fact that *fealty* is a somewhat unusual word, that i
sounds slightly Shakespearean doesn't bother our headline
writer. In his world of counted-out spaces, it fits. (Besides, he
can put *allegiance* in the sub-head and everything will be all
right.) Through this happy necessity of space limitation,
copyreaders * have breathed life into words that long ago
were on the way out in general American usage—such words
as *wax* (for grow, related to the German word *wachsen*) in

G.O.P. BACKING SEEN WAXING

lore (a word related to *learn* and the German word *lehren*) in

HELGOLAND BLAST ADDS SCIENCE LORE

collier (for coal miner) in

5-Day Week for Colliers
Is Considered in Britain

albeit (for although) in a typical *Variety* headline:

B'way Spotty Albeit "Egg" Cracking

anent (for inrespect to, concerning) in

U.S. Prestige Issue Raised
Anent Holland and Portugal

soothsayer (for fortune teller) in

SOOTHSAYERS IN HIDING

and *bruit* (for report, related to *the* French word *bruit* meaning noise) in

---

* The trade word for the man who composes headlines is *copyreader* or
copy-desk man.

AMNESTY PROGRAM
BRUITED IN GREECE

Headline writers have popularized such words as *onus*, *parley*, *impasse**, *bloc*, *pact*, *impugn*, *decry*, and *score* (criti-

> KOREAN IMPASSE
> BRINGS DEADLOCK
> OVER STALEMATE

cize severely).

By placing a word in a headline, headline writers have given quick currency to words like *genocide, isotope, brinkmanship, astronaut, sputnik, beatnik, automation, automated,* and *apartheid*.

Here's a headline that scores three times:

PARLEY LEADERS
SCORE APARTHEID

Headline writers have their lighter moments, too, when they vie with one another to achieve a headline that has interest and novelty. In such a mythical contest one newspaper changed its column headings for Births, Marriages, and Deaths to Hatched, Matched, and Snatched. That looked like a winner until another newspaper came along with Yells, Bells, and Knells. It's hard to improve on that kind of rhymed compression unless you're on the staff of *Variety*. Then you come up with

STIX NIX HIX PIX†

and startle the world. And the French were even more startled when one of their journalists translated it as, "Morceaux de bois nient paysans au cinéma," which hastily translated back to English means, "Pieces of wood disown farmers in the cinema."

Even conservative papers like the New York *Times* and *Herald Tribune* will occasionally gag up their headlines:

G.I.'s Beef Over Pork Puts Officer in Stew
As Eisenhower Settles a Messy Dispute

---

* The *New Republic* quotes a headline in the Norfolk, Va., *Pilot:*
† Translation: Inhabitants of rural districts (STIX) are not enthusiastic about (NIX) moving pictures (PIX) dealing with bucolic themes (HIX).

or

BRITONS REFUSE EWES
FIT FOR GLUES, NOT STEWS

or

KISS AND HISS DIDN'T MISS

(If you're puzzled, Kiss and Hiss were two motorists whose cars collided.)

But a headline writer's lot is not always a happy one. Into the limited space given him he must compress the gist of the news and he must try to do it without ambiguity. It is a great tribute to his ability and ingenuity that only occasionally do you stare and stare at a headline like

EYES LABOR IN RUMANIA

and in a startled sort of way wonder what it can mean.

The first sentence of the news item explains all: "Desperately surveying the European horizon for labor with which to remedy her manpower shortage, France is expected soon to lay claim to 400,000 men and women in the Banat region of Rumania."

Or your eyes labor over this one:

ANTI-REDDATARULE
HITS LOCAL UNIONS

until you realize that you're not looking at a new *anti* word but at three words ANTI-RED, DATA, and RULE. The headline writer got himself into this jam, because one of the rules set down for him is never to let a word run into the next line.

The reason for this restriction on headline writers was called to our attention one day last summer. We were driving from the Adirondacks to Pittsfield, Massachusetts. On Route 22 a mile or two out of Petersburg, N. Y., we came upon this road sign:

When we first saw it, we were going rather fast, and we thought perhaps we hadn't read the sign right, but there, two or three miles farther on, was another just like it.

There must be other motorists passing this sign who think,

72

TOM COURTOS

as we did, that they are passing through the quaint, sun-drenched town of Little Hoo—with a sick river on its hands. (The SLOW caution adds to this feeling.) Later, of course, we discovered that the supposedly ailing stream is the Little Hoosick River.

A headline writer cannot afford this kind of misinterpretation. He can't afford to separate words. He doesn't use hyphens.

The true story (vouched for by *Parents Magazine*) about the little girl belongs here. On Saturday her class had gone to visit the town reservoir. On Monday, composition day, the teacher assigned the topic, "An interesting place I visited over the weekend." Much scratching of heads and pens and then the little girl raised her hand. "Miss Finch," she asked, "is *waterworks* all one word or do you spell it with a hydrant?"

It has been said that we are a nation of headline readers. That may be bad for our general awareness, because headlines often contain an editorial slant and don't tell us the whole story. But it can be good, if what we want is to increase our store of words painlessly.

When you see a new or familiar word in a headline, read on. You're sure to have it explained in the subhead or in the first sentence of the news story. Then again, as pointed out in Chapter 2, you will be learning new words throug contact and context.

ARE YOU A HEADLINE READER?

Here's a test we have prepared on words that stare up a you regularly from the headlines.

Next to each number below you will find a word in capitals followed by four words or phrases. In each case select the word or phrase that has most nearly the same meaning as the word in capitals. Answers will be found on page 363.

1. AMBIGUOUS   (a) clear (b) doubtful (c) large (d) complicated

2. AMENABLE   (a) religious (b) responsive (c) kind-hearted (d) cruel

3. AMITY   (a) linen (b) strife (c) friendship (d) enmity

4. AUGURY   (a) foretelling (b) increase (c) boring tool (d) sickness

5. AUSTERITY   (a) style (b) poverty (c) calmness (d) severity

6. CASTIGATION   (a) projectile (b) driving force (c) punishment (d) insulting

7. CONDONE   (a) surround (b) pardon (c) bring together (d) rule together

8. CONTENTION   (a) deep satisfaction (b) self-restraint (c) competitive struggle (d) convincing reason

9. DECRY   (a) denounce (b) catch sight of (c) weep (d) spy on

10. DEFALCATION   (a) desertion (b) embezzlement (c) emigration (d) branching off

11. DEMUR   (a) to be coy (b) grumble (c) object to (d) remove

12. DENIZEN   (a) agent (b) police (c) underworld (d) inhabitant

13. DISSENTIENT   (a) not agreeing (b) abstaining (c) odorless (d) unfeeling

14. DISSERTATION   (a) praise (b) food (c) sprinkling (d) essay

15. DISSIPATE   (a) concentrate (b) squander (c) speak foolishly (d) drink slowly

16. DISTAFF   (a) musical scale (b) female (c) left (d) shepherd

17. ESCHEW   (a) eat slowly (b) to go wrong (c) avoid (d) lose

18. ETHNIC   (a) moral (b) foreign (c) legal (d) racial

19. FRESCO — (a) painting on fresh plaster (b) cooling drink (c) Italian vegetable (d) fresh fruit

20. HARBINGER — (a) safe port (b) forerunner (c) drunken revel (d) warrior

21. HIRSUTE — (a) cheap (b) juicy (c) hairy (d) smoky

22. HOLOGRAPH — (a) chart (b) table of contents (c) deep cavern (d) handwritten document

23. ILLICIT — (a) free (b) easy (c) spotless (d) not legal

24. IMBROGLIO* — (a) decoration (b) quarrel (c) scandal (d) harem

25. IMPROMPTU — (a) offhand (b) tardy (c) precise (d) not proper

26. IMPROVISE — (a) impoverish (b) supervise (c) arrange suddenly (d) overlook

27. IMPUGN — (a) bother (b) hunt (c) attack (d) uphold

28. INTERIM — (a) meantime (b) entrance (c) burial (d) step

29. INUNDATE — (a) flood (b) insulate (c) make an entry (d) go under

30. LETHARGY — (a) energy (b) sluggishness (c) inability (d) permission

31. MITIGATE — (a) soften (b) copy (c) send away (d) fight against

32. MORES — (a) additions (b) nationalities (c) customs (d) conflicts

33. MULCT — (a) take away by trickery (b) pasture cows (c) soften with soap (d) think over

34. NEBULOUS — (a) starry (b) cloudy (c) intoxicated (d) clear

35. OBSOLESCENCE — (a) destruction (b) opposition (c) consolation (d) going out of use

36. OPULENT — (a) soothing (b) wealthy (c) hopeful (d) attacking

37. PANACEA — (a) cure-all (b) vital organ (c) oceanic island (d) international agreement

38. PENURIOUS — (a) poor (b) imprisoned (c) stingy (d) hardy

39. PEREMPTORILY — (a) promptly (b) decisively (c) exorbitantly (d) thoroughly

40. PRELATE — (a) army officer (b) geometric curve (c) college head (d) church official

41. PRESAGE — (a) grow old (b) publicize (c) send ahead (d) predict

42. PROXY — (a) neighbor (b) president (c) fraud (d) substitute

---

* Also written erroneously as *embroglio* because of relationship to *embroil*.

43. PUNGENT   (a) pugnacious (b) erasing (c) biting (d) wild

44. QUIXOTIC   (a) fleet-footed (b) visionary (c) protective (d) foreign

45. RENEGADE   (a) partisan (b) villain (c) deserter (d) adherent

46. RESCIND   (a) confirm (b) go back (c) change (d) cancel

47. RESTIVE   (a) quiet (b) patient (c) resisting (d) submissive

48. SEMINAR   (a) graduate course of study (b) conservatory (c) agricultural board (d) sewing-circle

49. SHALE   (a) type of rock (b) head covering (c) oil (d) fish

50. TRUCKLE   (a) convey (b) domineer (c) drag along (d) yield subserviently

"Does 'ex' take the ablative or the dative?"*

7. Pre-Fixing Words

IN HIS BOOK, *Gilbert and Sullivan*, Hesketh Pearson relates the following incident:

"Oh, Mr. Gilbert," said a wealthy lady at some dinner

party, "your friend Mr. Sullivan's music is really too delightful. It reminds me so much of dear Baytch (Bach). Do tell me: what is Baytch doing now? Is he still composing?"

"Well, no, madam," Gilbert returned, "just now, as a matter of fact, dear Baytch is by way of decomposing."

What a difference that little prefix *de* made! In this case it marked the difference between life and death! Prefixes and combining forms are those important little syllables coming at the beginning (*pre*) of a word, which often control the destiny of the word. Wedded to a word, a prefix affects it for good for ill, for weal for woe, for better for worse.

Prefixes can determine how you feel about a person or an idea. If you are against (*anti*) somebody you have a decided *anti*pathy (*pathos*, feeling) toward him. If you like him you'll be in *sym*pathy with (*sym*) him, and if you don't care one way or another, you are *a*pathetic (*a*, not). If you completely identify yourself emotionally with him, have a shared *in*side feeling, then you are *em*pathic (*en, em*, in).

Prefixes can be *con*structive or *de*structive. They can build up or *con*solidate your faith in yourself and make you *con*fident, or they can weaken your faith in yourself and make you *dif*fident. Prefixes can *di*vide and *se*parate people or bring them together in *co*operation.

They may work for or against you; they are *pro* (for) or *con* (*contra*, against). You engage in *contro*versy with your *op*ponents (*op* for *ob*, against, in the way) and are a *pro*ponent of the ideas you stand for (*pro*, for).

Prefixes can *e*levate or *de*press, *ad*d (*ad*, to + *do*, give) or *sub*tract, *in*crease or *de*crease. They can make your golf game *sub*normal or transform a film that is already colossal into a *super*colossal epic. They can turn mere man into a *super*man attaining *ultra*sonic speeds or drag him down as an *infra*human into *sub*terranean depths. A change of prefix turns man's cosmos, or universe, into a small world, a *micro*cosm, or into a large universe, a *macro*cosm.

Prefixes are *multi*lingual and *poly*glot, for they speak in many tongues, having come down to us through the Greek and Latin, French and Anglo-Saxon. They also speak the language of love and hate. You will come across *male*volent *mis*anthropes, men of ill (*mal, male*) will who hate (*mis*)* mankind, and *bene*volent *phil*anthropists who love (*phil*) their

---

* Not to be confused with MIS, badly, an Anglo-Saxon prefix found in *mis*spell, *mis*take, *mis*inform, etc.

fellow men and wish them well (*bene*).

Often the prefix is the master key that unlocks the meaning of a word. If you meet a word like *juxta*position, you don't need to go beyond the prefix *juxta*, meaning near, to know that the word contains the idea of nearness or "along-sidedness." All's well with words that begin with the prefix *eu*. You know immediately that *eu*phony must mean something pleasant, in this case a pleasant sound. All's right with words that begin with *ortho*. An *ortho*dontist corrects the *mal*formation of the teeth.

You'll find that in some words all you have to know are the prefixes to get at the meaning. For example, there's the word *intransigent* that occurs so often in newspaper accounts of world events. Some individual, organization, or country is constantly taking an *intransigent* position or is showing *intransigence*. Precisely what is meant by an intransigent position? The answer is found in the prefixes *in* (not) and *trans* (across). Somebody is unwilling to come across to the other side. An intransigent person or nation is *un*compromising and *un*yielding. *Intransigent* accentuates the negative.

We have limited ourselves here to a treatment of prefixes coming into English from Greek and Latin; those coming from Anglo-Saxon are relatively simple. In addition, we have included some word elements attached to the beginnings of words and called combining forms or fused elements, like *ortho*. Some dictionaries do not consider them to be technically prefixes, but these forms do perform the same functions. That is why we have included them. You will find more combining forms in the next two chapters.

THE MIGHTY PREFIX

The prefix is small but mighty. It is more than a mere addition to a word or root; it is often a dynamic aid in prying loose the meaning of a word. We guarantee that your knowledge of words and your ability to remember them will be greatly increased if you master the prefixes.

And that isn't too hard to do, because the method of approaching the word through the prefix has certain definite merits and advantages, among which may be numbered the following:

1. There are only a small number of important prefixes, less than a hundred compared with thousands of roots.

2. Prefixes are generally safer to handle and more dependable than roots because their meanings have undergone fewer changes.

3. Prefixes are more easily identifiable. Perhaps because of their position at the beginning of the word, their spelling has undergone fewer changes, the principal one being a rather easily recognized change made for the sake of euphony.

An example is found in the word *accord*, where *ad* has been changed to *ac* to blend with the *c* of *cord*. (For the same reason *in* + *logical* becomes *illogical* and *in* + *press* becomes *impress*.) Such changes in which the last letter of the prefix is changed to blend with the first letter of the root to which it is added are called *assimilation*, itself an example (*ad* + *similis*, like).

Someone asks you which of the heart actions is the *systole*, and which the *dia*stole. You don't have to be an M.D. to answer that; all you have to be is a C.P., a connoisseur of prefixes. The *sy* is *syn*, the prefix meaning together; *dia* means through or apart. The *systole* occurs when the heart *con*tracts; the *dia*stole when the heart *ex*pands.

We're going to try to help you become a connoisseur of prefixes. For your inspection we are listing a number of important prefixes. Once again we do not recommend memorizing lists—the hit-and-run method. We want you to stay with each of the prefixes for a while and associate it with its equivalent or its opposite or the words in which it is found.

PREFIXES FOR CONNOISSEURS

Latin	English Away, From, Off	Greek
AB, ABS		**APO**
*ab*jure: to swear *off from*, to abandon one's claim or right to. (A *jury* is sworn in.)		*apo*state: one who stands *away from* or forsakes a faith.
*abs*cond: to steal *off* and hide *away* from the law. (*Recondite* means hidden in the sense of being difficult to understand.)		*apo*gee: farthest point *away from* the earth (*ge*), therefore the highest point. (*Geology* is earth science.)

Both, Around, About

AMB, AMBI

ambivalence: a *two*-way pull; a simultaneous attraction toward and repulsion from an object, person, or action.

AMPHI

amphora: a jar or vase carried by *two* handles.

amphibious: able to live in *two* environments, on land and in water.

ANTE

antediluvian: antiquated; literally *before* the flood.

Before

PRO

proscenium: the part of the stage *(skene) in front* of the curtain.

Latin

BENE

benevolence: *good* will; desire to promote the *well*-being of others.

English

Well

Greek

EU

euphoria: a sense of *well*-being.

eupeptic: having *good* digestion.

CIRCUM

circumambient: surrounding.

circumlocution: a *roundabout* way of saying something.

circumference: line going *around* a circle.

Around

PERI

peripatetic: walking around from place to place; itinerant.

periphrastic: talking in a *roundabout* way.

periphery: line *around* a circle or other surface; outer boundaries.

A few years ago, the name *Circumferential* Parkway was proposed for the new highway going around part of New York City. Later, *Peripheral* Parkway was suggested as a more euphonious name. Finally, because it was feared that either name would be too hard to pronounce, a compromise was reached. And so it is known as the Belt Parkway, for doesn't a belt go around something too?

With, Together, Very

COM, CON, CO, COL, COR

concurrence; literally a running *together;* meeting; agreement.

colloquy: literally a talking *together,* informal conference.

SYN, SYL, SYM

syndrome: *symptoms* occurring *together* or happening *concurrently; drome* is also *run* as in *dromedary,* hippo-*drome.*

81

contemporaneous, happening at the same time or *together*.

convivial, from the Latin word *convivium*, a living *together*, dining *with* others, a banquet; hence joyous, festive.

synchronous; happenin at the same time.

symposium: originally drinking *with* others a a convivial banquet.

Speeches and entertainment followed or accompanied th dinner among the ancient Greeks. A symposium (literally drinking together) was the conversational part of the ban quet. Nowadays it refers to an exchange of ideas at a forum or in a publication where writers get *together* to exchang views.

Com is also an intensive meaning *very*, as in *con*geal, t change to very cold, hence to freeze, and in *con*dign, ver worthy, hence deserved, suitable, merited.

Against, Opposite

CONTRA (via French, COUNTER)

contravene: literally come *against;* oppose; disregard.

countermand: literally order *against:* issue a *con*trary order, revoke, recall.

counterpoise: a weight set *against* another; balance; equilibrium.

ANTI, ANT

antibiotic: literally *against* life; tending to destroy the life of micro-organ isms.

antidote: something given *against* an illness or poison; a remedy.

DE

demolition: tearing *down;* destruction.

Down

CATA(KATA

catastrophe: a turning up side *down;* a great misfortune.

Latin	*English*	*Greek*
	Out of,	
E, EX	From	**EC, EX, EXO**

elected: chosen *from* a group.

eclectic: chosen *from* various sources.

In, Within

IN

*im*bibe: *to drink in (bibulous,* addicted to use of intoxicating drinks).

*im*mure: to enclose within walls *(murus);* imprison; confine.

EN, EM

*en*caustic: burnt *in;* having the color fixed by heat; *(caustic* criticism, the kind that can "burn you up").

On, Upon

IN

*in*scription: writing *upon* something as on a hard surface.

EPI

*epi*taph: an inscription as *on* a gravestone.

(Epithets, however, are descriptive terms, names added *on* like William the *Conqueror,* or more usually unflattering names heaped *upon* someone. *Epitaphs* have been defined as the flattering descriptions of the dead and *epithets* as the unflattering descriptions of the living.)

Not

IN, IL, IM, IR

*in*corrigible: *not* capable of being corrected or reformed.

*im*mortal: death*less*.

*il*licit: *not* lawful.

*ir*refragable: *not* breakable; *un*deniable.

A, AN

*a*morphous: having *no* shape or form.

*am*brosia: literally *im*mortal but referring, of course, to the food of the gods which made them immortal.

The Greek gods fed on *ambrosia* and imbibed *nectar,* which also helped to ward off death. The word *nectar* may be derived from *necr,* a Greek root for dead and death, as in *necr*omancy, a form of magic in which there was pretended communication with the dead, and *necr*opsy, a post-mortem examination, an autopsy. The Latin root *nec (nic)* also spells death in such words as per*nic*ious, deadly in its effect, and inter*nec*ine, bringing death to both sides, causing mutual destruction *(inter,* between, among, mutual).

(Note that the prefix *in* is protean, assuming various shapes, forms, and meanings. A few others, like *com* and *ob,* are that way also, but in time and with practice and occasional thumbing of a good dictionary, you will learn to distinguish and recognize the different meanings and spellings. We have tried to give you as much help and briefing as space allows.)

Latin	*English*	*Greek*
MULTI	Many	POLY
*multi*lingual: comprising many languages.		*poly*glot: speaking *many* languages.

	Through,	
PER, PEL	Thoroughly	DIA (also meaning *apart*)
*per*egrination: a wandering *through* many lands. *Pilgrim* and *pilgrimage* are derived from the same root. *pel*lucid: *thoroughly* or crystal clear. *per*ennial: lasting the whole year *through* lasting for years; hence, eternal or sempiternal.		*dia*spora: a scattering of people *through* many regions like the dispersal of the Jews after the Babylonian exile. *Sporadic*, meaning scattered, or at intervals, is from the same root. *dia*phanous: allowing light to pass *through*; transparent.

OMNI	All	PAN
*omni*vorous: eating *all* things, as opposed to *carnivorous* and *herbivorous*. *omni*potent: *all* powerful, *al*mighty; a term often applied to God, the *Omni*potent and *Omni*scient (*all*-knowing).		*pan*oply: a complete suit of armor. *pan*acea: a cure-*all*. *pan*demonium: when capitalized, the home of *all* the demons; infernal tumult; wild uproar.

PRE, PRO *(forth)*	Before	PRO
*pre*lude: something said before a play. *pro*pound: to set *forth*.		*Pro*logue: a statement made *before* or prefacing a play or poem.

SEMI	Half	HEMI
*semi*circle.		*hemi*cycle.

Demi is another prefix meaning half. The three halves come together in a music column in the New York Sunday *Times* where assorted items are called HEMIDEMISEMIQUAVERS. That's a half of a half of a half of an eighth note (*quaver*) or a ¹⁄₆₄ note.

Latin	English	Greek
	Under	

SUB, SUC, SUF, SUG, SUP, SUR / **HYPO**

subcutaneous: *under* the skin. / hypodermic: *under* the skin.

supposition: a statement "placed *under*" to support a belief. / hypothesis: a *supposition*, a working explanation of some belief.

surrogate: *substitute*.

| | Above, Beyond | |

SUPER, SUPRA / **HYPER**

supererogatory: showily *super*fluous in that something is done *beyond* what is asked. / hyperbole: a throwing *beyond;* excess; exaggeration.

| | Across, Beyond | |

TRANS / **META**

transformation. / metamorphosis: change of form or shape (see *amorphous* above).

transmigration: the passing or migration (going *across*) of the soul into another body, human or animal. / metempsychosis: transmigration (Psyche was the Greek goddess of the soul).

trance: a daze or stupor, as if passing *beyond* life.

If you learn the influence of a prefix upon a word, your vocabulary will grow. Now go ahead or *pro*ceed to the questions to test and *ex*pand your knowledge of *pre*fixes and words. Answers to these tests will be found on page 363.

I. Accentuating the Negative

In a poem which appeared in William Rose Benét's column, the "Phoenix Nest," in the *Saturday Review,* Dwight Chapman complained that the negatives (really the negative prefixes) of English words baffled him. Enjoy the poem and then see how canny or uncanny an etymologist you are.

DISCOMPREHENSION

The negatives of English words
Conspire to baffle one:
Too few turn out predictably,
Too many turn out un-.

Of prefixes they take their choice
Unfettered and at will,
And some results are logical
But most are strangely il-.

The canny etymologists
Are seldom led astray,
To them each case looks typical
To me each case looks a-.

What sliver of orthography
Is left for us to grab
When nowhere is normality
And everywhere is ab-?

From the following list, select the twelve words in which the prefix has a negative force.

1. anomalous
2. atypical
3. incandescent
4. inflation
5. illogical
6. immure
7. insurrection
8. abnormality
9. ignoble
10. unpredictably
11. intoxicated
12. nonpolitical
13. aggressive
14. dissolution
15. irremediable
16. ascribe
17. immune
18. inflammable
19. inopportune
20. amoral

II. Prefixes in Opposition

In the left-hand column appear ten words with their meanings. On the right are the decapitated parts of the same words. Affix the prefix that will make each word whole again and will give it a meaning opposite to that of the corresponding word on the left. Each dot represents a letter.

1. *beni*gnant, well-disposed   . . . ignant
2. *caco*phony, harsh or bad sound   . . phony
3. *con*fident, sure of oneself   . . . fident
4. *ex*hibit, display   . . hibit
5. *homo*geneous, of the same kind throughout. . . . . . geneous
6. *hyper*thyroid, related to overactive thyroid. . . . thyroid
7. *intro*vert, one who turns thoughts inwardly. . . . . vert
8. *male*factor, evil doer   . . . . factor
9. *pre*natal, before birth   . . . . natal
10. *re*tract, draw back   . . . tract

III. Prefixes Help Your Spelling

Some prefixes change their spelling for the sake of euphony. *n* plus *literate* becomes *illiterate*. That's why *illiterate* has wo l's. It's as simple as adding 1 and 1. Now try these:

1. Sub + press   = _____
2. Ad   + locate   = _____
3. Ob   + cult   = _____
4. In   + palpable   = _____
5. In   + rational   = _____
6. Con + relate   = _____
7. Ad   + sign   = _____
8. Ad   + credit   = _____
9. Per + lucid   = _____
10. Dis + fusion   = _____

IV. Divide and Conquer

We'll divide the words and let you conquer them. We'll give you the roots and their meanings. You are to give the meanings of the prefixes and then of the entire word.

1. *ab*erration	_____	*erra*	wander	_____
2. *ac*cretion	_____	*cret*	grow	_____
3. *a*morphous	_____	*morph*	form, shape	_____
4. *ante*cedent	_____	*ced*	go	_____
5. *circum*vent	_____	*vent*	come	_____
6. *de*ter	_____	*ter*	frighten	_____
7. *di*late	_____	*lat*	wide	_____
8. *dis*cursive	_____	*curs*	run	_____
9. *dys*trophy	_____	*troph*	nourishment	_____
10. *im*maculate	_____	*macula*	stain	_____
11. *im*placable	_____	*placa*	appease	_____
12. *im*potent	_____	*pot*	able	_____
13. *inter*vene	_____	*ven*	come	_____
14. *intra*mural	_____	*mur*	wall	_____
15. *oc*clude	_____	*clud (claud)*	shut	_____
16. *per*meate	_____	*mea*	go	_____
17. *poly*chrome	_____	*chrom*	color	_____
18. *retro*gress	_____	*gress*	step	_____
19. *se*dition	_____	*it*	go	_____
20. *syn*thesis	_____	*the*	put, place	_____

V. Pure Delight

Finally, here is David McCord's famous and delightfu
little poem* for you to have fun with. It shows what happen
to some words when they have no prefixes to guide them. Ca
you ___sert the proper ___fixes?

GLOSS

> I know a little man, both ept and ert.
> On intro-? extro-? No, he's just a vert.
> Sheveled and couth and kempt, pecunious, ane,
> His image trudes upon the ceptive brain.
> When life turns sipid and the mind is traught,
> The spirit soars as I would sist it ought.
> Chalantly then, like any gainly goof,
> My digent self is sertive, choate,** loof.

---

* Copyright 1954 by David McCord. From *Odds Without Ends*, by permis
sion of Little, Brown & Co.
** Pronounced KO-ate.

8. Count Off!

"TO GET along anywhere on the Continent," a cynical traveler once said, "all you need to know of any man's language are the words 'How much?' and 'Too much!'" The casual European tourist, however, has discovered that to get full value to really know "how much too much" anything is, it's also a good idea to learn how to count.

When you set out to enrich your vocabulary, you become a tourist in the ancient world of Greece and Rome. You will find, too, that you'll be getting more value out of many words that you come across if you learn how to count from one to ten.

If you do, unlocking the mysteries of such words as (1) *monolithic* (2) *dichotomy* (3) *triptych* (4) *quadrennial* (5) *quintessence* (6) *hexagon* (7) *hebdomadal* (8) *octavo* (9) *novena* and (10) *decalogue* will be child's play—as easy as counting from one to ten. For that's exactly what we just did—using Latin and Greek numbers.

Besides, if you know your numerical prefixes, you won't be counted out the next time the life of the party turns to you and asks, "How many sides has a paragon?"

COUNTING OFF IN LATIN AND GREEK

(We are using the forms that count in English—those that appear most frequently as numerical prefixes.)

Latin No.	Combining Form	No.*	Greek	Combining Form
unus	uni	I	ΜΟΝΟΣ	mono (alone, only)
duo	du, bi	II	ΔΥΟ, ΔΙΣ	dis, dy, di
tres	tri	III	ΤΡΕΙΣ	tri
quattuor	quadr	IV	ΤΕΤΤΑΡΕΣ	tetra
quinque	quint	V	ΠΕΝΤΕ	penta
sex	sext	VI	'ΕΞ	hexa
septem	sept	VII	'ΕΠΤΑ	hepta
octo	octo	VIII	'ΟΚΤΩ	octo (okto)
novem	nov, non	IX	'ΕΝΝΕΑ	ennea
decem	decim	X	ΔΕΚΑ	deca (deka)

* No. is an abbreviation of *numero,* Latin for "by number."

Don't try to learn them as a list. You'll get to know them better as we enumerate the words and combining forms in the slow count we're going to make now.

UNUS, UNI   I   *MONO*   ΜΟΝΟΣ

One is an awesome, *uni*que number. It stands for the smallest number—one of any kind—and for the largest number—everything rolled up into one *uni*fied whole, one *uni*verse. It gives us our beautiful word at*one*ment (being *at one* with God and man) and our much sought-after ideal of *unity* —expressed so well in the motto of our country, *E pluribus unum.* Out of many—one! For out of thirteen colonies and ultimately fifty states was forged one mighty nation—one *union.*

A thing is *unique* when it is the only one of its kind. When we sing in *unison*, all of us try to sing one (and the same) sound. But Johnny-one-note is just a *mono*tone. *Uni*lateral actions are *one*-sided. *Uni*, from the Latin, and *sphere*, from the Greek, were combined to form *Unisphere*, the name of the symbol of the 1964 New York World's Fair.

A *mono*lith is a single huge stone (*lithia* water is mineral water and a *litho*graph is first designed on a stone block). *Mono*lithic is a stronger and more picturesque word than *uni*fied because of its stone base. For instance, the substitution of the word *unified* in the following sentence from the New York *Herald Tribune* would make the idea much less formidable:

> On the other hand, the formation of
> a *monolithic* labor organization would
> represent an awesome concentration of
> power.

A *mono*poly is a single control of sales. And a *monk* is one who lives al*one* in a *mon*astery!

Putting first things first is what we do when we use *prim* or *proto* at the beginning of a word. Both mean first, *prim* from Latin, *proto* from Greek. A *Prim*ate is a top-ranking church dignitary, an archbishop. A *prim*er is a first reader. "The forest *prim*eval" goes back to the *first ages* of the world, just as medi*eval* refers to the Middle Ages and co*eval* to things existing at the same time.

Proto gives us the word *protocol*, so often seen on page one of our newspapers. It means literally the first gluing, referring to the leaf which was glued to the rolls of papyrus and which contained an account of the manuscript. From this original meaning we get the two meanings most frequently found today. Here is one from the New York *Herald Tribune:*

> An official announcement said today
> that Poland and Czechoslovakia had
> signed a *protocol* that would open their
> frontiers immediately for normal com-
> mercial transactions.

Obviously, this *protocol* means a group of first, or preliminary negotiations discussed and agreed upon. But these days the word is more often used in another sense. Here's another sentence from the New York *Times:*

> In the official haste, the advance notice
> to the United Nations which *protocol*
> required was overlooked.

Here *protocol* deals not with the contents but with the *order* of procedure prescribed by diplomatic etiquette.

A *protagonist* is the first or leading character in a play, the chief participant in any action. The prefix is *proto*, not *pro;* *protagonist* should, therefore, not be used to mean *proponent.*

DUO, BI, DIS   *II*   *DI, DY*   ΔTO, ΔIΣ

We say that two is company but historically two is a *divisive* number. It immediately destroys the unity of one. We, therefore, find *dou*bt entering and *dis*sension rife.

To be *dou*btful or in a state of *du*biety is to be of two minds about something. The German word for doubt is *Zweifel*—with *Zwei,* the German word for two, sticking right out of it.

If the doubt is very serious, it may even be a *di*lemma, on the two horns of which one is usually impaled.

The word *di*plomacy has been unable to escape this taint of two-ness. The word itself comes from *diploma* which merely meant a paper folded double. Such a folded paper served as the credentials of a *diplomat.* So it's not really the *two* that's to blame but the *double*-talk or *du*plicity of diplomacy.

Bi gives us *bi*cameral, having two chambers (*camera*)—legislative—like our own Congress. *Bi*noculars are two (additional) eyes, and to com*bine* (*bini,* two at a time) is to put two and two together. *Bi*gamy literally means being married to two people at the same time. The following limerick shows how a young fellow who disliked *mono*gamy took advantage of his knowledge that *bi* = two:

> There was a young fellow of Lyme
> Who lived with three wives at a time;
> When they asked, "Why the third?"
> He replied, "One's absurd,
> And bigamy, Sir, is a crime!"

The most difficult of the words that stem from two is *dicho*tomy, but as soon as you recognize that it means a cutting into two, it's easy. Where there is a *dichotomy,* there are two divisions—two opposite schools of thought exist. The cutting is done by *tomy.* (See page 2).

TRES, TRI, TER   *III*   *TRI*   ΤΡΕΙΣ

Most of the words with three in them are fairly obvious. A three-footed stand for holding a camera is a *tri*pod; if it holds a kettle it's a *tri*vet. A *tri*ad is a group of three. When the three are pictures or carvings on folding panels, side by side, you have a *tri*ptych (pronounced *triptick*). A major work of literature or music in three parts is a *tri*logy, although the word *triptych* is used when they are all presented together in one volume.

The Latin word for a crossroad is *trivium* (*ter*, three together + *vium*, from *via*, a road). The meaning of this word was extended to denote a public square, street, or highway. What was said and heard there was *trivialis*, of little consequence, ordinary, commonplace, whence our word *trivial*. *Trivia*, a plural form of *trivium*, has been taken over into English directly in its late Latin meaning of trifles, insignificant details.

A word one reads often these days in connection with free elections and a free press is un*tram*meled. A *trammel* is a net of three layers, which like any net can enmesh or entangle the *feet*. Untrammeled elections are, therefore, un*fet*tered.

QUATTUOR, QUADR   *IV*   *TETRA*   ΤΕΤΤΑΡΕΣ

Four is a square, yielding *quadr*angle, *quadr*ilateral, *squadr*on, and *quadr*ille, a square dance. *Quadr*ennial (four + annual) elections are held every four years. A *quatr*ain is a four-line stanza, like the famous *Rubaiyat* of Omar Khayyam (*Rubaiyat* is Persian for *quatr*ains).

Stop at any gas station, and the pump containing the more expensive gas will have the word TETRAETHYL on it. *Tetra* appears in hundreds of chemical and geometrical combinations.

Tetra is the combining form, but another word for four via Latin is *tessera* which brings us back to the square we started with. Whatever is formed of little squares as in mosaic work or marked like a checkerboard is *tessella*ted.

QUINQUE, QUINT   *V*   *PENTA*   ΠΕΝΤΕ

As the numbers become larger the harvest of words, excluding the technical, becomes smaller.

Five yields *quin*quennium, a handy word to indicate a recurring period of five years, and *quint*essence, literally the fifth or highest essence, because the Greeks recognized only four elements (earth, air, fire and water). The word therefore means the purest, finest form or expression of anything. When Hamlet speaks of man he says, "And yet to me what is this quintessence of dust?"

From *penta* we get *penta*gon, a five-sided figure, the *Penta*teuch, the first five books of the Bible, and the *penta*thlon Olympic events in which each athlete takes part in five athletic contests: leaping, foot racing, wrestling, throwing the discus, and hurling the javelin.

SEX, SEXT	VI	HEXA	EΞ

Sex and *hex* sound alike and are English words, but here they are just six of one (Latin *sex*) and a half a dozen of another (Greek *hex*). To the naked eye most snowflakes are exquisitely patterned *hexa*gons.

A *sext*ant, that very important navigator's instrument, gets its name from the fact that its arc is one-sixth of a circle. A *sem*ester is a six months' period, now generally used for a school term of any length.

And what is the word for someone in his sixties? We'll let Helen Westley, veteran Theater Guild actress, answer that one. While she was working on a set in Hollywood, an extra gushed up to her.

"Why, Miss Westley, what are *you* doing in this picture?"

"My dear, haven't you heard," replied Miss Westley, "I furnish the *sex*agenarian appeal."

SEPTEM	VII	HEPTA	ΕΠΤΑ

Of course, there's always *Septem*ber, and the mystery of why this pleasant ninth month masquerades under the number seven is cleared up when we recall that the Roman year used to begin in March. In 153 B. C., January became the first month, probably in honor of Janus, the Roman god of beginnings. *Quint*ilis and *Sext*ilis, the names of the fifth and sixth months under the old system, were kept, just as we keep the names *Septem*ber, *Octo*ber, *Novem*ber, and *Decem*ber. Eventually, in honor of *Juli*us Caesar and *August*us Caesar, Quintilis and Sextilis became July and August respectively. And a good thing too. Can you imagine the prosecutor in one of those TV courtroom scenes pointing an accusing finger at the glamorous defendant and asking, "And where were you on the night of Sextilis the sixteenth?"

The famous translation of the Old Testament into Greek is called the *Septua*gint, because seventy scholars (not all of them *septua*genarians) are said to have worked on it.

Hepta (hept) is the form that appears in scientific words, as for example *hepta*ne, a hydrocarbon containing *seven* atoms of carbon to sixteen of hydrogen in a molecule. *Hebd*omadal, which comes to us from Greek via Latin, is a word that was once more frequently used. All this imposing word means is "occurring every seven days" (i.e. weekly).

OCTO	*VIII*	*OCTO*	OKTΩ

Octo (Greek) gives us *octa*gon, eight sides, and *octo*pus, eight feet. In San Francisco recently a biologist discovered that Willie, the aquarium octopus, had only seven tentacles—with no stump to show that it ever had had an eighth. The reporter of this news item asks, "Does that make Willie a septopus?" No. To keep the record straight it makes Willie a *hepta*pus, because *pus* is really *pous*, the Greek word for foot, and should be preceded by *hepta*, the Greek word for seven.

NOVEM, NON	*IX*	*ENNEA*	ENNEA

We have lots of phrases with *nine* in them like "a nine days' wonder," "a cat's nine lives," "nine points of the law," but very few words.

There's *nove*na, a nine days' religious devotion, and of course, *Novem*ber. Sports headlines tell us that the annual athletic meets held at Princeton are called the *Nona*gonal Games, because nine colleges take part.

DECEM, DECIM	*X*	*DECA*	ΔΕΚΑ

But ten gives us a spate of words—from the simple or obvious like *dime* and *decim*al to one that tells a story—*dicker*. The Latin word *decuria*, a set of ten, was applied to the units of trade in hides and skin between the Romans and "barbarian" tribes. History repeated itself on this continent when the same word in its changed form *dicker* was used in the sense of *haggle* in the fur trade between the settlers and the Indians. "To *dicker* and to swap" occurs in the writings of James Fenimore Cooper.

If we want to refer to the Ten Commandments in one word we have the word *Deca*logue.

To *decimin*ate originally meant to kill one in ten, generally as a punishment for mutiny. Today our newspapers use it in the sense of an*nihil*ate, to reduce to nothing.

Corresponding to the pentathlon, there is an even mightier

athletic feat, the *deca*thlon, which tests an athlete's skill i
ten events.

NIHIL (nothing), NULLUS (none)   OTΔEN *(nothing*

Nihil is the Latin for nothing. Compress it a little and you
get our word *nil*. Expand *null* a little and you get *nullif*
and an*nul*. *Utopia* (*ou*, not) means *No Place* (see p. 000)

A report in the *Times* tells us of "a wave of *nihilism*
among the youth of Germany and other defeated countries,"
and then helpfully goes on to explain that "there is a tend
ency to believe in nothing." With a capital letter Nihilisn
refers to a terrorist organization in Czarist Russia given :
name and fame in Turgenev's *Fathers and Sons*.

CENTUM   *C*   *HECATON, HECTO*   EKATON

Centum gives us the words *cent, century, centenary*, an
*centi*pede.

From the Greek word we get *hecatomb*, the slaughter o
sacrifice of a large number of people. Originally it meant the
sacrifice of a hundred cattle, usually bulls (the *b* is from *bous*
bull, ox, cow). A *hecto*graph is a duplicating machine that
turns out a hundred copies or more.

MILLE   *M**   *KILO*   XIΛIOI

Mille gives us *mile* (a thousand paces in the Roman mile
and *millennium*. *Millennium* or *chiliad* may be used literally
to mean a period of one thousand years. But more often
it is used for some far-off year when man will have re
molded "this sorry scheme of things entire . . . nearer to
the heart's desire." At any rate the child was wrong whe
said, "A millennium is something like a centennial only i
has more feet." We, who know that *ped* is the root for foot
recognize that the child was thinking of *mille*pede and *centi*
pede.

And that gives us the cue for our last paragraph, in which
we feature the word sesqui*ped*alian—*sesqui* means one and :
half as in sesquicentennial. A writer who is addicted to the
use of words that seem a foot and a half long is culpable o
sesquipedality! The *Literary Digest* invented a term for ex
cessive use of long words: *hyperpolysyllabicsesquipedalianism*

---

* The Roman numbers C and M are not related to the words centum o
mille. It's just a coincidence. The symbol for one thousand was CƆ, resem
bling an M. Half (the right half) became D, five hundred.

I. Can You Figure These Out?

After reading the sentences below, answer the questions by using numbers. Answers for these tests will be found on page 364.

A. When General Dwight D. Eisenhower received the Navy's Distinguished Service Medal, he jokingly remarked, "I'm now really triphibious."

To how many branches of the service did he imply that he belonged?

B. Therefore, if ancient Greek can be stretched to describe this political situation, the President was confronted with a trilemma or even a tetralemma, by the Senate votes today.

How many choices or doubts confronted the President?

C. Up until 1947 the Nonagonal meet was known as the Heptagonal Games.

How many colleges competed until 1947? How many were added to the competition in 1947?

D. In 1947, Trinity Parish celebrated its quarter millennium.

Select the figure showing how long Trinity had been in existence: (a) 500 (b) 1000 (c) 250 (d) 400.

E. Philadelphia held a sesquicentennial exposition in 1926.

In what year did the event that was being celebrated occur?

F. John Masefield's "Cargoes" opens with the magnificent line:

"Quinquireme of Nineveh from distant Ophir."

A quinquireme (more properly quinquereme) was an ancient galley propelled by oars. How many banks of oars or rowers to a bench did it have?

II. Assorted Numbers

Fill in the blanks with the correct number-words or number-prefixes. Each dot represents a letter.

A. When G. B. Shaw was now in his nineties, he was often referred to as a hardy . . . .

B. The . . . . . . centennial of Cervantes' birth (1547–1616) was celebrated in 1947.

C. *Animus* means mind. A measure agreed upon without a dissenting vote is passed . . animously and a condition of perfect agreement is called . . animity.

D. *Zoon* (plural *zoa*) means a living thing. Very small animals which represent early or first forms of life are called . . . . . zoa.

97

III. Count the Impostor Out!

One of the words in each group is masquerading as a number. It looks like a word whose root is a number, but it is only an impostor. Cross off the word in each group which doesn't *count*.

1. (a) unit (b) unison (c) unify (d) monitor (e) monotheism
2. (a) duplex (b) dupe (c) bicameral d) biscuit (e) dilemma
3. (a) triad (b) trinity (c) trireme (d) tripe (e) tertiary
4. (a) quart (b) squadron (c) quarrel (d) quarry (e) quadrilateral
5. (a) cinquefoil (b) quinquennium (c) quince (d) quintessence (e) quintet
6. (a) sextet (b) siesta (c) sexton (d) sextuplet (e) sextant
7. (a) septum (b) heptarchy (c) hebdomadal (d) septet (e) September
8. (a) oculist (b) octagon (c) octopus (d) octave (e) October
9. (a) nonagon (b) nonentity (c) noon (d) novena (e) enneasyllabic
10. (a) decalogue (b) decimal (c) decade (d) decadent (e) dime

IV. Treasure Hunt

You may not believe it but the numbers one to ten are concealed in these words. We've added two supernumeraries, one meaning 14 and the other 40. Can you file them in their numerical instead of their alphabetical order?

a. farthing
b. fortnight
c. nonce
d. noon
e. octavo
f. punch (the drink)
g. quarantine
h. septentrional
i. siesta
j. tithe
k. troika
l. zwieback

NUTBURGER
CHEESEBURG
FISHBURGER
VEALBURGE
MUTTONBUR
PORKBURG
CHICKENBUR
SAUSAGEBU

REA

"We've got some made with ham, too—but we don't know what to call them."

---

9. Attachable-Detachable Parts

DO YOU remember the name of the Hunchback of Notre Dame? It is a peculiar name, strangely appropriate to the weird occupant of the cathedral bell-tower. Victor Hugo named him Quasimodo after the opening words of a service sung on the first Sunday after Easter: *"Quasi modo geniti*

---

* Drawing reproduced courtesy *Collier's.*

infantes . . ." (In the same way as new-born babes . . .) Quasimodo's intelligence remained that of an infant almost all his life. One-eyed, hunch-backed, bow-legged, he was hardly anything but "an-almost-but-not-quite-there" person— a *quasi*-human being.

In this chapter we deal with attachable and detachable parts like *quasi, pseudo, crypto,* and *neo.* Since these parts are added to already existing words, the only problem is to know what *quasi, pseudo, crypto,* and *neo* do to words—how they affect the meaning of words we already know.

QUASI

A rose is a rose is a rose, but when it's only "mighty lak a rose" it's a quasi-rose. When you feel that something is almost but not quite the real thing you can use the attachable part *quasi.* That's what a New York City magistrate did when he remarked, "Garages are *quasi*-public utilities." What he meant was that if garages weren't legally public utilities like the railroads, they were public utilities in all but name.

In the same way a *Times* correspondent who didn't want to call the Greek government an actual dictatorship defined it as a *quasi*-dictatorship. Another *Times* writer had similar reservations about the freedom of Trans-Jordan, which, he wrote, had enjoyed "twenty-five years of *quasi*-independence under Britain's mandate." *Quasi* itself has the same type of independence. It comes under the mandate of other words. It's a free lance like the professional soldiers who sold their services. They were *quasi*-independent, too, going wherever they wished but effective only when they attached themselves. They had no roots. So, all you can do with *quasi* is to attach it but you can't form any new words with it as a root.

PSEUDO

Pseudo, false, is close to *quasi* in meaning. You can attach it to other words to indicate that here we have something masquerading as the real thing, the genuine article. A magazine editorial states:

> Another few years of the archpragmatic [*arch* is another attachable-detachable part meaning chief, principal] New Deal, for example, and we too might have slid sideways into *pseudo*socialism, like England.

Pseudo can be used as a word by itself meaning pretended, feigned, counterfeit, spurious or it can be fused into a word like *pseudo*nym, a false or pen name.

CRYPTO

The words to which *crypto* is attached become not false, but hidden or secret. Winston Churchill gave prominence to this attachable part in April, 1947, when he started a controversy by stating publicly that "a visitor from the United States . . . has foregathered with that happily small minority of *crypto*-Communists." In October, 1947, Senator Pepper declared, "The *crypto*-Fascists may as well know that the people of America throw down before their evil feet the gauntlet of defiance." A *crypto*-anything is one who is accused of working secretly for an objective he is unwilling to declare.

A *crypt* is an underground or secret vault. *Cryptic* remarks conceal their meaning. A *crypto*gram is a message whose meaning is unlocked or deciphered by a secret code. You'll find *crypt* hidden in apo*crypha*l which once meant secret but now means of doubtful authenticity, fictitious, spurious. Apo *crypha* are certain books of the Bible which are additions to the generally accepted canon. *Krypton* is an element forming part of the air, a hidden element because it occurs in the ratio of one part in a million.

NEO

An element discovered in the same year as krypton was named *neon* or the new element. Those orange-red lights on signs were named after the gaseous element in the bulbs, an element discovered by the French scientist G. Claude. *Neo* is attached to words to indicate a new form or development. *Neo*-Gothic refers to a style of Gothic architecture which was used in this country and England a century ago. *Neo*-classic and *neo*-Greek architecture imitated the Greek and Roman style of building. The term *neo*-Fascists is used a great deal in newspapers to describe those who are attempting to revive fascist ideology.

Neo may attach itself as a free-lance prefix or it may combine with other roots. The *Neo*lithic inhabitants of Europe lived during the latter or new part of the Stone (*lithos*) Age.

A *neo*phyte is a beginner or novice. A *neo*logism is a newly coined word (*logos*, word).

AUTO

Auto (from the Greek *autos*), found in so many words as a free lance (as in *auto*mation is a mechanical contrivance that

means *self*. An *auto*maton is a mechanical contrivance that is *self*-moving like a man. A man who acts in a mechanical fashion is also called an *automaton* or a *robot*, the name given to the mechanical men created in Capek's play *R.U.R.* Too new for our unabridged dictionary are *automated* and *automation*, words coined to keep pace with the marvels of an age in which machines, mechanical brains, and accelerated systems of procedure and calculations do the work of many men in so much less time. The prophecies of *R. U. R.* have come true in reverse: the machines have become the mechanical men. (See *robot*, p. 237.)

AUTOMATION BY ROBOTS
But Human Brains Produced It

When colonies want *auto*nomy, they seek the right of *self*-government. Sovereign states seek *self*-sufficiency; their goal is *aut*archy (also *aut*arky). An *auto*psy is the act of seeing with one's own eyes, more specifically the examination of a dead body to ascertain the reasons for death. *Auto*chthonous (from *autos*, self, and *chthon*, earth) means arising from the earth or the land it*self*, hence not coming from elsewhere but native, indigenous, aboriginal.

CIDE

An autopsy may determine that the cause of death was sui*cide*. Here we have another *self* word, the Latin *sui*. However, we are not interested here in the beginning of the word, for *cide* is attached at the end of a word. When so attached *cide* spells Murder! Our whodunits deal not only with homi*cide* but with infanti*cide*, patri*cide*, parri*cide*, matri*cide*, sorori*cide*, uxori*cide*, etc. About the house and garden we can use germi*cide*s, insecti*cide*s, and pesti*cide*s. The Nazi crime of wiping out national, racial, and religious groups needed a new word. Dr. Ralph Lemkin added *cide* to a Greek word element meaning nation or group and produced the now much-used word geno*cide*.

Dr. Oliver Wendell Holmes, poet and essayist, also used *cide* to coin the word verbi*cide*, a crime he described in these words:

> Life and language are alike sacred. Homicide and verbicide
> —that is, violent treatment of a word with fatal results to its
> legitimate meaning, which is its life—are alike forbidden.

PHIL

One who treats words with love and affection, is a *philolo-gist* (*phil*, love). *Phil* and *phile* are used either at the beginning or end of words. Anglo*philes* admire England, and Russo*philes* like all things Russian. A Franco*phile* is not a follower of Franco but a person devoted to France. *Phil* is a favorite with word coiners, or *neo*logists. Christopher Morley once described Sir Arthur Conan Doyle as an "infracanino-phile." Divide that up into *infra* (below), *canin* (dog), and *phile* (love), put the parts together again and you have "a lover of the underdog."

One who loves all his fellow men and helps them is a *phil*anthropist (*anthropos*, man, as in *anthropo*logy). A *phil*anderer is also in love but he plays at love-making. A *phil*atelist loves stamps as a *phil*osopher loves wisdom.

PHOBE AND PHOBIA

A *phobia* is a morbid dislike or an unreasonable dread or fear,* and the people who have it are *phobes*. So we have Russo*phobes*, Anglo*phobes*, and Franco*phobes*. A person who fears strangers and the people of all nations not his own is suffering from *xeno*phobia (*xenos*, strange).

Some people are afraid of high places. Their fear is called *acro*phobia (*acros*, highest, as in *acro*bat and *Acro*polis, the high hill of the city—*polis*—of Athens.) Richard Maney wrote of the 1947 Brooklyn Dodgers that they were suffering from *acro*phobia because they slumped so often after reaching the dizzy heights of first place.

There are at the time of this writing some two hundred catalogued phobias. Do cats bother you? Then you are suffering from *ailuro*phobia. There is or there can be a word for each specific fear. When President Roosevelt in his First Inaugural Address said, "The only thing we have to fear is fear itself," there was a word for that—*phobo*phobia.

PSEUDO-ATTACHABLES

A *hamburger* was originally a Hamburger steak, getting its name from the city in Germany where these chopped steaks became famous. It is therefore obvious that *burger* is not a real ending and that it certainly doesn't mean "chopped," but that didn't stop the neologists, who needed new names for the

* So, rabies is called *hydrophobia* because the victim is unable to swallow or even bear the sight of water.

103

delights they were chopping up and putting between two slices of bread. We soon had cheeseburgers, chickenburgers, clamburgers, spamburgers, barbecueburgers, nutburgers, and even oomphburgers. The English began doing it too. A dispatch from London tells us that "whale meat was served in the form of chopped steak with sauce. Those who ate it claimed that it tasted like chopped steak. There was no flavor of fish. That was why they called it 'whaleburger.'"

The name of another place that has been chopped up to give us an attachable part is the ancient village of Marathon, from which Pheidippides is said to have made his famous 22-mile run to bring news of victory to Athens. *Athon* has been added to words as if it meant "endurance contest." So we see such words as *walkathon, danceathon, pushathon, telethon, guessathon, write-a-thon, readathon,* and *talkathon,* a handy word to describe what happens when Senators stage a filibuster.

I. What Do the Following Kill?

Choose the proper word from Column B to match the words in Column A. Answers for these tests will be found on page 364.

A.	*B.*
1. regicide	a. snakes
2. vermicide	b. parents
3. sororicide	c. dandruff
4. parricide	d. bees
5. canicide	e. wife
6. apicide	f. dogs
7. herpicide	g. birds
8. uxoricide	h. children
9. filicide	i. worms
10. avicide	j. monkey
	k. sister
	l. king

II. Who Are These Ologists?

A. In medicine *ologist* denotes a specialist in a specific type of disease. Try to match the name of the specialist in the left-hand column with his specialty on the right.

1. otologist	a. skin
2. rhinologist	b. nerves
3. ophthalmologist	c. women's diseases

4. neurologist   d. nose
5. cardiologist   e. heart
6. dermatologist   f. ears
7. gynecologist   g. eyes
8. pathologist   h. old age
9. gerontologist   i. nature and origin of disease
10. endocrinologist   j. glands of internal secretion

B. And here are some other *ologists* in other branches of science and learning.

1. psychologist   a. insects
2. ornithologist   b. words
3. archaeologist   c. caves
4. speleologist   d. earthquakes
5. herpetologist   e. poisons
6. paleontologist   f. reptiles
7. toxicologist   g. fossils and other forms of
8. etymologist   early life
9. seismologist   h. birds
10. entomologist   i. former history through ex-
                               cavations
                            j. mind and behavior

When you learn these words, you not only fix the meaning of the ending but you also add some useful roots and word elements to your word-building stock! Check with the dictionary for the unfamiliar ones.

III. Who Is the Ruler?

Cracy is an element meaning *rule*. We are most familiar with the word *democracy* or the *rule* of the people (*demos*), but there have been many other types of rule in history. See how many you can identify by matching the two columns. Once again check with a dictionary. You'll find some useful roots in these words.

Form of Government	*Rule by*
1. theocracy	a. women
2. gerontocracy	b. nobility or elite
3. plutocracy	c. the worst citizens
4. bureaucracy	d. mob
5. gynecocracy	e. church authorities
6. aristocracy	f. desk officials
7. ochlocracy	g. wealth
8. kakistocracy	h. old men
9. timocracy	i. absolute monarch
10. autocracy	j. love of honor

IV. What Are We Afraid of?

Fears may be magnified by the long technical names given to them but their names may not seem so formidable if you learn their roots. Match the names in the left-hand column with the specific fears on the right.

1. astrophobia	a. closed space
2. ballistophobia	b. light
3. claustrophobia	c. hair
4. ergophobia	d. celestial space
5. nyctophobia	e. missiles
6. ochlophobia	f. food
7. panophobia	g. crowds
8. photophobia	h. everything in general
9. sitophobia	i. night
10. trichophobia	j. work

10. Every Word Has a History

WHAT made history almost 2,500 years ago made news again only yesterday. This is how the New York *Times* reported the story:

> ATHENS, Aug. 15—Archaelogists of the American School of Classical Studies at Athens finished today the twelfth season of excavations in the Agora, the main public square of ancient Athens and one of the oldest continuously inhabited places in the world. On the site of the museum the archaeologists this year found several hundred ostraka, pieces of pottery on which the Athenians of the fifth century before Christ scratched the names of persons they wished exiled for ten years. Themistocles, Hippocrates and Aristides were among the names.

And this is how a reporter of an earlier age, the famou
Greek historian and biographer Plutarch, handed down th
story of Aristides and the ostraka.

> "As therefore they [the Athenian voters] were writing the
> names on the sherds [*potsherds* or *shards,* pieces of pottery]
> it is reported that an illiterate clownish fellow, giving Aris-
> tides his sherd, supposing him a common citizen, begged him
> to write *Aristides* upon it; and he being surprised and asking
> him if Aristides had ever done him any injury, 'None at all,'
> said he, 'neither know I the man; but I am tired of hearing
> him everywhere called the Just.' Aristides, hearing this, is
> said to have made no reply, but returned the sherd with his
> own name inscribed."

Because in voting the Athenian citizens voted by castin
oyster shells (*ostraka*) or potsherds into an urn, we have th
words *ostracism* and *ostracize* today. The Athenians use
ostracism as a method of exiling citizens who might becom
dangerous to the state. Those whose names appeared on
majority of the shells, with a minimum of 6000 adverse vote:
were banished. Today, ostracism is generally a social rathe
than a political act. When we ostracize a person, we avoid hi
company or bar him from our society.

Every English word has a history if, like the excavators o
the Agora, we know where and how to look for it. Diggin
up the past of a word and tracking down its origin is calle
etymology. In Chapters 3 and 4, when we took words apar
and uncovered their roots, we were doing spadework i
etymology.

Now we're going to set out on an etymological tour throug
history, shuttling back and forth in time and space, stoppin
here and there for words that tell interesting stories or revea
customs and institutions of bygone days. We shall find tha
when we know the story behind a word, when we can tie th
word to the kite of history, we can hold on to it more firml
in our minds.

IN THE MARKET PLACE OF ATHENS

So, without further rambling, we'll begin our etymologica
journey in the Agora of Athens, where the citizens gathere
to ostracize Aristides. This public square, like the villag
green and commons of our New England towns, is one o

he milestones on man's road to democratic thought and
ction. Here the freedom-loving citizens of Athens assembled
o exercise their democratic rights, to listen to their great
rators and statesmen, and to discuss freely the affairs of the
ay.

Although the word *Agora* is generally associated with the
idea of a market or open space, it really means a place for
iscussion. *Agora* is derived from a Greek verb meaning to
peak or discuss. On the one hand, the idea of a public square
s kept in the word *agora*phobia, a fear of open spaces; and
n the other hand, the idea of *to speak* appears in such words
s cate*gory*, pane*gyric*, and par*egoric*.

Let's stay a moment with the last of these three words.
You'll find the other two in the exercises.) A *paregoric* is a
oothing medicine or anodyne. How does a verbal root mean-
ng to speak find its way into medicine? Etymology resolves
uch problems. The Greek verb *paregoreuein*, containing the
refix *para*, beside, literally means to be at one's side with
vords, to offer advice or comfort. Now think of a mother's or
loctor's comforting bed*side* manner. Words of encourage-
ment are often as good as medicine. So, even among the
Greeks, their word corresponding to *paregoric* meant a sooth-
ng and comforting medicine.

COME TO THE FAIR!

From the Agora or market place of Athens, we travel in
ime and space to another market. We arrive at the cathedral
own of Ely, England, where a famous fair is taking place.
Let's call the century the sixteenth and the day, October 17,
St. Audrey's Day. People have come from miles around to
ttend the fair to purchase the gay finery on display.

St. Audrey's Fair is particularly noted for its fine silk neck-
aces or neckties worn by the girls of the time. At first they
vere called St. Audrey's laces but soon the clipped speech of
he people turned *St. Audrey* laces into *tawdry* laces just as it
urned *St. Denis* into Sidney. Many a swain found that a
awdry lace was the way to a girl's heart. An old ballad tells
us of the complaint of one luckless lad:

> One time I gave thee a paper of pins
> Another time a tawdry lace;
> And if thou wilt not grant my love
> In truth I'll die before thy face.

Cheap and showy imitations of the fine tawdry lace soon found their way into the market places and fairs of England. And so the word *tawdry* took on its present connotation of cheap and showy.

Not all who came to the fair came to buy. Fairs were ready-made for the traveling quacks of the period. Arriving at a fair, these "pitchmen" would mount a platform and attract a crowd with stories, tricks, or juggling. When the crowd was sufficiently large and interested, they would sell their remedies. These traveling players and salesmen, the counterpart of our "grifters," were called *mountebanks*, from the Italian phrase *montare in banco*, to get up on a bench. Today we apply the word *mountebank* to a buffoon or to one who uses cheap tricks to gain attention or notoriety.

Sometimes, to build up interest and increase sales, the mountebank or charlatan employed a young attendant as part of the act. This "shill" would eat or pretend to eat toads which were considered poisonous by the superstitious people of the time. Soon the lad, a good actor, would be writhing in pain. At this moment his master would try out his bottle of medicine on his *toadeater* or *toady*. The remedy worked like magic, and the toady was soon smiling gratefully. Anyone who performed such servile work for a master or superior came to be called a *toady*, a cringing, fawning person, a servile flatterer, a *sycophant*.

And *sycophant* takes us back to Greece again, to Athens in the district of Attica. Although etymologists are of the opinion that the explanation of how this word got its meaning is not certain, we are including it because the interesting story helps fix its meaning. According to Plutarch, "the exportation of figs was once unlawful, and the informer against the delinquents [was] called a sycophant." Literally, *sycophant* means one who shows (*phan*, to show, as in dia*phan*ous, showing through) figs (*sycon*, a fig, as in *syca*more, a tree allied to the fig and mulberry family). Because of the informer's cringing and servile manner, *sycophant* was next applied to a toady or parasite, a meaning which it has today.

SPARTAN SHORT CUT

For the origin of our next word, *laconic*, we travel to Athens' great rival, Sparta in the district of Laconia. The Spartans have left us no great speeches as the Athenians did. They were noted for their military discipline and achievement and for their sparing use of words.

Many collections have been made of their short answers and terse expressions. In this etymological excursion we have time to listen to only two of them.

Plutarch tells us about an exchange of messages between Philip of Macedon, father of Alexander the Great, and the Spartans. When Philip invaded Greece, he asked the Spartans whether they wished him to come as friend or foe. This was brief enough but the Spartans upheld their reputation for not wasting words when they returned the one-word answer, "Neither!"

Erasmus, the great Renaissance scholar, tells another story about Philip and the Spartans. Philip had sent a long list of demands. The Spartans sent it back and at the bottom wrote the single word, "No."

In our own times we have had another example of these short defiant thrusts at an enemy. We refer of course to the historic answer given by General Anthony C. McAuliffe at Bastogne in December, 1944, when the Germans called on him to surrender. We give it to you in General McAuliffe's own words:

> On the afternoon of December 22, when German shells were hacking Bastogne to bits and all my men were holed in cellars, two blindfolded kraut officers arrived with surrender demands. There were two written demands for surrender, one in English and the other in German. They told me there was only one possibility to save my troops from annihilation—surrender.
> I read the message in English and used the first word that came to my head, "Nuts." Then one of my officers pointed out that the Germans had submitted a formal document and would want a formal reply. We thought it over and decided, why not. And so we wrote a formal reply, "Nuts."

The Spartans would certainly have applauded General McAuliffe's reply, a true descendant of their defiant answers hurled at Philip. The Spartans have set their trademark upon these sharp and pointed statements, so like the short swords they themselves used. Expressions of this kind are called *laconisms*, after Laconia, the name of the district inhabited by the Spartans. A *laconic* reply or statement is one that is direct and to the point, pithy, terse, concise and succinct.

BY THE RIVER JORDAN

The story of another word is connected with a habit o speech. For this one we go back to Biblical times and to the banks of the River Jordan. The Gileadites, fighting under thei leader Jephthah, have defeated the Ephraimites. To distinguish the fleeing enemy from his own men, Jephthah takes advantage of a speech difference between the Gileadites and the men o the routed enemy who are trying to escape. Here is the story as it is told in Judges 12:5, 6—

> And the Gileadites took the passages of Jordan before the Ephraimites: and it was so, that when those Ephraimites which were escaped said, Let me go over; that the men of Gilead said unto him, Art thou an Ephraimite? If he said, Nay;
> Then said they unto him, Say now Shibboleth; and he said Sibboleth: for he could not frame to pronounce it right. Then they took him, and slew him at the passages of Jordan: and there fell at that time of the Ephraimites forty and two thousand.

Shibboleth (a Hebrew word meaning an ear of corn or a stream) was the test word chosen to separate friend from foe The Ephraimites, unable to pronounce the sound *sh*, were recognized by that test and slain.

Thousands of years later on the peninsula of Bataan his tory repeated itself. The Japanese were successfully infiltrat ing our lines by learning the password and posing as friendly Filipinos. On January 20, 1942 the Americans put a stop to this practice by the simple expedient of choosing *lollapaloosa* as the password. Since the Japanese are unable to pronounce the sound of *l*, of which *lollapaloosa* has its share, the sentrie were ordered to fire upon anyone who could not say the word. The closest the Japanese got to our lines was "rorra paroosa."

Nearer home, American citizens were entering Canada to escape the draft. Immigration officials found it difficult to distinguish between Canadian and American citizens. This time a language difference was used as a shibboleth. When they were in doubt, officials asked the tourist to name the last letter of the alphabet. Americans always called it "zee" but the Canadians, like the French and British, called it "zed."

These tests based on speech and language differences are true and literal shibboleths, but today the word *shibboleth* is used in a different sense to mean a watchword or oft-repeated slogan rather than a password used as a test. A book reviewer in the *Saturday Review* used it in this sense: "the ancient American *shibboleths* of success—save your money, keep your shoes shined, and get to work on time." Often the word *shibboleth* is used to characterize a phrase to which only lip service is given. "What we need today," someone has said, "are not the *shibboleths* of democracy buts its dynamic practice."

ROME, THE ETERNAL

Democracy, as we all know, means the rule of the people—all the people. But there have been times in the world's history when great sections of the people were looked on with contempt by their rulers as unfit to take part in the duties of citizens. So it was in the very early days of Rome. A king, Servius Tullius, divided the people into five classes to contribute to the state's defense. He reasoned that those who had the most property should be called upon to contribute the most to its defense. However, he omitted one group, the class having little or no wealth. Later writers called this sixth group *proletarii*, "a name," says Aulus Gellius, "derived from their duty and function of producing offspring, for although they could not greatly aid the state with what small property they had, yet they added to the population of their country by their power of begetting children."

Because *proles* is a Latin word for offspring and because the poor were *prolific* "and served the state not with their property but with their offspring" they were given the name *proletarii* from which come our words *proletarian* and *proletariat*.

However, when Rome became a world power it called on the *proletarii* and others to aid it. Before that time, without the services of its poorer members, the Roman state waged small wars with neighboring tribes to extend its power over the Italian peninsula. In one of these wars, in the year 458 B.C., the Romans inflicted a crushing defeat on a tribe called the Aequi. Cincinnatus, the commander and legal dictator of the Romans, said

> . . . he did not require the blood of the Aequi; they might go, but, that they might at last be forced to confess that their nation had been defeated and subdued, they should pass beneath the yoke as they departed. A yoke was fashioned of three spears, two being fixed in the ground and the third laid across them and made fast. Under this yoke the dictator sent the Aequi.*

---

* Livy's *History of Rome* translated by B. O. Foster in the Loeb Library.

This custom of making a defeated army pass under a yoke was called *subjugatio* (*sub*, under and *jugum*, a yoke). The defeated soldiers were made to crawl in single file under the improvised yoke. The Roman commander had achieved his purpose—he had *subjugated* the enemy.

We still keep the picturesque ceremony of passing under a yoke but apply it under more pleasant and romantic conditions. Pictures of West Point weddings show the bride and groom marching under "an arch of swords." At a ski wedding couples have been photographed passing under upraised skis; at weddings of baseball players, under crossed bats. Of course, the symbol of the yoke here has nothing to do with *subjugation*. The relationship is purely *conjugal*—the bride and groom are joined together (*jug*, join, and *con*, together).

Some still doubt whether the man who wanted to build a military empire greater than the Roman Empire, who tried to *subjugate* the whole world is really dead. But if you read *The Last Days of Hitler*, by H. R. Trevor-Roper, there can be little doubt. "The characters in this latter-day Götterdämmerung," an advertisement tells us, "include Hitler's fantastic court of toadies, quack doctors, astrologers and would-be betrayers. Enacted against a grotesque background —an underground bunker in the heart of Berlin—the story culminates in the suicides and ritual burning" of Hitler and some of his entourage. A reviewer refers to this manner of Hitler's death as his self-*immolation*. And that is precisely what Hitler wanted his death to mean to the Germans, an act of martyrdom and sacrifice.

Immolation, a sacrifice, comes from the Latin word *mola*, ground grain or meal. In Roman religious practices, the priest would sprinkle sanctified ground grain and salt on the animal's head. The sprinkling with meal or ground grain was technically the *immolatio*. It was a preparatory act but later came to mean the sacrifice itself.

We linger on in Rome but we let the years roll by, years that see Rome lose her military supremacy. However, she remains the Eternal City; for she has become the religious capital of the western world. At the head is the Pope, and our next word is concerned with the election of a Pope. In the year 1274, in order to hasten the election of a new Pope and to prevent outside interference, the procedure in use today was officially adopted.

After the death of a Pope, the College of Cardinals is convened and meets in a walled-off section of the Vatican. The

Marshal locks the door from the outside, and a designated cardinal locks it from the inside. The door is not opened again until a new Pope has been elected. Each morning and evening the cardinals vote. If no candidate gets the required two-thirds vote, the ballots are burned in a stove whose chimney extends through a window of the Sistine Chapel. Straw is added to show the spectators outside by its thick smoke that the new Pope has not yet been chosen. This meeting is called a *conclave*, literally a meeting locked with (*con*) a key (*clav*). The word *conclave* is today applied to any large or important meeting.

MONASTERY BELLS

To other customs and institutions of the church centuries ago we are indebted for additional interesting words. During the dark ages of Europe's history the monks kept learning alive through their devoted labors in the monasteries. They copied by hand the manuscripts of the great works of ancient authors and set down the services and holy books of the Church.

The monks adorned their manuscripts, especially those made for use in church services, with beautiful decorations painted in bright colors and gold. They followed the practice of Roman scribes who used red ink for headings and special parts of chapters. Such a special heading or initial letter in red was called a *rubric* (from *ruber*, Latin for red). Since the heading in red often gave instructions, the word *rubric* came to mean a directive or a rule of conduct. More recently the meaning of the word has been still further extended until today writers use it to mean a special motto, pet phrase, or even a shibboleth, meanings not yet recorded in our dictionaries.

The monks illuminated manuscripts not only of sacred books and secular literature but also of musical compositions used in the church services, such as masses and hymns. Guido d'Arezzo, a Benedictine monk of the eleventh century, a teacher of singing, invented a Great Scale which is the basis of our modern musical notation. He used letters to indicate the notes and corresponding to each letter he used a syllable which can be sung, since it is impossible to sing single consonants. He started his scale with the Greek letter Gamma, which is G, and called its corresponding note Ut.

Guido d'Arezzo took the syllables *Ut, re, mi, fa, sol, la* from a hymn to St. John the Baptist:

> UT *queant laxis* REsonare *fibris*
> MIra *gestorum* FAmuli *tuorum*
> SOLve *pollutis* LAbiis *reatum*
> *Sancte Iohannes.*

("That thy servants may sing out thy wondrous acts strongly and freely, remove the guilt from their polluted lips, St. John.")

Later *ut* was changed to *do,* which is easier to sing since it ends in a vowel, and *si* was added, probably from the initial letters of *Sancte Iohannes* (St. John).

The entire scale was known as the gamma-ut or *gamut* from the first note and its equivalent syllable, just as *alphabet* is derived from the first two Greek letters, *alpha* and *beta. Gamut,* the complete scale of notes, is applied to fields other than music and means the entire range or compass of any activity.

Another word which comes from a hymn is *dirge,* a funeral song. *Dirge* is a contraction of the first word of a Latin funeral service which begins, *"Dirige, Domine, Deus meus, in conspectu tuo viam,"* (O Lord, my God, *direct* my way in Thy sight.) This is based on Psalms 5:8—"... make Thy way straight before my face."

IN THE DAYS OF CHIVALRY

During the period when the monks were keeping alive the heritage of learning, knighthood came into flower. We stop for only one word, *accolade.* The *accolade* was the final step conferring knighthood. The early kings of France were etymologically correct when they placed their arms around the neck (*ad,* to, and *collum,* neck) of the newly-made knights in order to kiss them. French generals and officials still keep up the custom of the accolade when they kiss the cheeks of the men whom they honor with an award.

William the Conqueror, a man's man, is said to have used his fist in conferring knighthood. Later a gentle stroke with the flat of the sword on the side of the neck (we get back to *ad* and *collum* again) or on the shoulder was substituted for a blow with the fist. Supposedly the words that accompanied the tap were, "And now I dub thee knight." Originally, *dub* meant to call or name, but because of its association with the stroking act in the ceremony, it came to mean *hit gently.* So, a poor golfer who dubs a shot merely taps the ball on the neck or shoulder instead of swinging through cleanly.

The word *accolade* has made a full circle from its original literal meaning to its modern figurative meaning of "crowning praise." Here are two examples which show how the word is now used to mean the honor bestowed rather than the physical act of bestowing an honor.

> One hesitates to quarrel with a book that comes with the *accolade* of such diverse thinkers as John Dewey and Donald Ogden Stewart and Albert Einstein and Dorothy Parker.

> The report, however, characterized Justices Parella and Shimmel as "qualified" while for Justice Coleman it reserved the *accolade* of "exceptionally qualified."

JOURNEY'S END

And so we too complete a circle and come to the end of our etymological *junket*, a word which has come a long way.

Junket is from the Latin *juncus*, a twig resembling a rush. Originally a junket referred to a basket made of rushes and twigs. Preparations of cheese and cream used to be served on these mats just as in India and other tropical lands foods like betel-nut paste are served on plantain leaves. Soon a junket came to mean any preparation of cream and cheese or any delicacy served on the mats. Finally it was applied to a feast or banquet, especially when served out-of-doors. That's the usual meaning of *junket* in England.

But in the United States *junket* took on an additional meaning—a pleasure excursion or a picnic. The more recent political use of the word probably stems from the clambakes, the oyster-fries, and the beer and pretzel feasts which were the natural climax of the free excursions once offered by political clubs and parties to their followers. So, any pleasure excursion is called a junket.

We hope that this etymological junket has been a joy ride for you, a joy ride that has helped to convince you that:

1. Words have an interesting history.
2. Their history makes the meanings of words more vivid.
3. Words change with the times and adapt themselves to new surroundings.
4. Learning the history of the words makes you know them better and makes it easier to remember them.

I. Synonym Families

In each of the following ten groups you'll find at least one word whose history you have learned in this chapter. Around each is a cluster of three synonyms and *one* word whose meaning is not related to the other words in the group. Select the word in each cluster that does not belong. Answers for this section will be found on page 365.

1. (a) gaudy (b) tawdry (c) delicate (d) showy (e) pretentious
2. (a) mendicant (b) buffoon (c) mountebank d) charlatan (e) quack
3. (a) toady (b) sycophant (c) counterfeiter (d) hanger-on (e) parasite
4. (a) laconic (b) pithy (c) succinct (d) terse (e) verbose
5. (a) slogan (b) watchword (c) shibboleth (d) wordiness (e) pet phrase
6. (a) gamut (b) harmony (c) scope (d) range (e) purview
7. (a) dirge (b) elegy (c) lamentation (d) threnody (e) eulogy
8. (a) affection (b) accolade (c) ceremony (d) salutation (e) award
9. (a) junket (b) trip (c) expedition (d) popularity (e) journey
10. (a) prolific (b) poor (c) fertile (d) propagative (e) fruitful

II. Can You Match These?

The words on the left were formed from the roots of some of the words appearing in this chapter. From the column on the right select a definition to match each of the words on the left.

1. panegyric
2. proliferate
3. rubicund
4. enclave
5. category
6. phase
7. clavicle
8. maelstrom
9. phenomenon
10. molar

a. a strip of land enclosed within foreign territory
b. an aspect of a problem or situation
c. an observable fact
d. a tooth that grinds food
e. reddish, ruddy
f. a speech of praise
g. to reproduce rapidly
h. classification
i. a grinding whirlpool
j. a condition of slavery
k. the collarbone

SOME FAMOUS LACONISMS

1. One day in March, 1942, David F. Mason, chief aviation machinist's mate, USN, saw a Japanese submarine while he

was on patrol duty. He dropped several depth charges, observed the wreckage, and radioed:

SIGHTED SUB. SANK SAME.

2. An Athenian candidate spoke for a few hours making a brilliant speech full of promises. His opponent arose at the end and declared, "All that he *said*, I will *do*."

3. Shortly after the appearance of *Les Misérables* Victor Hugo and his publisher carried on the shortest correspondence on record. Hugo's letter contained only the following:

?

His heart was gladdened when the publisher replied with:

!

4. The celebrated English surgeon, John Abernethy, (1764–1831) was a man of few words. A lady patient who knew this came into his office one day, bared her arm, and said: "Burn." Dr. Abernethy replied, "Poultice." She returned the next day and said „Better." He answered, "Continue treatment." A few days later she returned and asked, "Fee?" At last Dr. Abernethy became talkative. "Nothing. You are the most sensible patient I ever met in my life."

5. About 2,500 years ago, a barber asked Archelaus, a Macedonian king, how he wanted his hair trimmed. Archelaus answered, "In silence."

"No. I tell you this is a stalagmite and that is a stalactite!" *

---

11. Something to Remember Them By

THE REAL problem in vocabulary building is not to find words to add to your store or to find out what they mean. The problem is to find a way of remembering them—so you don't have to go back to the dictionary time after time to check on a memory that has failed you.

At this point let us remind you of the various methods we

---

* Drawing reproduced courtesy '47 *the Magazine of the Year.*

have suggested of fixing and clinching the meanings of words. These methods are based on the principle that to fix something in our minds we must *associate* the specific thing we want to remember with something we know or something we can learn easily.

We have made five principal suggestions:

1. Since the normal way of meeting a new word is to come across it in what we read and hear, we can sometimes remember the meaning of the word if we can recall the context or the situation in which the word occurred. (See Chapter 2, "The Company Words Keep.")

2. Often we can clinch the meaning of a word by concentrating on and properly identifying the prefix, especially when it strongly colors the meaning of the word. (See Chapter 7, "Pre-Fixing Words," and Chapter 8, "Count Off!")

3. Sometimes just dividing words into recognizable shorter units will unlock and fix the meaning of a word. (See Chapter 3, "Divide and Conquer.")

4. Frequently we can attach the meaning of a word firmly to our minds by its root and the words that cluster around it. (See Chapter 4, "Deep Are the Roots," and Chapter 5, "Brief Encounters.")

5. Finally, knowing the story behind the word, knowing something of its historical past can enable us to fix its meaning. (See Chapter 10, "Every Word Has a History.")

TRICKS OF MEMORY

There are other methods that apply to fewer words; there are tricks and devices that can help us in specific cases. We consider no trick or device too low when a larger vocabulary is the goal. Sometimes we must stoop to conquer.

One of the time-tested ways of remembering a series of items is known as a mnemonic device. *Mnemonic* (the *m* is silent) comes to us from the Greek root MNE, to remember. We can fix the meaning of this word right away by associating it with words that cluster around the root MNE. A person who suffers from a*mne*sia has lost his memory, the prefix *a* uttering a decided, "No!" A government that offers a*mne*sty to a group of rebellious citizens is really saying, "Let's forget it." The Greek goddess of memory was *Mne*mosyne, a fickle lady!

A bright little school lad found that out. He was told he

could remember the date of Columbus' discovery of America
by memorizing:

> In fourteen hundred ninety two
> Columbus sailed the ocean blue.

The next day he had forgotten the couplet, but remembering that there was a rhyme involved boldly recited:

> In fourteen hundred ninety three
> Columbus sailed the dark blue sea.

Despite such occasional mishaps the system of remembering with rhyme's artful aid has been an accepted teaching method since early times. Many of us spell *believe* and *receive* correctly because we remember that it's

> *i* before *e*
> except after *c*
> or when sounded as *a*
> as in neighbor and weigh.

It's a good rhyme but not a good rule. It's more useful to say:

> *i* before *e*
> when sounded like *ee*
> except after *c*.

Students in colleges and universities learn long lists of names and facts with the aid of mnemonics. You may recall the scene in *Arrowsmith* * in which the fraternity boys of Digamma Pi get together for a bull session. Sinclair Lewis writes:

> No discussion at the Digamma Pi supper was more violent than the incessant debate over the value to a doctor . . . of remembering anatomical terms. But no matter what they thought, they all ground out at learning the lists of names which enable a man to crawl through examinations. . . . Unknown sages had invented rimes which enabled them to memorize. At supper—the thirty piratical Digams sitting at a long and spotty table, devouring clam chowder and beans and codfish balls and banana layer-cake—the Freshmen earnestly repeated after a senior:
>
> > On old Olympus' topmost top
> > A fat-eared German viewed a hop.

Thus by association with the initial letters they mastered

---

* By Sinclair Lewis; copyright 1925, Harcourt, Brace and Company, Inc.

the twelve cranial nerves: olfactory, optic, oculo-motor, trochlear, and the rest. To the Digams it was the world's noblest poem, and they remembered it for years after they had become practicing physicians and altogether forgotten the names of the nerves themselves.

WORDS OF MANY LETTERS

Rhymes are not the sole basis of mnemonic devices. Sometimes we use the first or first few letters of the separate items we have to remember and try to make a pronounceable word of them, very much the way certain many-worded bureaus, agencies, or organizations are called UNESCO, UNICEF, NATO, SEATO, etc. Words formed in this way are called *acronyms*. So, *radar* is formed from *ra*dio *d*etecting *a*nd *r*anging; *Loran* (*loran*) from *Lo*ng *Ra*nge *N*avigation, and *sonar*, *so*und *n*avigation *r*anging.

And there are some other interesting ones. WAVES, for instance, are *W*omen *A*ppointed for *V*oluntary *E*mergency *S*ervice in the U. S. Navy. Their British sisters are WRENS, *W*omen's *R*oyal *N*aval *S*ervice plus an inserted E. How many who generously send CARE packages know that they are doing so through the *C*ooperative for *A*merican *R*elief *E*verywhere?

One of the most interesting and viable acronyms was originally military slang—SNAFU (*s*ituation *n*ormal, *a*ll *f*ouled *u*p). On March 2, 1961, the New York *Herald Tribune* gave this word status and respectability by using it on Page 1 in a headline!

KENNEDY-ON-TAPE RESULTS IN SNAFU

The news story used the word *confusion*, thus implying that a *snafu* is a chaotic situation that is not altogether unexpected.

UP OR DOWN

The tricks of mnemonics are useful when we want to distinguish between words we sometimes confuse. Every day thousands of visitors to the Carlsbad Caverns of New Mexico and the Luray Caverns of Virginia marvel at the truly magnificent formations known as *stalagmites* and *stalactites*. And every day hundreds of these visitors wonder which is which, which are the stalagmites and which the stalactites. A mnemonic device does the trick—and does it forever. Stalactite, the word with the *c* in it comes down from the *c*eiling of the

:ave. Stalagmite, which has the g in it, grows up from the
ground.

Sometimes we even have trouble distinguishing such simple terms as *bulls* and *bears* as used in the stock market. What
is "bearish" and what is "bullish"? Which is up and which is
down? Again the artifice of mnemonics comes to our aid.

1. A bull is an optimistic speculator who buys because he
expects prices to go *up*. His opposite is the bear who expects
them to go down and sells.

2. A bull, who tries to "up" prices, can be associated with
the animal's habit of tossing *up* with his horns; a bear, who
tries to depress prices, with that animal's habit of clawing
down.

3. Finally, you can remember the meaning of *bear* from
the most authentic story of its origin. There's an old English
proverb, "to sell the skin before one has caught the bear." In
Exchange Alley, London, during the eighteenth century, the
phrase "bear-skin jobber" was applied to a certain type of
stock speculator. He sold the "bear-skin" or "bear," that is,
he sold for future delivery stock which he did not own at the
time of sale. He hoped that the price would drop by the time
of delivery so that he could profit to the extent of the difference between the price on the day of sale and the lower
price on the day of delivery.

MORE SINNED AGAINST . . .

We'll stoop a little lower for the next one. There's an
English expression "to cry peccavi," which means to admit
one's guilt, to confess an error or wrongdoing. *Peccavi* is a
Latin verb meaning "I have sinned." How can we fix that?
How can we remember that beyond the moment?

Let's turn to an item that appeared in *Punch* on May 18,
1884:

> It is a common idea that the most laconic military dispatch
> was that sent by Caesar to the Horse Guards at Rome, con-
> taining the three memorable words, *"Veni, vidi, vici,"* and
> that perhaps, until our own day, no like instance of brevity
> has been found. The dispatch of Sir Charles Napier, after
> the capture of Scinde, to Lord Ellenborough, both for brev-
> ity and truth, is however, far beyond it. The dispatch con-
> sisted of one word, Peccavi—I have Scinde (sinned).*

* This pun, like so many other sayings attributed to famous persons, was
not the work of its reputed author. However, before the truth about its
authorship could be discovered, it stirred up intense feeling in England because the taking of Scinde had involved much bloodshed and the pun was
considered in poor taste.

Scinde is now spelled Sind which makes the pun even better. This district in India has figured in the news in recent years because its largest city, Karachi, became the capital of the newly-created country of Pakistan.

This story from *Punch* fixes the meaning of *peccavi* through a pun and a striking account of a historical event. We can still further clinch its meaning and that of related words if we apply our method of clusters to the root PECC. The idea of sin runs through *peccant*, im*pecc*able (also im*pecc*ant), and *pecc*adillo. *Peccant* of course means sinning; *impeccable,* flawless or faultless; and *peccadillo* a small or trifling sin or failing.

And so we urge you to apply all the principles of association we have summarized and repeated in this chapter and any other tricks or devices that will help you fix and remember elusive words.

HOW MANY CAN YOU REMEMBER?

I. Look Them Over Again

Do you remember the preliminary test you took at the end of Chapter 1, page 20? You have met many of those words in the chapters following that test. You might be interested in taking that test over again to compare your score now with your score then.

II. How Many Words Have You Learned?

Here's another test containing words chosen from the many words we've discussed in the preceding eleven chapters.

In each line below you will find one word in small capitals followed by four words or phrases. In each case select the word or phrase that has most nearly the same meaning as the capitalized words. Answers will be found on page 365.

1. ABROGATION   (a) promulgation (b) repeal (c) extension (d) investigation

2. ABSTEMIOUS   (a) temperate (b) superstitious (c) hesitant (d) careful

3. ACCOLADE   (a) affection (b) award (c) arrival (d) welcome

4. ACROPHOBIA   fear of: (a) dogs (b) high places (c) going out (d) thunder

5. AMENABLE   (a) religious (b) cruel (c) responsive (d) kindhearted

6. AMNESTY   (a) pardon (b) hiding place (c) rebellion (d) farewell

7. ANTIPODES   (a) foot ailment (b) exact opposite (c) hatred (d) aborigines

8. APATHY   (a) suffering (b) curiosity (c) patience (d) indifference

9. AUGURY   (a) increase (b) boring tool (c) sickness (d) foretelling

10. AUTONOMY   (a) quick action (b) inquest (c) machine (d) self-rule

11. BANE   (a) potion (b) wickedness (c) detestation (d) ruin

12. BICAMERAL   (a) having two chambers (b) photographic (c) antique (d) double-jointed

13. BUCOLIC   (a) lush (b) rustic (c) sunny (d) quiet

14. CLANDESTINE   (a) hand-written (b) subversive (c) secret (d) daily

15. COGNOSCENTI   (a) experts (b) ball players (c) perfume dealers (d) teachers

16. CONDONE   (a) contribute (b) surround (c) pardon (d) bring together

17. CORROBORATION   (a) great crime (b) defense (c) rusting (d) confirmation

18. CRUX   (a) outcome (b) weakness (c) critical point (d) candle-holder

19. CRYPTIC   (a) metallic (b) secret (c) open (d) stolen

20. DAIS   (a) easy chair (b) district (c) raised platform (d) after-dinner speaker

21. DENIZEN   (a) police (b) underworld (c) inhabitant (d) agent

22. DEPLETE   (a) fill again (b) mock at (c) empty out (d) unfold

23. DICHOTOMY   (a) division (b) plant (c) religious office (d) struggle

24. DILEMMA   (a) expanse (b) twisting (c) deliberation (d) quandary

25. DIRGE   (a) song of mourning (b) instructions (c) wave (d) scarcity

26. DIVA   (a) sculptress (b) temptress (c) prima donna (d) dancer

27. DOUR   (a) insulting (b) stern (c) vigorous (d) stingy

28. EGREGIOUS   (a) agreeable (b) separated (c) outstanding (d) assembled

29. EGRESS   (a) strange animal (b) exit (c) foreign woman (d) great desire

30. ELDRITCH   (a) loud (b) eerie (c) prolonged (d) aged

31. ELUCIDATE   (a) untie (b) escape (c) sharpen (d) make clear

32. ENCLAVE | (a) fortified area (b) conquered territory (c) free city (d) district enclosed within alien territory

33. EPHEMERAL | (a) short-lived (b) everlasting (c) shoddy (d) flimsy

34. ESCHEW | (a) eat slowly (b) avoid (c) cheat (d) lose

35. ETHNIC | (a) foreign (b) moral (c) legal (d) racial

36. EXCULPATE | (a) free from blame (b) cut out (c) drive away (d) shatter

37. EXPEDITE | (a) get in the way (b) hasten (c) send away (d) treat the foot

38. EXTORT | (a) twist out (b) answer (c) decrease (d) do wrong

39. FACTITIOUS | (a) historical (b) fictional (c) artificial (d) natural

40. FEALTY | (a) swearing (b) softness (c) faithfulness (d) sensitivity

41. FEASIBLE | (a) practicable (b) impossible (c) deceptive (d) financial

42. FETISH | (a) unreasoning affection (b) headdress (c) style (d) magic cure

43. FIAT | (a) failure (b) message (c) decree (d) success

44. FLUX | (a) fall (b) conclusion (c) change (d) icy

45. GELID | (a) frightful (b) soft (c) tense (d) icy

46. HARBINGER | (a) forerunner (b) drunken revel (c) safe position (d) dock worker

47. HECATOMB | (a) cemetery (b) great slaughter (c) beehive (d) geometric figure

48. HOMOGENEOUS | (a) manly (b) assorted (c) creamy (d) similar

49. ICON | (a) glass (b) old book (c) image (d) Russian coin

50. ILLICIT | (a) easy (b) free (c) not legal (d) spotless

51. IMBIBE | (a) drink in (b) learn (c) enter (d) deposit

52. IMBROGLIO | (a) quarrel (b) decoration (c) harem (d) scandal

53. IMMACULATE | (a) stainless (b) beautiful (c) ornamental (d) well-dressed

54. IMMUTABLE | (a) unchangeable (b) yielding (c) dumb (d) short

55. IMPECCABLE | (a) unbreakable (b) tightly packed (c) unable (d) faultless

56. **INDURATE** — (a) burn in (b) suffer (c) grow hard (d) promise

57. **INTRANSIGENT** — (a) complex (b) uncompromising (c) sleepless (d) traveling

58. **KILN** — (a) pot (b) small cave (c) crate (d) large oven

59. **LACONIC** — (a) statuesque (b) terse (c) talkative (d) lingering

60. **LAVE** — (a) heat (b) dislike (c) wash (d) defeat

61. **LOGISTICS** — (a) results (b) diplomacy (c) reasoning (d) supplying and quartering troops

62. **LUCUBRATE** — (a) polish (b) oil (c) illuminate (d) study hard

63. **MENDICANCY** — (a) bartering (b) habit of begging (c) self-improvement (d) repairing destruction

64. **MIEN** — (a) compromise (b) Chinese vase (c) bearing (d) anger

65. **MIMICRY** — (a) imitation (b) shouting (c) plant (d) insect

66. **MULCT** — (a) think over (b) soften with soap (c) pasture (d) take away by trickery

67. **NADIR** — (a) zenith (b) common level (c) disgrace (d) lowest point

68. **NEBULOUS** — (a) cloudy (b) clear (c) starry (d) intoxicated

69. **NEOPHYTE** — (a) branch (b) beginner (c) warrior (d) limb

70. **NEXUS** — (a) insect (b) vein (c) link (d) neighbor

71. **OBSOLESCENCE** — (a) destruction (b) consolation (c) going out of use (d) opposition

72. **ONUS** — (a) shame (b) piece of music (c) hardship (d) burden

73. **OPULENT** — (a) soothing (b) hopeful (c) wealthy (d) attacking

74. **PANACEA** — (a) cure-all (b) oceanic island (c) international agreement (d) vital organ

75. **PAREGORIC** — (a) soothing medicine (b) great praise (c) oratory (d) market place

76. **PEDIATRICIAN** — (a) teacher (b) children's doctor (c) statesman (d) foot specialist

77. **PENURIOUS** — (a) imprisoned (b) lonely (c) hardy (d) stingy

78. **PERIPHERY** — (a) wordiness (b) territory (c) circumference (d) winding road

79. **PLETHORA** — (a) overabundance (b) sadness (c) musical instrument (d) seasickness

129

80. POLYGLOT   (a) speaking several languages (b) foreign (c) manysided (d) wealthy

81. PRESAGE   (a) grow old (b) send ahead (c) publicize (d) predict

82. PROCRASTINATE   (a) put off (b) make progress (c) prefer (d) thicken

83. PSEUDONYM   (a) convenience (b) pen name (c) deception (d) novelist

84. PUNGENT   (a) erasing (b) wild (c) pugnacious (d) biting

85. QUIXOTIC   (a) fleet-footed (b) foreign (c) protective (d) visionary

86. RENOVATE   (a) begin (b) make new again (c) clean thoroughly (d) acknowledge

87. RESCIND   (a) change (b) cancel (c) climb (d) confirm

88. SALIENT   (a) salty (b) prominent (c) valuable (d) considerate

89. SATE   (a) drink (b) declare (c) glut (d) ridicule

90. SERRATED   (a) bright (b) tough (c) dull (d) saw-toothed

91. SHIBBOLETH   (a) ancient soldier (b) slogan (c) wordiness (d) vegetable

92. SUBTERFUGE   (a) prearrangement (b) bribery (c) compulsion (d) evasion

93. SUPEREROGATORY   (a) pertaining to a will (b) non-essential (c) at a high altitude (d) inquisitive

94. SYCOPHANT   (a) counterfeiter (b) parasite (c) customs official (d) epicure

95. SYSTOLE   (a) slow motion (b) theory (c) heart contraction (d) arrangement

96. TOME   (a) monument (b) book (c) statue (d) tool

97. TRIVET   (a) kettle-holder (b) golf stick (c) camera (d) cheap jewel

98. TYRO   (a) rich man (b) beginner (c) cruel person (d) absolute ruler

99. UNTRAMMELED   (a) slow (b) quick (c) free (d) pure

100. VILIFY   (a) honor (b) settle in the country (c) enrich (d) malign

II. I'D RATHER BE RIGHT

"You will please address me as 'Librarian,' Sir—I am not a 'Bookie'!"

12. Mistaken Identities

A TAXI-DRIVER whose fixed fee is fifty cents for the trip from the Mayflower Hotel in Washington to one of the government buildings received just that amount from a prosperous looking customer.

"That's correct, isn't it?" the man asked as the cabby stared at the two quarters in the palm of his hand.

"It's *correct*," answered the cabby, "but it ain't *right*."

We're not going to make any such fine distinctions between what is *correct* and what is *right*. Nor are we going to go as far in the other direction as Josh Billings did. "When

* Drawing reproduced courtesy *Reader's Scope.*

a man sets down a poor umbreller," he once wrote, "and he takes up a good one, he makes a *mistake,* but when he sets down a good umbreller and takes up a poor one, he makes a *blunder.*"

Such distinctions matter only for the punch line of a good story or the phrasing of a witty retort. We are dealing here with broader distinctions that that. We are dealing here with words whose identities are sometimes mistaken and which are therefore confused with other words or misused for them.

THESE LOOK OR SOUND ALIKE

There are many words that are similar in spelling or pronunciation and sometimes we mistakenly reach for a word because it seems to have the right sound or look.

ABJURE, ADJURE
  Abjure: "swear off" the use of, to renounce, to give up.
  Adjure: appeal to earnestly, entreat.

UNESCO IS ADJURED
TO DEFINE FREEDOM

Adjuration, the noun formed from *adjure,* means an earnest appeal.

AMEND, EMEND
  Amend: modify, alter by adding something *to* an original resolution or plan.
  Emend: to take *out* errors and make corrections.
  The corresponding nouns are *amendment* and *emendation.*

BASILICA, BASILISK
  SHERLOCK HOLMES: Miss Cartwright? She gives me the shivers. She has an eye like a *basilisk.*

(from broadcast on ABC)

These two words are probably never confused by those who use them, but we list them here as we do many others in this section because they are interesting and because we have come across them in our newspaper reading.

Actually, the two are related, for both are derived from the root of *basileus,* the Greek word for king. The idea of power and royalty resides in them, as in the name of the plant basil and the masculine name Basil.

Basilisk: "little king"; a fabulous lizard, dragon, or serpent whose hissing drove other reptiles away and whose very look was thought to be fatal. Shakespeare often refers to this supposed power of the basilisk, as in the exchange between Gloucester and Lady Anne (*Richard III*, Act I, Scene 2):

Gloucester: Thine eyes, sweet lady, have infected mine.
Lady Anne: Would they were basilisks, to strike thee dead!

Basilica: "royal portico." In ancient Rome the basilica was a building used for social and commercial meetings. It had a nave or long central hall rising higher than the colonnaded aisles and an apse or projection, generally semicircular. The early Christian churches were modeled after the basilicas. The title *basilica* is given to certain Roman Catholic churches and carries with it special liturgical privileges.

BESIDE, BESIDES
Beside: alongside.
Besides: in addition to.
Archie of Duffy's Tavern used to say "and further *besides*" just to make sure you didn't misunderstand him.

BIANNUALLY, BIENNIALLY
Biannually: twice a year.
Biennially: every two years.

In 1927 the difference in meaning was strongly brought home to the members of the New Jersey State Legislature, when they discovered with a start that they had passed a bill providing, according to the printed version of the law, that members to the Assembly be elected *biannually* (twice a year). There was taxpayers' money to pay! A special session had to be called to correct the "typographical error."

CAPRICIOUS, CAPTIOUS
Capricious: adjective from *caprice*, a whim; *capricious* (second syllable rhymes with *wish*) means apt to change suddenly, unpredictable.
Captious: from Latin *cap, capt*, meaning to seize or catch; therefore, eager to catch others at mistakes. A *captious* critic is faultfinding to a fault, carping, caviling.

CENSOR, CENSURE
Censor: to suppress, forbid, delete.
Censure: to criticize adversely, reprimand, rebuke.

The adjective *censorious*, however, is, in meaning and use, more closely related to *censure*. A *censorious* person is severely critical of the action and behavior of others, captious and condemnatory at the same time.

135

CHAOTIC, INCHOATE

Chaotic: adjective from *chaos;* in a state of complete confusion.
Inchoate (inKOate): from a Latin word meaning to begin; just beginning, therefore still rudimentary or undeveloped.

These words come close in meaning because things in their early stages (*inchoate*) may also be in a state of confusion (*chaotic*).

CHARY, WARY

Though similar in meaning *wary* stresses suspiciousness, an alertness against being taken in (like *beware*), whereas *chary* stresses carefulness, great reserve and discretion.

If you are *chary* of praise, you give it sparingly; if you are *wary* of praise you take it sparingly because you are on guard against it.

In the headline

NAM CHARY OF PRICE CONTROLS

WARY would have been better.

CLIMACTIC, CLIMATIC

Climactic: from *climax;* therefore, the *c* must appear in the word and be pronounced. A *climax* is a crowning effect. Something that is *anticlimactic* knocks the crown awry or knocks it off altogether.
Climatic: from *climate.*

COMPLACENT, COMPLAISANT

Though they may be pronounced alike, they are very different in meaning. Both are derived from the same root, *plac,* to please. *Complacent* is closer to the Latin; *complaisant* made a detour through French to get to us. In both words the prefix *com* is intensive, meaning very.
Complacent: very pleased (with oneself); self-satisfied, smug.
Complaisant: willing to please others; therefore, obliging, compliant, affable, gracious.

CONTINUAL, CONTINUOUS

Continual: recurring at intervals.
Continuous: going on without a break.

DEDUCE, DEDUCT

P. Moran, Percival Wilde's comedy detective and "deductor," always "deducts" when he should be *deducing.* "Annabel," he says, "I can *deduct* that man is a stone-mason."
Deduce: to conclude or infer something from the evidence given.

Deduct: to subtract.

To *deduct* (*subtract*) is, therefore, almost the opposite of *deduce,* which means to put two and two together.

DEFINITE, DEFINITIVE

A *definite* statement is specific, concrete, precise, and exact; a *definitive* statement is final and conclusive, the last word on the subject. A definitive edition or biography is so complete that it's the edition to end all editions.

DEPRECATE, DEPRECIATE

Our files are bulging with clippings from newspapers, magazines, and books, in which *deprecate* and *deprecatory* are used where *depreciate* and *depreciatory* are called for. At this late date there's nothing much that can be done about it except to tell you how they differ in meaning and how they should differ in use.

To *deprecate* an action is to disapprove of it strongly. The idea of regret that the action has occurred is generally implied.

To *depreciate* an action is to belittle it, to deflate it and lessen it in value—opposed to the word *appreciate* which means to value properly or to increase in value.

Here's a mnemonic device that may help to keep the distinction straight: When the meaning is to bel*i*ttle or bel*i*ttling, use the word with the *i* in it, either depreciate or depreciatory.

But it's a lost cause, either way. Here's our most recent exhibit from an editorial in one of our largest and most influential newspapers (written before Astronant Alan B. Shepard went up into space):

> The United States, having sent into
> space and safely recovered an anthropoid,
> and having successfully employed solid
> fuels in Polaris and Minuteman missiles,
> need not view this Soviet achievement
> with undue self-*deprecation.*

DISCOMFITED, DISCOMFORTED

We have seen and heard the first of these two words often used in the sense of being made uncomfortable or embarrassed. *Discomfited* means literally to be completely "undone," to be defeated, to be frustrated.

DISINTERESTED, UNINTERESTED

Disinterested does not mean not interested, although an increasing number of writers are using it in that sense.

To be *disinterested* is to be without selfish motives or interest therefore, objective and impartial, unbiased. *Uninterested* mean not interested, bored, indifferent.

However, one writer who is not indifferent to this distinction and says so is Richard Watts, Jr., who in his theater column of February 12, 1961, in the New York *Post*, wrote: "A very easy mistake to make in writing is to say 'disinterested' when you mean 'uninterested.'" We have inscribed his name on our Roll of Honor.

Joining him on our Roll of Honor is Orville Prescott of the New York *Times*, who began his book review on March 13, 1961, with the sentence, "Most supposedly civilized people are *uninterested* in the wonders of nature and indifferent to the beauty, charm, and fascination of wild animals."

ENORMITY, ENORMOUSNESS

The distinction usually made between these two words has become blurred.

Enormity emphasizes the abnormality, the outrageousness of something.

> The *enormity* of the crimes becomes all the greater after visiting the camps. But displays and photographs of the camps in actual operation are necessary to bring home to the visitor the essential depth of the crimes.

Enormousness refers to hugeness or size.

> When one sees the difficulties still facing England and other countries which suffered less physical destruction during the war than Greece, one realizes the *enormity* of the task ahead.

Since the huge size of the task is referred to, *enormousness* would be better here.

EQUABLE, EQUITABLE

Equable: steady, uniform, even-tempered. A country may have an *equable* climate; a person, an *equable* disposition.

Equitable: just, fair. A division or distribution of profits or goods may be *equitable,* i.e. in accordance with *equity.*

ESOTERIC, EXOTERIC, EXOTIC

Esoteric: secret in the sense of being only for the initiated, or those in the inner circle (*eso*, within; *esoteris*, inner).

> Many people think the robots are still
> used only in a limited way and at such
> *esoteric* places as M.I.T. and the Pen-
> tagon.

Exoteric: opposite of *esoteric;* therefore, popular, easily understood, suitable for the general public.

Exotic: foreign, strange (*exo*, outside); unusually colorful in appearance.

EXIGENT, EXIGUOUS

Exigent: urgent, requiring immediate attention.

Exiguous: small, trifling.

The *exigencies* of a situation are the urgent needs.

FACTIOUS, FACTITIOUS, FRACTIOUS

Factious: tending to promote internal dissension through formation of *factions* or cliques.

Factitious: artificial, sham, unreal.

Fractious: refractory or unruly, apt to break into a passion (*fract*, broken).

FLAUNT, FLOUT

Our files also bulge with examples of writers who *flout* correct usage by using *flaunt* where *flout* is called for.

Flaunt: make a show of, display proudly.

Flout: defy, contemptuously pay no attention to, disregard.

> There can be nothing but ultimate
> confusion and chaos if court decrees are
> *flaunted*, whatever the pretext.

Since the meaning intended is obviously one of disregarding and defying rather than displaying proudly, *flouted* should have been used.

FORTUITOUS, GRATUITOUS

Fortuitous: happening by chance, accidental. (*Fortuitous* does not mean fortunate or lucky.)

Gratuitous: for no good reason, uncalled for (a *gratuitous* insult); unwarranted (a *gratuitous* assumption).

INFLAMMABLE, INFLAMMATORY

> The Senator denounced Mr. John-
> son's statement as "*inflammable*."

Inflammable: capable of being set on fire, combustible.

Inflammatory: likely to inflame passions, rouse strong emotions.

Speeches or statements may be *inflammatory;* the paper they'r written or printed on is *inflammable.* That's why the Senator' denunciation would have been more effective if he had use *inflammatory.*

INGENIOUS, INGENUOUS

Ingenious: clever, resourceful. (A genius is likely to be clever and resourceful.)

Ingenuous: frank, candid, unsophisticated, naive. The opposite is *disingenuous,* insincere, not frank.

JUDICIAL, JUDICIOUS

Judicial: disinterested, fair, like a judge.

Judicious: wise, prudent, sensible.

A *judicial* decision is one handed down by the court. If it is a wise decision, it is also *judicious.*

LIE, LAY

We decided to include these words in a vocabulary book because their misuse is probably the most common error we in America make. Even those who know how to use these two troublesome verbs fear them.

We once heard a very charming Southern novelist say to an audience of teachers of English:

I don't know why you asked me to speak to *you.* Why, I've never been able to learn the difference between *lie* and *lay.* The characters in my stories always *sit* or *stand.* I never let 'em get near a bed. People in my stories just never get a rest.

What makes the already difficult distinction between *lie* and *lay* even more difficult is the existence of another *lie,* meaning to tell an untruth.

Lie means to recline.

(Correct: I'm tired. I'm going to rest. I'm going to *lie* down.)

Lay means to put down or place.

(Correct: Put that pistol down, Babe. *Lay* that pistol down.)

But that's only the beginning. The fact that other forms of these verbs overlap makes things worse. Watch carefully!

	Recline	Put Down	Tell Untruth
Present:	I am *lying* down.	I am *laying* the book on the desk.	He is *lying.*

ast:	I *lay* down yesterday.	I *laid* the book on the desk.	He *lied* yesterday.
resent erfect:	I've *lain* in bed all day.	I have already *laid* the book on the desk.	He's *lied* all his life.

Here's a rule of thumb and a mnemonic that may help.

When you can substitute *is*, use *lies*: The book lies (or is ying) on the desk now.

When you can substitute *was*, use *lay*: The book lay on the lesk yesterday.

When you can substitute has *been*, use *lain*: The book has ain on the desk all week.

Christopher Morley once wrote a clever limerick paying ribute to the difficulty of these two words and offering an musing way of remembering how to distinguish between hem. We reprint it here with "the blessing" he graciously estowed upon us.

> LIE and LAY offer slips to the pen
> That have troubled most excellent men.
> You may say that you *lay*
> In bed, yesterday;
> If you do it today, you're a hen.

And here finally is an example of a sentence that is correct, a note the early milkman found one morning:

Dear Milkman: Please lay a dozen eggs on my front porch.

To which our milkman, like our cab driver, might have said,

"It's correct, lady, but it ain't right."

LUXURIANT, LUXURIOUS

Luxuriant: growing profusely.
Luxurious: sumptuous, suggesting comfort and ease.

Advertisements that tell of apartments for rent or houses for sale that are *luxuriantly* furnished are likely to scare away prospective customers—for *luxuriantly* suggests an oppressive jungle splendor and hardly the comfort and ease that the word *luxuriously* does.

141

MILITATE, MITIGATE

Militate: to work against, hinder, fight against. (In origin related to the word *military,* from *miles,* Latin for soldier.)
Mitigate: reduce severity of, make milder.
Militate is sometimes used incorrectly for *militate.*
Militate should always be followed by the word *against.*
Mitigate never should.

OFFICIAL, OFFICIOUS

Official: having authoritative standing.
Officious: going beyond one's *official* duties and authority, meddlesome, interfering.

As used and understood by most people the word *officious* has gone beyond the meanings found in our dictionaries. Today it is often used with the added meaning of domineering and "bossy."

PERSPICACITY, PERSPICUITY

Those who care know that *perspicacity* is the quality of *seeing* clearly, while *perspicuity* is the quality of *being* clear.
They also know that *perspicacious* means shrewd, and *perspicuous* means clear.

PRECIPITATE, PRECIPITOUS

Discriminating users of the language see a distinction between these two words, using only the word *precipitate* for what is hasty or rash (as a *precipitate* flight or *precipitate* action), reserving *precipitous* for what is steep or abrupt (a *precipitous* drop or climb).

In the motion picture *The Ghost and Mrs. Muir* the real-estate agent warned Mrs. Muir not to be "*precipitous* in renting the house." Although the house is atop a *precipitous* cliff, the word *precipitate* would be better applied to her hasty decision.

A discriminating user of words is the *Times* sports columnist, Arthur Daley. In a recent column he wrote:

> The *precipitate* expansion of the American League to ten clubs a few months ago saw Calvin Griffith switch his base from Washington to the twin cities of Minneapolis and St. Paul.

Mr. Daley joins Mr. Watts and Mr. Prescott on our Roll of Honor.

PRESCRIBE, PROSCRIBE

Prescribe: lay down the rules for, order.
Proscribe: prohibit, forbid, outlaw, interdict.
Prescribe and *proscribe* are almost opposites. If a course of action is *prescribed*, the blueprint for it is furnished. If a course of action is *proscribed*, it is forbidden.

Sulla, an early Roman dictator, issued a general order condemning to death all who had fought against him. Such terror resulted that a Senator asked Sulla to list those whom he meant. Sulla then had a list posted in a public place on which the names of eighty persons were inscribed. So began the *proscriptions*—lists on which winning leaders in Rome's many civil wars wrote (*script*) down before (*pro*) the public the names of those they wanted "rubbed out."

SPECIE, SPECIES

In preaching a sermon on charity, Sydney Smith (1771–1845), Dean of St. Paul's, frequently repeated that, of all nations, the English were most distinguished for their generosity and for the love of their species. That Sunday, however, the collection was particularly disappointing. Thereupon, Smith remarked that he had made a great mistake, for he should have said that they were distinguished for the love of their specie.

Both *specie* and *species* are singular.

Specie refers to hard coin. *Species* indicates a distinct class or variety (a strange *species* of birds, not *specie*).

TORTUOUS, TORTUROUS

Tortuous: winding or twisting.
Torturous: painful.

TURBID, TURGID

Turbid: muddy, roiled, clouded.
Turgid: swollen, inflated, pompous.
An author's writing may be either muddied (a *turbid* script) or pompous (a *turgid* style) or both. When water is roiled, muddy, or cloudy it is *turbid*.

This newspaper excerpt obviously contains a typographical error, but it points up the difference in meaning:

> Not even the fact that in some homes the new water was slightly *turgid* for the first few hours dampened their enthusiasm.

(Typographical error: *turgid* for *turbid*.)

143

UNEXCEPTIONABLE, UNEXCEPTIONAL

Something that is *unexceptionable* is above reproach; no objection or exception can be taken to it.

Unexceptional means not exceptional, ordinary.

Using *unexceptional* for *unexceptionable* may result in a meaning contrary to that intended, as in the following:

> I haven't seen the new one [script of radio address], and it's entirely possible that, under proper coaching, it could turn out to be very good, or at least *unexceptional*.

VENAL, VENIAL

Venal: that can be bought or bribed; therefore, mercenary, corrupt.

Venial: forgivable, excusable, trivial (*venial* sins).

Venal is sometimes misused for *venial* as in the following:

> He is not much of a hand at characterization either, and is particularly inept when it comes to heroines. But these are *venal* literary sins.

And vice versa:

> Equipped with a fierce mustache, Robert Chisholm makes the part of a *venial* headmaster seem funny by playing it aggressively.

Associating *venial* with *trivial* may help you to remember which is which.

Exercises for this and the next chapter will be found at the end of Chapter 13.

*'Miss Jones—under 'Experience' could you be a little more
specific than just 'Oh, Boy!'?"* *

13. The Right Word

THIS is a continuation of the search for the right word begun
in the previous chapter; so just to keep your spirits up, we're
going to tell you a story that shows how important it sometimes is to know the right word. It happens to be a true story.
It happened to a friend of ours whom we'll call Joe. It's a
story about a traffic cop who embarrassed himself out of
giving a ticket. Joe, as he admitted to us later, had started his
car a split second before the red light dropped to green. He
moved ahead and was just about to shift into high when a
police car drew alongside and edged him over to the curb.

Feeling that his sin at worst was venial, Joe decided to
brazen it out. "What's wrong, officer?" he asked innocently.

"What's wrong?" By this time the officer was standing be side his car. "What's wrong? At that last traffic light you mad a pre . . . a pre . . . You know, a pre . . ."

"A premature start?" suggested Joe helpfully.

"Yeah, that's the word. And now get the heck out of here— FAST!"

THESE ARE SIMILAR IN MEANING

ACRID, ACRIMONIOUS

Both come from the same Latin root and mean bitter, but *acrid* is reserved for taste or smell, *acrimonious* for quarrels or discus sions.

> Both issues are expected to cause *acrid* debates tomorrow.
> (Better: *acrimonious*)

AGGRAVATE, ANNOY, IRRITATE

Connoisseurs use *aggravate* only in the sense of making a situa tion worse or more severe.

> He warned the workers against sup porting these anti-social policies, which he declared would *aggravate* rather than *alleviate* their plight.

Alleviate is the actual and the etymological opposite of *aggravate* (*levis*, light; *gravis*, heavy).

Many use *aggravate* when they really mean *annoy, exasperate,* or *irritate.*

AMBIGUOUS, EQUIVOCAL

Though generally used interchangeably to mean having two or more possible interpretations (*ambiguous*: "going off in two, *ambi,* directions"; *equivocal*: equal voice, "double talk"), the nice dis tinction made is that while *ambiguity* is always unintentional, *equivocation* may be purposeful, intended to deceive.

In other words, an *ambiguous* statement is made by someone who doesn't know how to make himself clear, while an *equivocal* statement is made by someone who doesn't want to make himself clear, who wants to use "double talk." Anybody can be *ambiguous;* you have to be clever to be *equivocal*—a diplomat, for instance, an official spokesman, a Delphic Oracle, or the witches in *Macbeth.*

The following sentence shows the distinctiveness of the word *equivocal:*

> The majority of them [hotel owners] use an *equivocal* phrase such as "near Christian churches," but some of them are more frank.

In the negative *unequivocal* is used almost exclusively. The press is constantly telling us that some official's answer was an *unequivocal* "no."

AVENGE, REVENGE

To discriminating users of the language *avenge* refers to a social and *revenge* to a personal emotion. You can *revenge* yourself, but you *avenge* the wrongs of others. *Revenge* contains the idea of retaliation on a selfish basis; *avenge,* a just retribution.

BRING, TAKE

Bring: carry *toward* the speaker or to his home.
Take: carry *away from* the speaker.

COMMON, MUTUAL

Mutual: felt by two or more persons for one another (*mutual* admiration or distrust).
Common: shared equally (*common* cause, a *common* enemy).

According to this distinction a friend shared by two or more people should be a *common* rather than a *mutual* friend, but because of the overtones of the word *common,* people use *mutual friend.* The horns of this dilemma can be side-stepped neatly by just saying "a friend of ours."

IMPLY, INFER

Imply: suggest indirectly, insinuate.
Infer: to draw a conclusion, deduce.
The same distinction holds true for their respective nouns, *implication* and *inference.*
In general the speaker *implies;* the listener *infers.*

> Earlier, Martin held Holt in contempt
> for *inferring* that the court was "aiding
> and abetting" the state because the court
> clerk's office permitted the designation of
> Negro to be placed against the names of
> Negroes selected for the jury panel.

Obviously, the word *implying* should have been used here.

MUNDANE, SECULAR

Though these words are sometimes used interchangeably, *mundane* generally refers to the transitory occurrences of this workaday world (*Sic transit gloria mundi*).
Secular is contrasted with religious (*secular* schools, *secular* buildings). It often stresses the materialistic as contrasted with the spiritual. *Secularism* is used as a synonym for materialism.

OBFUSCATION, OBSCURANTISM

Of these two, *obscurantism* (sometimes seen as *obscruranticism* is the much stronger word).

To *obfuscate* means to darken where there is already some light and thus confuse and bewilder. *Obfuscation* is therefore the act of confusing others or the state of being confused oneself.

An *obscurantist* is one who wants to keep things dark (*obscure*), who strives to prevent enlightenment and is opposed to progress in knowledge and to new ideas and methods. The word is often used to describe one who is both bigoted and reactionary. *Obscurantism* therefore means a bigoted opposition to enlightenment.

> In his first prepared statement since his course was dropped by the city school officials, Dr. Stern said that their action was "a retreat from reason in the face of *obscurantists* who have consistently opposed any teaching in this intercultural field."

PRONE, SUPINE

Though often used interchangeably (incorrectly), these words, as seen from a reclining position, are opposites.

Prone: flat on one's face; thrown forward (cf. *pro*, forward); lying face downward.

The misuse of *prone* for *supine*, its opposite, often causes a writer to place people in a rather contorted position, as in the following excerpt:

> In this picture Miss Stanley lies *prone* on a couch in several episodes with her eyes fixed upon the ceiling.

Supine: lying on one's back, face upward; inactive.

Shall we acquire the means of effectual resistance by lying *supinely* on our backs and hugging the delusive phantom of hope, until our enemy shall have bound us hand and foot?

Patrick Henry

RECOMMEND, REFER

Perhaps you, too, have heard the nurse in a doctor's office ask a new patient, "And who *recommended* you to Dr. Blank?" The word that should be used is, of course, *referred*, for it is Dr. Blank who was *recommended* for his skill, not the patient.

The expert is *recommended;* the person who wishes to consult the expert is *referred*.

THESE WORDS CAN FOOL YOU

These slips will show only when you write. When you are

peaking, no one will be able to notice the error.

AFFECT, EFFECT
Affect, always a verb, means to influence.
Effect, as a verb, means to bring about as a result.

CARAT, CARET
Carat: unit of weight (for diamonds, gold).
Caret: the mark ∧, actually the Latin word *caret,* which means
it is lacking.

COMPLEMENT(ARY), COMPLIMENT(ARY)
Complement: that which fills up or completes, also a full allowance.
Compliment: flattering tribute, praise.
An amusing story told by Lt. Col. H. P. Agnew in *The Reader's Digest* may help you to remember the distinction.

A State Selective Service Headquarters in the South was being inspected by a brassy young officer from Washington. Noting that the number of typewriters and desks far exceeded the number of typists, he asked one of the girls, "What is the normal complement of this office?" "Well, suh," she replied, "Ah reckon the most usual compliment is 'Howdy, honey chile, you're sure luscious-lookin' this mawnin'.'"

DISCREET, DISCRETE
Discreet: careful, prudent.
Discrete: separate, distinct, unrelated.
Discreet statements are tactful and prudent; *discrete* statements have no relation to one another.

ELICIT, ILLICIT
Elicit: call forth (*elicit* a reply or information).
Illicit: illegal, not lawful.

FLAIR, FLARE
Flair: a knack or aptitude.
Flare (noun): a flaming light burning a short while, generally used as a signal.
Flare (verb): to blaze up.

INDICT, INDITE
Though pronounced exactly alike and though they are identical in origin, these words have very different meanings.

To *indict* is to make a formal accusation against. In legal procedure a grand jury *indicts,* draws up the formal charge; the case is then tried before a petit (petty) jury, which may acquit or convict the person against whom the *indictment* has been brought. *Indict* does not mean to convict—although many people have the mistaken idea that it does.

To *indite* is a literary term meaning to compose, express in words, write. In the spring a young man's fancy sometimes turns to *inditing* verses to his love.

INTERPELLATION, INTERPOLATION

Interpellate: to call for a statement or explanation from a member of a parliamentary government.

> Behind the conflict started by *interpellations* today on the governement's economic policy is the question whether France can go on toward recovery.

Interpolate: insert a remark, throw something into the body of a text.

> The walls are papered with copies of songs the Kennys have written, on which many generations of flies have *interpolated* new notes.

PALATE, PALLET, PALETTE

Palate: roof of mouth.

Pallet: hard mattress, or bed made of straw (French *paille* straw).

Palette: artist's mixing board.

PRINCIPAL, PRINCIPLE

Principal may be an adjective or a noun. In either case it means chief: the *principal* reason, the *principal* of a school.

The disgusted pupil who said, "It's not the school I don't like it's the princip?? of the thing!" could spell it either way and still be right.

Principle means a rule of conduct (against the *principles* of a man of *principle*).

THESE WORDS CAN FOOL YOU TOO

These slips will show only when you say them. When you write them you're sure to be right.

CON'JURE, CONJURE'

Con'jure: practice sorcery, to call up by magic.

A *conjurer* is one who practices this art, often used for a magician or juggler.

Conjure': to appeal to solemnly and earnestly, to beseech, to implore.

ead these aloud now:

MERCUTIO: The ape is dead, and I must conjure him.

> I conjure thee by Rosaline's bright eyes. . . .
> That in thy likeness thou appear to us!
>
> *Romeo and Juliet*, Act II, Scene I

Did you pronounce it *con'jure?*)

HAMLET: What is he whose grief
Bears such an emphasis? Whose phrase of sorrow
Conjures the wandering stars, and makes them stand
Like wonder-wounded hearers?

> (*Hamlet*, Act V, SceneI)

(Did you pronounce it *conjures?*)

OR'TE, FORTE

Forte, when pronounced for*teh*, means loud or loudly. In music
t is represented by   *f* ; very loud, *fortissimo,* is represented
y *ff.*

Forte, when pronounced *for'teh*, means loud or loudly. In music
accomplishment in which one excels.

Read This Aloud Now:

> Her [Katharine Cornell's] *forte* is
> sentiment and sensibility rather than
> cunning animality and passion. What
> we look to her for is warmth, not heat.

(Did you say *fort?*)

SLOUGH, SLOUGH

Slough, when pronounced to rhyme with *bough,* is a noun
meaning a marshy, muddy place.
Slough, when pronounced to rhyme with *tough,* is both a
noun and a verb. As a noun it means an outer skin that is shed.
The verb is generally used with off and means to cast or throw.
In bridge, a losing or useless card is sloughed, thrown off, or
discarded.
Slough, when pronounced to rhyme with *through* and sometimes
spelled *slew* and *slue,* means a bog or swamp and also an inlet or
bayou.

Read This Aloud Now:

> They drew near to a very miry slough. . . . The name of
> the Slough was Despond.
>
> John Bunyan, *Pilgrim's Progress*

(Did you rhyme it with *bough?*)

TO SAVE YOU EMBARRASSMENT

These Are "Bad" Words:

BATHOS, PATHOS

Pathos is a legitimate praiseworthy emotion.

Bathos, which etymologically means depth, has the meaning of emotionally "jumping off the deep end," descending from the sublime to the ridiculous. Bathos, therefore, refers to something that is insincere, mawkish, overdone, ridiculous, or anticlimactic. The adjective is *bathetic*.

CAVALIER (n.), CAVALIER (adj.)

A cavalier (noun) was originally a horseman, at a time when owning a horse was the hallmark of a knight and courtier. A cavalier is therefore a gay, courtly gentleman, one from whom we expect chivalrous (French *cheval*, horse) conduct.

The adjective *cavalier*, however, though it has the same origin and is actually the same word, has come to have an altogether different meaning. A cavalier was evidently chivalrous only to others who rode on horseback or to beautiful ladies. Those on foot, who were literally beneath him, he treated in a curt (not courtly), offhand, unceremonious manner. To be treated *cavalierly* is, therefore, to be given a supercilious "brush-off."

EGREGIOUS

Egregious means outstanding. It is almost always used in an unflattering sense, with a strongly depreciatory and disparaging meaning (an *egregious* liar, an *egregious* blunder).

FULSOME

This word is frequently misused. It no longer means full or abundant; it now has only an unfavorable meaning. It means excessive or overdone to the point of being in bad taste or disgusting.

> Perhaps the political observers will
> offer some interesting speculations, but
> it is doubtful that Mr. Average Citizen
> will find in this film anything other than
> a warmhearted, *fulsome* tribute to one
> of the great men in history.

There is no doubt that the writer wished to praise, not damn, the film he was reviewing.

MERETRICIOUS

Meretricious is not a synonym for meritorious. Quite the contrary. Coming from *meretrix*, the Latin word for harlot, it means tawdry, flashy, showily attractive.

NOISOME

Noisome has nothing to do with noise. It is a shortened form of *annoysome*. It is used to describe an offensive odor. Its synonyms are *smelly, stinking, fetid, disgusting, offensive,* and *mephitic.* We added *mephitic* (used to refer to an offensive or poisonous smell) only to point out that it has nothing to do with Mephistopheles. The adjective for him is *Mephistophelean.*

POETASTER

Some writers "damn with faint praise" but some unwittingly find themselves praising with a loud damn when the word they meant as praise backfires. For example:

Poetaster is a term of contempt describing a second-rate would-be poet, a mere scribbler of verses. The attachable part *aster* does that to words; it cuts them down in size and quality. A critic*aster* is an inferior critic, one held in contempt. A pil*aster* is a false pillar or column that is part of the wall, a projection of it made to look like a column.

Poetaster is a word that should not be taken lightly. It was so taken recently by two of our newspapers. An essay entitled, "Now I Sing of Summertime" by one of our leading poets had this subhead:

> One of our leading *poetasters* rises
> to defend hot weather—and gets a bad
> case of nostalgia.

Another newspaper making a spread of nationally known literary figures now living in Brooklyn characterized one of them as a "novelist and poetaster."

The faces of the caption writers who thought those up should be a deep shade of red.

THESE WORDS AREN'T

Sometimes we are embarrassed because we mishandle a word by giving it a twist that makes it wrong.

PRESUMPTIOUS (Wrong!)

The word is *presumptuous* with the "choo" sound clearly heard, not *presumptious*. It means impertinently bold or forward, taking too much for granted.

The verb *presume,* from which it comes, may have two meanings, as this anecdote about Sir James M. Barrie aptly illustrates. One day, he opened the door on a reporter he didn't want to see.

"Mr. Barrie, I presume," said the reporter.

"Yes!" snapped back the usually calm Mr. Barrie and slammed the door closed.

The meaning of *presumptuous* is aptly illustrated in Mr. Barrie's unspoken use of the word.

PORTENTIOUS (Wrong!)

The word is *portentous,* coming from the noun *portent* (*strange portents,* signs or omens). It means ominous, threatening, presaging something extraordinary and solemn.

It is probably confused with *pretentious,* a word meaning showy.

UNCTIOUS (Wrong!)

The word is *unctuous* with the "choo" sound clearly heard. It generally means oily in a suave, insincere and gushing manner— the way we sometimes use the word "dripping."

The words *ointment* and *anoint* (notice the one *n*) come from the same root as *unctuous.* Compare the word *point* from Latin *punct.*

UNEQUIVOCABLY (Unequivocally wrong!)

The word is *unequivocally,* from *unequivocal,* already considered on page 000. We list it because it seems to be a fairly common misapprehension.

A similar mistake is made by those who use *undoubtably.* There's no such word; the word is *undoubtedly.*

I. Does It Make Any Difference to You?

Answer the questions that appear in *italics.* Answers for these tests will be found on page 365.

1. (a) A large glass of brandy at this time may *affect* his recovery.
   (b) A large glass of brandy at this time may *effect* his recovery.
   Which did the doctor order?

2. (a) *Lie* down, Fido!
   (b) *Lay* down Fido!
   Which should you say to a dog?

3. (a) I *lied* in the hammock all afternoon.
   (b) I *lay* in the hammock all afternoon.
   Which was more restful?

4. (a) He *adapted* the plan.
   (b) He *adopted* the plan.
   Which required more ingenuity?

5. (a) One twin *brought* Toni home.
   (b) One twin *took* Toni home.
   Which twin has the Toni?

6. (a) Joe *flouted* his father's authority.
   (b) Joe *flaunted* his father's authority.
   In which case was Joe trading on his father's reputation?

7. (a) The judge was *disinterested.*
   (b) The judge was *uninterested.*
   In which case did the lawyers apparently put on a dull show?

8. (a) On the opening night a gun refused to fire and a premature curtain cut off a *climatic* speech.

   (b) On the opening night a gun refused to fire and a premature curtain cut off a *climactic* speech.

      In which sentence did the first-nighters miss a speech about the weather?

9. (a) The townspeople *lay* down on the highway in an attempt to slow up the advancing enemy tanks.

   (b) The townspeople *laid* down on the highway in an attempt to slow up the advancing enemy tanks.

      Which townspeople were more effective in their attempt?

10. (a) *Besides* Khrushchev we saw Chiang Kai Shek and Maria Callas.

    (b) *Beside* Khrushchev we saw Chiang Kai Shek and Maria Callas.

      Which was an unlikely seating arrangement?

II. The Right Word

We are limiting our exercises to sentences taken from newspapers and magazines in which the wrong word appeared. We are giving you a choice.

1. But there is already considerable evidence that animals do talk (inter-specie, inter-species) languages that are sufficient for their purposes.

2. This magazine did not mean to (imply, infer) that Metropolitan makes a profit on its policy holders.

3. [The star] returned to finish the performance to a sympathetic, (fulsome, enthusiastic) reception.

4. It is said that the original script made the American a foolish, (venial, venal) fellow, interested only in looting and black-marketing.

5. The handicap of geography alone has (militated, mitigated) against adequate solutions for the problems of poverty, ignorance and disease.

6. He (deprecated, depreciated) the importance of his work at Scribner's but in the literary world he was held to be the dean of editors and the greatest of his generation.

7. (Beside, Besides) the three police officers whom he accused of negligence, Bergeret picked up several figures of some prominence.

8. In the main, he regards the press and radio as primarily (complementary, complimentary) rather than competitive.

9. I never realized the (enormity, enormousness) and rich variety of this land of almost 200 millions of people.

10. Thirty-three per cent of the respondents (unequivocably,

unequivocally) said "Yes."

11. Mr. Tozzi sang the title role impressively, while the secondary singers and the chorus were also (unexceptional, unexceptionable).

12. The tourist group met the United States Ambassador early in their journey. His only advice to them was not to (flaunt, flout) their wealth.

13. The Experimental Theater's third production of the season was somewhat less (fortuitous, fortunate) than its predecessors.

14. In this store you can buy pickled walnuts, chocolate-covered grasshoppers, rattlesnake meat, rose-petal preserves and other (exotic, esoteric) delicacies.

15. Mrs. Eugene O'Neill's brief part in a long story is incomplete and disorganized, humorless and largely (disinterested, uninterested) in the theater, which was the center of her husband's life.

16. Perhaps the new Lincoln Theater group, Phoenix, and Stratford can be induced to (participate in, partake of) such an arrangement.

17. He is capable of great patience, as illustrated by his recent feat of sitting in silence for two hours when asked a question by Admiral Joy, without any apparent (discomfiture, discomfort).

18. Within three weeks of their meeting he had proposed to her; it was very (precipitous, precipitate).

19. Once more they have shown themselves prepared to defy justice and reason, ready to (flaunt, flout) an arrangement which many had thought unduly favorable to them.

20. Obviously satisfied, he (lay, laid) down his welding torch.

"Don't say 'curl,' say 'coil.' "

14. How Do You Say It?

My favorite story concerns my favorite person, James (Nozzle-Nose) Durante. I had brought him a hunk of script for that week's program and Jim was reading it over for the first time. One of the lines went, "I shall endeavor to do so, Junior"—only Jim pronounced it "endeever." And I said, "Jim, don't mispronounce that word; it'll louse up the joke. Say it right—say 'endeavor'..." His eyes bugged out of his head, and he said, "Is that endeavor?" ... And pointing to the script, he turned to Eddie Jackson and said, "Hey, Jackson! Come, look at endeavor!"

Along the same lines, at a later date, I corrected him again on the pronunciation of some word, and he said, "Go ahead—educate me and we'll both be out of a job!" (Garry Moore, *Variety*)

* Drawing reproduced courtesy the *Saturday Review*.

MISPRONUNCIATIONS bring laughs, and to a comedia laughs mean security. If anyone else should mispronounc a word he may get a laugh too. But that kind of laugh means insecurity.

Sometimes you know just the word you want to use. Let's say you've decided that the word *schism* exactly expresse what you mean. What happens? In that split second befor your brain telegraphs the word to your vocal cords you won der whether it should be pronounced *shizm, sizm,* or *skizm* and the word that comes out isn't *schism* at all but a less forceful and less accurate word that your insecurity has made you compromise on.

The purpose of this chapter, then, is to help you remove another basic fear that may stand in the way of developing a larger and more effective vocabulary, the fear of mispronouncing words.

Obviously we can't do this for all the words that are likely to be mispronounced. To take care of emergencies that may arise, you must get into the habit of using a dictionary to check and determine correct pronunciations. But unless you know how to use a dictionary, the diacritical marks (— ∪ ∧ ··) will be just so many black spots before your eyes.

In this chapter therefore we're going to do two things:

1. Take up a number of useful, moderately difficult words that are often mispronounced and
2. Present them to you as a dictionary might so that you will grow accustomed to the habits of a dictionary and so acquire the dictionary habit more easily.

NEED FOR DIACRITICAL MARKS

It's the vowels that make the most trouble. Any one of them has more sounds than you can shake a stick at. Take the vowel *o* for example. It has a different sound in each of the nine simple words in this very moral sentence. Read it aloud slowly:

---

a—hat, ā—hāte, â—bâre, ä—bär, e—hen, ē—hē, i—hit, ī—hīde, o—hot, ō—hōme, ô—bôrn, u—hut, ū—hūge, û—bûrn, oŏ—hood, ōō—hōōt, ou—out, oi—oil, ng—sing, ngg—finger, th—thin, th—then, zh—vision, and ə which equals a in dial, e in model, i in pupil, o in method, u in circus, or y in martyr.

MoST WoMEN Do NoT LoVE A "WoLF'S" WoRDS oR METHoDS.

A dictionary might *fix* the vowel sound in each word by writing it like this:

Mōst wimən doo not lŭv ə Woolfs wûrdz ôr mĕthədz.

To read this you need a key. That's why we supply a list of key words on the right-hand page of this chapter and chapters 21 and 22.

Key words are simple words that easily identify a sound for you. We are using these:

ā—hāte	ē—hē	ī—hīde	ō—hōme	ū—hūge	ōō—hōot
ă—hăt	ĕ—hĕn	ĭ—hĭt	ŏ—hŏt	ŭ—hŭt	ŏŏ—hood
â—bâre			ô—bôrn	û—bûrn	
ä—bär					

and ə which equals
a in dial, e in model, i in pupil, o in method, u in circus or y in martyr.

SCHWA

Schwa is the name given to the symbol ə. In Hebrew the word *shewa* is the name given to certain diacritical marks placed under letters to indicate *the slightest possible vowel sound*—the kind of vowel sound that makes the difference between *prayed* (prād) and *parade* (pərād) and between *cress* (krĕs) and *caress* (kərĕs). Although there is no etymological connection, you can associate the *schwa* with the German word *schwach*, meaning weak. For the symbol ə indicates a vowel so weak that it is nothing more than a short grunt. The vowels *a, e, i, o, u,* and *y* in the words di*a*l, mod*e*l, pup*i*l, meth*o*d, circ*u*s, and mart*y*r have completely lost their identity and have become the same indistinguishable neutral sound for which the symbol ə is used.

---

a—hat, ā—hāte, â—bâre, ä—bär, e—hen, ē—hē, i—hit, ī—hīde, o—hot, ō—hōme, ô—bôrn, u—hut, ū—hūge, û—bûrn, ŏŏ—hood, ōō—hōot, ou—out, oi—oil, ng—sing, ngg—finger, th—thin, th—then, zh—vision, and ə which equals a in dial, e in model, i in pupil, o in method, u in circus, or y in martyr.

ACCENT MARKS

In indicating syllables that are given special stress or promi‐
nence in pronunciation we are going to abandon the metho‐
used so far of capitalizing the accented syllable and use th‐
more mature dictionary method of the accent mark ('). T‐
avoid confusion, however, we are going to underline th‐
accented syllable as well:

ho' tel <u>lob</u>' by

In some words, two syllables may be given prominence. I‐
such words we shall indicate the stronger stress (primary ac‐
cent) with accent mark and with underlining; the weake‐
stress (secondary accent) with accent mark only:

dis' tri <u>bu</u>' tion <u>sec</u>' re ta' ry

WORDS FREQUENTLY MISPRONOUNCED

To help you get accustomed to using the dictionary we ar‐
making dictionary entries for a few representative words.

OUR OWN DICTIONARY ENTRIES

intrepid (in·<u>trep</u>'id), adj. [Lat. *intrepidus*, unshaken, undaunted: *in*,
not + *trepidus*, alarmed, agitated.] *not to be frightened*,
fearless; undaunted. **intrepidity**, n.; **intrepidly**, adv.
Synonyms: adventurous, audacious, bold, courageous, daunt‐
less, doughty, fearless, heroic, resolute, undaunted, valiant,
valorous.
Antonyms: afraid, apprehensive, cowardly, craven, cringing,
fearful, frightened, poltroon, pusillanimous, timid, timorous.
From same root (TREP): **trepidation, trepidant.**

irrevocable (i·<u>rev</u>'ə·kə·bl), adj. [Lat. *irrevocabilis*, unable to be re‐
called: *in*, not + *re*, back + *voca*, call + *bilis*, able.] beyond
recall; final; unalterable, as an *irrevocable* promise, an *ir‐
revocable* fate.
From same root and stem (VOC, VOCAT): **revoke, invoke, con‐
voke, evoke, provoke, avocation** (a calling away from one's

a—hat, ā—hāte, â—bâre, ä—bär, e—hen, ē—hē, i—hit, ī—hīde,
o—hot, ō—hōme, ô—bôrn, u—hut, ū—hūge, û—bûrn, ŏŏ—hood,
ōō—hōōt, ou—out, oi—oil, ng—sing, ngg—finger, th—thin,
th—then, zh—vision, and ə which equals a in dial, e in model,
i in pupil, o in method, u in circus, or y in martyr.

regular profession or trade; hence a hobby), to **advocate** (to call for support of).

ongevity (lon·jev′ə·ti), n. [Lat. *longus* + *aevum*, age.] length of life; prolonged duration of life.
From same root (AEV, EV): **coeval, primeval, medieval** or **mediaeval.**

minutiae (min·nū′shi·ē, mi·nōō′shi·ē), n. almost always used in this plural form. [Lat. *minutia*, smallness, small particle, plural *minutiae*, insignificant details.] small details; trifles; precise details of small consequences, as the *minutiae* of exact scholarship.
From same root and stems (MIN, MINU, MINUT): **diminish** (make smaller), **diminutive,** adj., (small), **diminutive,** noun (a suffix like *let, ule,* etc. denoting smallness or affection), **comminute** (break into small particles; reduce to dust or powder; pulverize).

posthumous (pos′·choo·məs), adj. [Lat. *postumus*, latest or last, superlative degree of adj. formed from preposition *post*, after. *Postumus* referred to a late-born child, or the youngest child, and also to a child born after the father's death. It was also written *posthumus* through confusion with *humus*, ground, since the late-born child (*postumus*) was born after the father had been laid in the ground.]
1. born after the death of the father, as a *posthumous* child; published after the death of the author, as *posthumous* letters; **2.** achieved after death, as *posthumous* fame; after death, as in Whistler's retort that he was asking "posthumous prices" for his paintings.
From same prefix (POST): **posterity** (generations that come after), **preposterous** (hind part front; therefore, utterly silly, contrary to reason; fantastic); **postern** (back gate or entrance).

prescience (prē′shi·əns, presh′i·əns), n. [Lat. *praescientia*, foreknowledge: *prae*, before, *scire*, to know.] knowledge of events before they happen; foresight; foreknowledge, **prescient,** adj.
From same root (SCI): **omniscient** (all-knowing), **sciolist** (one who pretends to knowledge—*ol* has a diminutive force), **adscititious** ("added to what you know"; hence, additional, supplemental).

a—hat, ā—hāte, â—bâre, ä—bär, e—hen, ē—hē, i—hit, ī—hīde, o—hot, ō—hōme, ô—bôrn, u—hut, ū—hūge, û—bûrn, ŏŏ—hood, ōō—hōōt, ou—out, oi—oil, ng—sing, ngg—finger, th—thin, th—then, zh—vision, and ə which equals a in dial, e in model, i in pupil, o in method, u in circus, or y in martyr.

rudiment (rōō'də·mənt), n., usually found in the plural. [La *rudimentum*, beginning, from *rudis*, imperfect, rude.] **1.** first principle of an art or science, as the *rudiments* of math ematics; a beginning or first step to any knowledge. **2.** tha which is yet in an undeveloped state. **rudimentary,** adj.
From the same root (RUD): **erudite** (freed from rudeness therefore very learned or scholarly); **erudition.**

succinct (suk·singkt') adj. [Lat. *succinctus,* girdled, concise: *sub* under + *cinctus,* girded, encircled.] expressed in a few words brief, concise.
Synonyms: compact, concise, condensed, laconic, pithy, sum mary, terse.
Antonyms: diffuse, lengthy, loquacious, prolix, verbose, wordy
From same stem (CINCT): **cincture** (a girdle or belt), **cinch** (via Spanish, a strong belt or strap for a saddle; colloquially a tight grip or an easy task), **precinct** (a district, an enclosure)

vagary (və·gâ'ri, və·gā'rē), n., pl. *ies.* [Lat. *vagari,* to wander roam.] **1.** a rambling excursion; a roaming about [obsolete **2.** an eccentric or extravagant notion or act; whim.
Synonyms: caprice, crotchet, fancy, quirk, whim.
From same root (VAG): **vague, vagabond, extravagant, diva gation** (a wandering or straying away; a digression).

WHICH DICTIONARY SHALL I USE?

You may wonder why there is no chapter called "How To Use A Dictionary" in this book. There is none because we believe that the best way to learn is by doing. And using a dictionary (or a "reasonable facsimile" thereof) is what you've been doing in this chapter.

Of course we have simplified things a little, but if you've read this far without too much difficulty, you'll find diction-aries, abridged or unabridged, easier to handle. This is a good place to take a quick look of appraisal at dictionaries which you may want to use or own.

Every unabridged dictionary is an abridged encyclopedia. **Webster's New International** (Merriam-Webster). This is

---

a—hat, ā—hāte, â—bâre, ä—bär, e—hen, ē—hē, i—hit, ī—hīde, o—hot, ō—hōme, ô—bôrn, u—hut, ū—hūge, û—bûrn, ŏŏ—hood, ōō—hōōt, ou—out, oi—oil, ng—sing, ngg—finger, th—thin, th—then, zh—vision, and ə which equals a in dial, e in model, i in pupil, o in method, u in circus, or y in martyr.

America's best unabridged dictionary, practical, scholarly, authoritative. Becuse it contains cross-references for words that have the same or related roots, its use can become an exciting adventure for anyone interested in etymological treasure hunts.

Funk and Wagnalls Standard Dictionary. This is an excellent dictionary which has a single alphabetical listing of all important entries except selected foreign phrases, which are placed in a special section. It is scholarly and authoritative, containing a great deal of important and extensive information under many of its entries. It lacks the cross-references and detailed etymological treatment of the *New International*. Moreover, it employs a double pronunciation key which is confusing to some users.

Oxford English Dictionary (also known as the OED, and also as the *New English Dictionary* or NED). This is a monumental work of scholarship which took thousands of scholars more than seventy years to complete. And it was worth the time and trouble. It is the greatest dictionary ever compiled, designed for scholars and research workers rather than for the casual dictionary user. It contains no pictures, maps, or encyclopedic material. Its distinctive features are a detailed study of the origin and etymology of each word and an abundance of quotations which trace its changes in meaning through the years. There are two shorter versions: a two-volume edition (*The Shorter Oxford*) which retains many of the characteristics of the larger edition, and a one-volume *Concise* eddition.

The New Century Dictionary and Cyclopedia (10 volumes of dictionary, 2 volumes of cyclopedia) is the most handsomely printed and the most literary of the unabridged dictionaries. It is valuable for its illustrative quotations and its extended, essay-like treatment of definitions. The more recent two-

---

a—hat, ā—hāte, â—bâre, ä—bär, e—hen, ē—hē, i—hit, ī—hīde, o—hot, ō—hōme, ô—bôrn, u—hut, ū—hūge, û—bûrn, o͝o—hood, o͞o—ho͞ot, ou—out, oi—oil, ng—sing, ngg—finger, th—thin, t͟h—then, zh—vision, and ə which equals a in dial, e in model, i in pupil, o in method, u in circus, or y in martyr.

volume edition retains many of the good features of the larger work.

ABRIDGED OR DESK DICTIONARIES

All College or Desk Dictionaries sell for about five or six dollars, but they are—for value received—worth many times that sum. There is no attempt here to single out any one of these as the best. If you have one of them, *it* is the best. There are no poor college or desk dictionaries. The only poor dictionary is one that is allowed to rust "unburnished, not to shine in use." All of them are scholarly, thorough, informative, and rewarding *when used*.

Webster's New Collegiate Dictionary. Since this is an offspring of *Merriam-Webster's New International* (Unabridged), it has many of the advantages of the famous parent volume. It comes in a thin India paper edition, which makes it easy to handle. The *Collegiate* contains comprehensive sections on punctuation, pronunciation, and foreign words. Its synonyms are carefully discriminated.

Funk and Wagnalls New College Standard Dictionary (Emphatype Edition). An authoritative, attractive volume, it is up to date in its entries, has more of them than any of the other desk dictionaries, and gives interesting encyclopedic information. Names of persons and places and foreign phrases are listed in the general vocabulary instead of in special sections or in appendices. Its synonym and antonym tables are very helpful.

American College Dictionary (The ACD). This is a newcomer which has many admirable features. The ACD gives current meanings first, archaic and obsolete meanings last. Its pronunciation key—it uses the schwa (ə) for unaccented, slurred vowels—is easy to follow. It is a heavy book but it is

a—hat, ā—hāte, â—bâre, ä—bär, e—hen, ē—hē, ĭ—hit, ī—hīde, o—hot, ō—hōme, ô—bôrn, u—hut, ū—hūge, û—bûrn, ŏŏ—hood, ōō—hōōt, ou—out, oi—oil, ng—sing, ngg—finger, th—thin, th—then, zh—vision, and ə which equals a in dial, e in model, i in pupil, o in method, u in circus, or y in martyr.

attractive, beautifully printed, and sturdily bound. Like the *Standard* it uses a single alphabetical arrangement for practically all entries. It is practical and scholarly.

Winston Dictionary: College Edition. Although this dictionary lacks the comprehensiveness of the other desk dictionaries, its entry words set in large capitals and its simpler definitions appeal to many dictionary users. This dictionary includes an atlas of the world, sixteen pages of maps in color, as well as a chronological table of the chief events in world history.

Webster's New World Dictionary (College Edition). This latest arrival among desk dictionaries is perhaps, like all new babies, the handsomest. Modern in every way, it is particularly useful to those seeking full etymological information and discriminating synonym tables. Its pronunciation symbols—it also uses the schwa (ə)—are perhaps the simplest and easiest to use. This dictionary also contains a section listing and giving information about colleges and universities in the United States and Canada, as well as junior colleges in the United States.

There is a paperback edition of this dictionary. Of the paperbacks we have seen, this is easily the best. It is the only one that gives derivations, and its pronunciation symbols, appearing at the foot of every right-hand page, are the easiest to use.

Because the smaller, abridged dictionaries are revised frequently, they should be consulted rather than the unabridged dictionaries if you are looking for latest meanings or changed pronunciations.

---

a—hat, ā—hāte, â—bâre, ä—bär, e—hen, ē—hē, i—hit, ī—hīde, o—hot, ō—hōme, ô—bôrn, u—hut, ū—hūge, û—bûrn, ŏŏ—hood, ōō—hōōt, ou—out, oi—oil, ng—sing, ngg—finger, th—thin, th—then, zh—vision, and ə which equals a in dial, e in model, i in pupil, o in method, u in circus, or y in martyr.

HOW DO YOU SAY IT?

OUR THANKS

We are grateful to all of the dictionaries mentioned for the help they have give us in the preparation of this book. We found it fun working our way around in each of them.

Considering the number of times we have consulted it, we should be ungrateful if we didn't mention an excellent dictionary, little known in America, Henry Cecil Wyld's *Universal English Dictionary*. This is a work of painstaking scholarship and clarity of definition by one of the great linguists and lexicographers of our time. It is British in its viewpoint and citations and uses phonetic symbols as well as diacritical marks.

A STRING OF FIFTY-FIVE

(We define them; you pronounce them)
Answers will be found on page 365.

How Do You Sound Your "A"?

1. UNSCATHED: Is one who has escaped uninjured (a) un skä thd′ (b) un skä thd′, or (c) un ska thd′?

2. ULTIMATUM: Is a final demand (a) an ultəmä′ təm, (b) an ultəmä′ tum, or (c) an ultəmat′ əm?

3. GRIMACE: When you make a face is it (a) a grimäs′ or (b) a gri′məs?

4. VERBATIM: Is a word-for-word account (a) a vûrbā′ tim or (b) a vûrbät′ im report?

5. DAIS: Is a raised platform (a) a dī′ is or (b) a dā′ is?

---

a—hat, ā—hāte, â—bâre, ä—bär, e—hen, ē—hē, i—hit, ī—hīde, o—hot, ō—hōme, ô—bôrn, u—hut, ū—hūge, û—bûrn, ŏŏ—hood, ōō—hōōt, ou—out, oi—oil, ng—sing, ngg—finger, th—thin, th—then, zh—vision, and ə which equals a in dial, e in model, i in pupil, o in method, u in circus, or y in martyr.

6. FRACAS: Is a noisy brawl (a) a frăk'əs or (b) a frak'əs?

7. DEPRAVITY: Is a state of corruption and moral degradation known as (a) dəpra'viti or (b) dəprā'viti?

8. MALTREAT: If one is roughly handled or abused, is he (a) maltrēt'əd or (b) môltrē' təd?

9. BAYOU: Is a sluggish channel of water (a) a bā'ōō or (b) a bī'ōō?

10. NADIR: Is the opposite of *zenith* (a) na'dēr, (b) na'dər, or (c) nā'dər?

Are You at Ease with "E's"?

11. ERA: Are we living in the atomic (a) er'ə or (b) ē'rə?

12. BESTIAL: Are acts that are uncivilized and degraded (a) bes'chəl or (b) bēs'chəl?

13. ALUMNAE: Should one refer to girl graduates as (a) əlum'nē or (b) əlum'nī?

14. HEINOUS: Is an atrocious offense (a) hānəs, (b) hē'nəs, or (c) hīnəs?

15. MISCHIEVOUS: Is a playful child (a) mischēv'iəs or (b) mis'chəvəs?

16. FETED: When a person is honored in a festive celebration, is he (a) fā'təd or (b) fē'təd?

17. PRELATE: Is a high church dignitary (a) a pre'lət or (b) a prē'lāt?

18. QUERY: Does one ask (a) a kwē'ri or (b) kwe'rī?

19. QUIETUS: Is Hamlet's word for death in his famous soliloquy (a) kwī e'təs or (b) kwī'e təs?

20. ERR: If you make a mistake do you (a) er or (b) ûr?

Do Your "I's" Bother You?

21. ITALICIZED: *Are words written as these are* (a) ităl'ə-sīzd or (b) ītal'əsizd?

---

a—hat, ā—hāte, â—bâre, ä—bär, e—hen, ē—hē, i—hit, ī—hīde, o—hot, ō—hōme, ô—bôrn, u—hut, ū—hūge, û—bûrn, ŏŏ—hood, ōō—hōōt, ou—out, oi—oil, ng—sing, ngg—finger, th—thin, th—then, zh—vision, and ə which equals a in diạl, e in modẹl, th—then, zh—vision, and ə which equals a in diạl, e in modẹl,

22. **RESPITE:** Is a welcome interval of rest (a) a res'pǐt or (b) a res'pīt?

23. **GENUINE:** Is something authentic (a) jen'ūǐn or (b) jen'ūǐn?

24. **RIBALD:** Is a coarse or off-color remark (a) rib'əld or (b) ri'bôld?

25. **DIVISIVE:** Are forces that attempt to split the unity of a country (a) dəvis'ĭv or (b) dəvī'sĭv?

26. **DINOSAUR:** Is one of the prehistoric reptiles called (a) a di'nəsôr or (b) a dī'nəsôr?

27. **ALUMNI:** Should male graduates be called (a) əlum'nī or (b) əlum'nē?

28. **STIPEND:** Is a fixed payment for services (a) a sti'pənd or (b) a stī'pěnd?

29. **SEISMIC:** Are earthquakes called (a) sīz'mik or (b) sēz'mik disturbances?

30. **WIZENED:** Is something that is withered and shriveled (a) wiz'ənd or (b) wīz'ənd?

Are You a Good G-Man?

31. **MIRAGE:** Is an optical illusion (a) a mǐ'rəj, (b) a miräzh', or (c) a mǐ'rəj?

32. **MALINGERER:** Should a person who feigns illness—who doesn't want to get well—be called (a) a maling'gərər, (b) a maling'ərər, or (c) a alinj'ərər?

33. **GIBBET:** Is a gallows in the shape of an inverted L called (a) a gib'ət or (b) a jib'ət?

34. **GEWGAWS:** Are baubles or trifling things (a) gū'gôz or (b) jōō'gôz?

35. **ORGY:** Is the word sometimes used for a wild, unrestrained celebration (a) ôr'gi or (b) ôr'ji?

36. **GIBBOUS:** Do we call a moon that is between half-full and full (a) gib'əs or (b) jib'əs?

---

a—hat, ā—hāte, â—bâre, ä—bär, e—hen, ē—hē, i—hit, ī—hīde, o—hot, ō—hōme, ô—bôrn, u—hut, ū—hūge, û—bûrn, ŏŏ—hood, ōō—hōōt, ou—out, oi—oil, ng—sing, ngg—finger, th—thin, th—then, zh—vision, and ə which equals a in dial, e in model, i in pupil, o in method, u in circus, or y in martyr.

And What About Ch's?

7. CACHE: Is a secret hiding place (a) a kash, (b) a kashā, or (c) a kach?

8. CHIROPODIST: Should one who treats minor ailments of the feet be called (a) a kirŏp'ədist, (b) a chirŏp'ədist, or (c) shirop'ədist?

9. SCHISM: Is a split or cleavage in an organization (a) a shizm, (b) a sizm, or (c) a skizm?

10. ARCHIVES: Are public records or the depository in which they are kept referred to as (a) är'chīvz or (b) är'kīvz?

11. CHAMELEON: Is the little lizard-like animal that can adapt its color to its surroundings (a) a shəmē'liən or (b) a kəmē'liən?

12. MACHINATIONS: Are the crafty schemings of evildoers called machinā'shənz, (b) mashināshənz, or (c) makinā'shənz?

13. CHICANERY: Is trickery or underhandedness referred to as (a) shikā'nəri or (b) chikā'nəri?

14. ARCHIPELAGO: Does a group of oceanic islands form (a) an ärchəpel'əgo or (b) an ärkəpel'əgo?

15. PENCHANT: Is a strong inclination or a partiality (a) a pen'shənt or (b) a pen'chənt?

16. CHARLATAN: Should we call a faker (a) a shär'lətən or a (b) chär'lətən?

Do You Keep Your Accents on Straight?

17. FORMIDABLE: Is an opponent who is to be feared or dreaded (a) fôr'mədəbl or (b) fôrmid'əble?

18. NONCOMBATANT: In time of war is a civilian (a) a non-kəmbat'ənt or (b) a nonkom'bətənt?

—hat, ā—hāte, â—bâre, ä—bär, e—hen, ē—hē, i—hit, ī—hīde, —hot, ō—hōme, ô—bôrn, u—hut, ū—hūge, û—bûrn, ŏŏ—hood, ōō—hōōt, ou—out, oi—oil, ng—sing, ngg—finger, th—thin, h—then, zh—vision, and ə which equals a in dial, e in model, in pupil, o in method, u in circus, or y in martyr.

49. DOLOROUS: Is something that is sad or mournful
                   (a) dəlôr'əs or (b) dō'lərəs?

50. OMNIPOTENT: Is one who is all-powerful (a omni'pətən
                   or (b) omnipō'tənt?

51. INTERNECINE: Is a civil strife deadly to both sides re
                   ferred to as (a) in tər nē'sin or (b) in
                   tûr'nə sin?

52. INTEGRAL: Is that which is essential to a plan (a) ar
                   inte'grəl, (b) an intē'grəl, or (c) ar
                   in'təgrəl part of it?

53. REMONSTRAT: If you plead with someone do you (a)
                   rem'ənstrāt or (b) rimons'trāt with him

54. CLANDESTINE: Is a secret appointment (a) klan'dəstin o
                   (b) klandes'tin?

55. ACUMEN: Should one's keenness or acuteness of mind
                   be called (a) əkū'mən or (b) ak'ūmən?

Of all language activities pronunciation is probably the most vulnerable to change. Hundreds of prounciations that were considered wrong ten or fifteen years ago are now acceptable.

A word suddenly leaps into prominence. An atom bomb is dropped and thousands of newscasters rush to their microphones and announce to their listening world that an atomic *era* has been ushered in. But most of them, not having had time to check their dictionaries, pronounce the word ĕrə Since then, many important and prominent people have adopted this pronunciation of the word. Yet of the five desk dictionaries—and dictionaries have listening posts everywhere and are very sensitive to pronunciation changes—only one has so far recorded ĕrə as a variant pronunciation. The others have held out valiantly for īrə or ērə.

Perhaps they've done so because they know what happened at the farewell dinner given to an important educational official in one of our large cities. The M. C., wishing to be gracious and flattering to the guest of honor, began with an introductory statement about his long period of service. What his audience heard was, "With the retirement of Superintendent Soandso, an educational *error* has come to an end"!

Don't let it happen to you!

"How many 🐾 *'s are there in* 〰〰𓏲𓏲𓆓𓏏 ?" ?"*

* Drawing reproduced courtesy *Look* Magazine.

---

15. Double Trouble

ONE NIGHT when Joel Chandler Harris, creator of Uncle Remus, was at his editorial desk, an old-time reporter looked over and asked, "Say, Joel, how do you spell *graphic?* With one *f* or two *f*'s?"

"Well," replied Harris in his gentle drawl, "if you're going to use any *f*'s, you might just as well go the limit."

That's the way many of our friends feel—some of them writers—when it comes to the question of double or single consonants. They just throw up their hands and say, "It doesn't make sense. Why one *r* in *iridescent* and two in *irresponsible?* Why one *n* in *anoint* and *inoculate* and two in *innuendo* and *innovation?* Why two *t*'s in *committed* and only one in *benefited?* No—I tell you there's no rhyme or reason for it."

But they're wrong. There is reason—a sound reason, and though there's no rhyme there's rhythm. Rhythm has something to do with doubling the consonant. We'll make that

---

clear a little later on, but first we'll tell you the true story of how one man's knowing his double consonants and knowing how to use a dictionary saved him a fine.

On October 13, 1945, a citizen of Durham, North Carolina, was brought before Judge Wilson of Traffic Court for parking his car on a restricted street right in front of a sign forbidding parking. But instead of pleading guilty, the defendant protested that he was not extracting ore from underneath the street.

This was not a facetious reply, for when the sign was brought in as evidence, the defendant triumphantly pointed out that it read "No Stoping" and *stoping*, he was able to prove with the help of an unabridged dictionary (p. 2,485, Webster's *New International*), means "extracting ore from a stope, or loosely, underground."

"Your honor," said the defendant, "I am a law-abiding citizen. When I saw that sign I noted it carefully. And being a law-abiding citizen, I said to myself, 'Bill, whatever you do, don't extract any ore—it's against the law.' Judge, I didn't do and stoping—and I move the case be dismissed."

The judge decided that the defendant had lived up to the letter of the law—the single letter—and the case was dismissed.

But we can't dismiss so easily the reason for single and double letters in spelling. We're going to try to chase the bugaboo of so many writers by beginning an enveloping operation and attacking the problem from three angles.

DIVIDE AND CONQUER

Our first approach is to go back to a technique we have already used in making long words easy—breaking them into recognizable units and then putting them together again. Spelling then becomes a simple problem in arithmetic; it becomes as easy as adding 1 and 1 and getting 2, or adding 1 and 0 and getting 1.

Let's see how it applies in actual cases. Words beginning with *dis* often cause trouble. Here are a dozen words. Should they have one *s* or two *s's*? You tell us. We'll divide them for you. You add up the *s's*:

dis + appoint

dis + solve

dis + satisfied

dis + service

dis + solution

dis + ease

dis + sent   dis + appearance
dis + similar   dis + aster
dis + illusion   dis + section
                dis + integrate.

If you have ever misspelled any of these words, hang your head in shame, because it means you weren't able to perform the simple arithmetical operation of $1 + 0 = 1$ or $1 + 1 = 2$

And it works just as well with other prefixes. If a prefix ends in a consonant and the word to which it is attached begins with the same consonant then the result is a doubled consonant:

mis + spell   but mis + apply
un + necessary   but un + answerable
in + numerable   but in + oculate (as in *oculist*).

When the first letter of the root is one that the last letter of the prefix must blend with, we also get a double consonant:

in + mobilize   = immobilize
in + legible   = illegible
in + relevant   = irrelevant
con + lateral   = collateral
con + mission   = commission
ad + commodate   = accommodate
sub + press   = suppress
sub + ceed   = succeed
syn + metrical   = symmetrical.

It is now easy to see that you won't get a double consonant if the prefix ends in a vowel:

re + commend   de + press
pro + fessor   a + cross
pre + paration   se + paration
        de + siccated (dried up).

Ah, but you say, "My trouble is not at the beginning of words, it's in the middle of words. Take the word *beginning*, for example. I know it has a double *n*, but why?"

THE ACCENT MAKES THE DIFFERENCE

Let's look carefully at these two columns of words:

A	B
prof'it	regret'
quar'rel	control'
trav'el	prefer'
wor'ship	begin'
hap'pen	rebel'
col'or	compel'.

The two columns are alike in every respect but one. The words in column A end in one consonant; so do the words in column B. The words in column A have a single vowel before the final consonant (*profit, quarrel*, etc.); so have the words in column B (*regret, control*, etc.). But whereas those in column A are accented on the first syllable, the words in column B are accented on the second syllable, *and that makes all the difference!*

The doubling of the consonant depends on the rhythm of the word; it depends on where the accent falls. Only when the accent falls on the syllable containing the single consonant that we're worried about is the consonant doubled as a rule. Let's see how it works. Add *ing* to each word in column A and nothing happens (*profiting, quarreling*, etc.). But add *ing* to each word in column B and the consonant is doubled (*regretting, controlling*, etc.):

Column A	Column B
prof'iting	regret'ting
quar'reling	control'ling
trav'eling	prefer'ring
wor'shiping	begin'ning
hap'pening	rebel'ling
col'oring	compel'ling.

Note that the consonant is doubled only when the accent falls on the syllable containing it. If the accent shifts from it, the consonant is not doubled:

ref'erence		refer'ring
pre'ferable	but	prefer'ring
con'ference	but	confer'ring
occur'rence.	and	occur'ring

176

No matter how many syllables the word has, the rule of accent works the same way:

unri'valed	uncontrol'lable
ben'efited	unforget'table
imper'iling	overstep'ping
tobog'ganing	noncommit'tal.

British writers and dictionaries such as the *Oxford English Dictionary* do not follow this rule strictly but prefer the double consonant except in a few words like *biased* and *caroled*. You can usually recognize a novel printed in England by the double *l* and double *p* spellings of words like *marvellous, travelled, woollen,* and *worshipped.* Some American writers occasionally follow this practice. Therefore, "to accommodate the English-speaking public," Webster's *New International Dictionary* gives both spellings but indicates its preference by putting the spelling with the single consonant first. Other American dictionaries follow the lead of Webster's. American editors and publishers prefer to streamline spelling and apply the rule strictly. Therefore we are asking you to conform with American practice by applying the rule strictly also in the exercises at the end of this chapter, after you have taken into account the following cautionary notes.

Cautions

1. This rule, good as it is, must not be applied indiscriminately. It operates only for words that follow the pattern: *one* final consonant, preceded by *one* vowel.

2. The rule operates only when the syllable that is added begins with a vowel (*ing, ed, age,* etc.):

equip'ping	but	equip'ment
commit'ting	but	commit'ment
prefer'ring	but	prefer'ment

3. The consonant is doubled in words like those on the left in 2, above, when the syllable before the added syllable is accented.

4. Like most rules of language, this rule does have a few exceptions. Here are the most noteworthy:

a. *chagrined'*: one *n* always.

b. *confer' able, infer' able, refer' able, transfer' able,* but note *defer' rable* and *defer' able.*

c. *cancella' tion, crys' talline, crys' tallize, ex' cellence* (from *ex cel'*), *met' allurgy*. These are, however, not true exceptions because the Latin words from which they are derived have two *ll*'s. For the same reason, *tranquil' lity* is preferred to *tranquil' ity*, but *tran' quilize* (formed from *tran' quil*) and *tran quil iz' er* are preferred to *tran' quillize* and *tran quil liz' er.*

d. *gas' sing* and *gas' sy*, but *gas' eous* and *gas' ify.*

e. A few words ending in *g*, like *humbug*, double the *g*, as in *humbugged*, to show that the *g* is not to be pronounced as a *j*. Moreover, there is an additional stress on the last syllable: *hum' bug'*.

f. Words derived from *kidnap* may have either one or two *p*'s even in American usage, because the last syllable may also be stressed: *kid' nap'*. So, the New York *Times*, a strict observer of the rule, prefers *kidnapped* and *kidnapper*. The English prefer the double *p* as in the title of Robert Louis Stevenson's novel *Kidnapped*.

MONOSYLLABLES

Words of one syllable like *stop* and *hop* have the same structure as the words we have discussed. *They end in a single consonant preceded by a single vowel.* It is obvious that if we apply our rule to a word of only one syllable the consonant will always be doubled when you add *ing*, *age*, or *ence*. *Stop*, therefore, becomes *stopping*, not *stoping*; and *hop* becomes *hopping*, not *hoping*. Neglecting to double the consonant can sometimes cause trouble. A literary critic found this out when he read his column one morning and discovered that the gripping novel he had reviewed had "griped" him intensely. Then there's the old, old one about a small-town editor who was very much embarrassed when his newspaper, writing a laudatory column about one of the town's leading citizens, called him a "battle-scared veteran." To make amends the editor wrote a correction for the next morning's edition. Unfortunately the typesetter got there first with "a bottle-scarred veteran."

A SOUND RULE

As we have seen, a double consonant has a tendency to shorten the preceding vowel sound (*hoping—hopping, dining*

—dinning). Therefore, where we cannot apply our rule, the sound or the pronunciation of the word may help us. For example, how many *s*'s are there in *occa ? ion*? Since we pronounce the second syllable *kay*, we can be pretty sure there's only one *s*. Two *s*'s would make the word rhyme with *passion*. This is a very crude test and should be used with circumspection.

However, there's another troublesome spelling situation in which the sound and a little detective work can help us.

WHICH VOWEL IS IT?

Often we are puzzled over the spelling of a word because a particular vowel has lost its identity. Words like *sed ? tive, friv ? lous, med ? cine, hypocr ? sy* offer such a problem. The unknown letters all represent the same indeterminate vowel sound—the schwa (ə). How do we solve the mystery of the disguised vowel? It's easy. We smoke it out. We find a related shorter or longer word in which the vowel comes out in the open because it is in an accented syllable.

See how it works by supplying the unmasked vowel. Answers to A and B will be found on page 366.

A

Problem Word	Clue Word	Unmasked Vowel
1. acadəmy	acad ? mic	....
2. affirmətive	affirm ? tion	....
3. authər	auth ? rity	....
4. conservətory	conserv ? tion	....
5. definəte	defin ? tion	....
6. ecstəsy	ecst ? tic	....
7. emphəsis	emph ? tic	....
8. exhilərate	hil ? rious	....
9. frivəlous	friv ? lity	....
10. grammər	gramm ? tical	....
11. hypocrəsy	hypocr ? tical	....
12. medəcine	med ? cinal	....
13. mirəcle	mir ? culous	....
14. monotənous	monot ? ne	....
15. narrətive	narr ? te	....
16. notəriety	not ? rious	....
17. nutrətive	nutr ? tion	....
18. omnivərous	v ? racious	....
19. repətition	rep ? titive	....
20. sedətive	sed ? te	....

SINGLE OR DOUBLE?

Answers will be found on page 366.

B

l's
1. chise ? ing
2. counse ? ing
3. exto ? ing
4. marve ? ous
5. mode ? ing
6. paralle ? ing
7. patro ? ing
8. shrive ? ed
9. unequa ? ed
10. unpatro ? ed

n's
11. becko ? ing
12. balloo ? ing
13. happe ? ing
14. pardo ? ing
15. trepa ? ing

r's
16. defe ? ing
17. diffe ? ing
18. occu ? ence
19. occu ? ing
20. offe ? ing
21. proffe ? ed
22. refe ? ee
23. refe ? al

t's
24. acqui ? al
25. acqui ? ing
26. allo ? ment
27. allo ? ing
28. ballo ? ing
29. benefi ? ing
30. profi ? able

III. WORDS ON PARADE

" 'Passé' might be the very word you're groping for." *

16. Do You Read the Sports Page?

DON'T GO away. This isn't a chapter about technical terms used in sports. It's about words most sports fans read and never see!

They don't see the words because their eyes are closed to everything but the exciting details of the game they're reading about. Mere words, no matter how difficult or unusual, can't slow up the action for them or dim the achievements of their heroes.

They go right past words like BELLWETHER, CUNCTATIOUS, DEBACLE, FLACCID, HIATUS, HOLOCAUST, IMPECCANT, JUGGERNAUT, LAGNIAPPE, OBSEQUIES, PALADIN, PANTHEON, PARAGON, PRESTIDIGITATION, PUISSANT, PULLULATING, PURLIEUS, RATIOCINATION, and TRANSPONTINE.

---

* Drawing reproduced courtesy *Collier's.*

We tried out twenty such sports words on a high school class of thirty-five bright seniors, and we opened their eyes wide—in amazement and unbelief. "I never found words like that in the sports pages," one pupil said. To which another, wiser student added, "But from now on you will."

And from now on we think you will too. If you want to enrich and increase your store of words pleasantly and enjoyably, you can do a lot worse than read the sports pages of your newspaper. Some of the best and certainly the most picturesque writing is being done day after day on the sports pages of our newspapers.

The style may occasionally be a bit jaunty and a little flamboyant. And why not? Dealing day after day with similar events and recurring situations, sports writers reach out for new ways of making their stories colorful and exciting. If in reaching for words that are somewhat different they occasionally overreach themselves—well, it's all done in good fun.

ALL IN SPORT

Even though some of the athletes whose names appear in the newspaper and magazine items quoted below are no longer active, we have nevertheless used the clippings from our long and active file for two reasons. In the first place, the choice of words in these clippings is still the best we have encountered for the particular words, and in the second place, we thought that it might give you a nostalgic thrill to see the names of some athletic heroes of the past. After all, to take only one example, the Brooklyn Dodgers are part of our folklore! That's why we retain the present tense—*now* for *then*.

When in midseason the Brooklyn Dodgers—leading the league—lose two games by the lopsided scores of 12-4 and 9-3 to a last-place team, the sports writer for a New York newspapers has to reach out. Stock words won't do. To Brooklyn fans this isn't just a defeat or a rout or even a catastrophe. So he writes: "There were 25,594 eye witnesses to this double *debacle*," and the gloom that has settled over Flatbush lifts a little.

Nor is the snapping of a winning streak, when it belongs to the Dodgers, something that can be passed over lightly. No, indeed. "*Obsequies*" are held" for the death of that Dodger winning streak before a Chicago crowd of 39,988, only a small minority of whom could be classed as mourners."

A pair of game-winning home runs become "a couple of *lethal* blows," but useless homers, punched out after the game has already been won, are "merely *lagniappe*."

A particular infielder who rarely makes any errors is referred to as the "usually *impeccant* Luis Aparicio." When a former hero erred, we were told that "that paragon of outfield perfection, jolting Joe DiMaggio, played it [a line drive] like a *tyro*."

A runless inning sandwiched between two innings when runs were plentiful becomes "a *hiatus* in the Giants' run-production department," and a puny batting effort is a "*flaccid* tap to the mound."

The 1947 World Series, with the opposing teams separated by the Brooklyn Bridge, was described as a "*transpontine* feud," while the frenzied master-minding of the rival managers in the sixth game of that series was characterized as "the longest and most intemperate orgy of *ratiocination*."

OTHER SPORTS

Goal posts that are not torn down after a smashing Notre-Dame victory over Army remain "*inviolate*." A week later we read that "the cadets came back from the Notre Dame *holocaust* with their best performance of the year." The forward-passing skill of a professional football player is nothing more or less than "the baffling *prestidigitations* of Sid Luckman, the master magician." And on a New Year's Day, Fritz Crisler's Michigan steamroller became "his *juggernaut*," which "whacked the bewhatsis out of Southern California by the tidy little count of 49 to 0."

In basketball, sports writers were practically unanimous in referring to the old New York University powerhouse as "Howard Cann's *puissant* performers," and to mighty Kentucky as "perennial *paladin* of the Southeastern Conference." Duke, another visiting team, out in front in its own section of the country, was referred to as "one of the *bellwethers* of the Southern Conference."

Outlying boxing arenas are called *purlieus*, a baseball player who is obviously stalling for time is *cunctatious*, the Hall of Fame at Cooperstown is "baseball's *pantheon*," and a headline for a story about the Kentucky Derby tells us that:

All Louisville Is Pullulating*

And that's a good place to stop!

Except to add that the next day, making good the prophecy of the student who said, "But from now on you will," another student in our bright senior class brought in one sports column (Dan Daniel in New York *World-Telegram*) that contained the words *proselyters, lagniappe, protean, ubiquitous, forensic,* and *peroration.*

ARE YOU A GOOD SPORT?

What is your batting average with these words we have taken from the sports pages? Here they are in a test for you. You ought to do well because the context is still fresh in your mind and because, if it isn't, you can go back and refresh your mind easily. Using the text to figure out the meanings will make you use your powers of *ratiocination.*

If you get all twenty right you are *impeccant;* if you get ten or fewer right you are a *tyro.* To consider yourself a big-leaguer you should get at least fifteen right.

I. Twenty Sports Words

Answers will be found on page 366.

1. *bellwether*   (a) high scorer (b) veteran team (c) leader (d) unpredictable performer
2. *cunctatious*   (a) obstinate (b) delaying (c) indifferent (d) domineering
3. *debacle*   (a) overwhelming disaster (b) error (c) mishap (d) encounter
4. *flaccid*   (a) stringy (b) flabby (c) slow (d) bounding
5. *hiatus*   (a) high spot (b) drawback (c) gap (d) total loss
6. *holocaust*   (a) disappointment (b) bruising battle (c) contest (d) wholesale destruction
7. *impeccant*   (a) well-groomed (b) faultless (c) graceful (d) usually dependable
8. *inviolate*   (a) unpainted (b) uncrossed (c) unharmed (d) firmly rooted

---

* Louisville, May 1—Derby week has flowered into the rich ripe beauty of its screwball phase and Louisville is *pullulating* with reasons why this horse race presents a spectacle unmatched by any other American sporting venture with the possible exception of a 42nd Street flea circus.

9. *juggernaut* — (a) avenger (b) irresistible force (c) lucky team (d) whip

10. *lagniappe* — (a) something for good measure (b) window dressing (c) futility (d) oilcloth for decoration

11. *obsequies* — (a) apologies (b) consequences (c) funeral rites (d) celebration

12. *paladin* — (a) representative (b) aggregation (c) surprise (d) knightly champion

13. *pantheon* — (a) temple (b) home town (c) place of origin (d) museum

14. *paragon* — (a) side show (b) veteran (c) student (d) model of excellence

15. *prestidigitation* — (a) master-minding (b) sleight-of-hand (c) skillful diagnosis (d) speed

16. *puissant* — (a) skilled (b) mighty (c) dependable (d) highly-regarded

17. *pullulating* — (a) apologizing (b) shouting (c) teeming (d) sprawling

18. *purlieus* — (a) places for tryouts (b) outskirts (c) money-makers (d) bandboxes

19. *ratiocination* — (a) second-guessing (b) delaying tactics (c) slow thinking (d) reasoning

20. *transpontine* — (a) traditional (b) across-the-bridge (c) everlasting (d) deadly

TAKING INVENTORY

Now it's time to take inventory again, for here in this chapter we are once more going through the cycle of the practical and sure way of increasing your vocabulary. As we see it, there are three steps.

STEP 1. You meet the word. You are introduced to it in context and get to know it. You try to size it up by stopping to take in the whole idea of which it is the unknown quantity. The words that accompany it, the general drift give you a vague or sometimes a pretty good notion of what it means. But if you don't meet the word frequently thereafter, it won't do you much good unless you take

STEP 2. You look the word up in a dictionary, selecting, from the several meanings given, the one that fits best into the context in which you found it. In this way you get an accurate definition and you learn the word, but you won't remember it unless you take

STEP 3. You must try to fix the word, whenever possible, by some logical association: origin, use, the story behind it, a fixed phrase. We are going to take this third step right now for a few of these words to show you once again how, when you fix a word, you learn much more than just the word itself.

THE THIRD STEP

BELLWETHER:

The bell rings in this word, because it is tied around the neck of the wether or male sheep that leads the flock. *Bellweather* is therefore often used to mean a leader.

CUNCTATIOUS:

This isn't a very useful word except to amaze your friends with, but if you're interested look at the entry under *Fabian Policy* on page 223. The word we usually use for one who employs delaying tactics is *dilatory*.

HOLOCAUST:

This word is made up of two Greek roots: *holo,* whole, entire, and *kaust,* burnt. Originally, a holocaust was a whole burnt offering or sacrifice. Then it came to mean a wholesale destruction, especially by fire. From the combining form *holo,* we get the word *holograph,* a document written entirely in the handwriting of the author. From *kaust* we get *caustic* (a caustic remark is one that sears) and *cauter*ize, to treat a wound by burning tissue through the use of heat or chemical caustics.

JUGGERNAUT:

Juggernaut is the name of the Hindu god whose idol is dragged in religious procession on an enormous car. The stories that vast numbers of devotees have thrown themselves in the path of the advancing car and been crushed under its wheels are untrue, but when the huge car pushes relentlessly forward through narrow streets crowded with frenzied worshipers, accidents can happen. The word *juggernaut* is frequently used today to describe an irresistible, ruthless force or machine that destroys everything that gets in its way. Some writers apply the word *juggernaut* to something unusually large or massive. In the February 28, 1961 issue of

Look, John Gunther effectively combined the two notions of the word, "World War II began a week later, when the Nazi legions crashed into Poland, now helpless and caught between two fires. So was set in ugly motion a *juggernaut* that, before it finally rolled to a stop, cost the world at least 20 million lives."

LAGNIAPPE:

This is a word that was born in the United States among the Creole population of Louisiana. Its original meaning is seen in this sentence written by a traveler in 1893 in *Harper's Magazine:*

"Take that for a lagniappe [pronounced lan-yap]," says a storekeeper in New Orleans as he folds a pretty calendar ino the bundle of stationery you have purchased.

Lagniappe is, therefore, a trifling present given when a purchase is made. It is also used in the sense of something given for good measure or something extra.

PALADIN:

This word is related to the word *palace*. It is the name specifically given to the twelve famous warriors of Charlemagne's court but is often applied to the Knights of the Round Table as well. Today the word is used for a noble defender of the right, or a renowned champion.

THE IDEAL WAY

And so the ideal and practical way to increase your vocabulary is to be on the lookout for new words in your reading, to get their meaning from the context, to check them in a dictionary, and, whenever possible, to fix them by associations that enrich the words and make you remember them.

II. *Some More Sports Words*

(in phrases from various newspapers)
Answers for these tests will be found on page 366.

1. *affluent* old age — (a) wealthy (b) doddering (c) wielding power (d) healthy
2. *callow* American youth — (a) unthinking (b) inexperienced (c) superficial (d) impetuous
3. *caparisoned* for battle — (a) eager (b) handicapped (c) reluc-

tant (d) decked out

4. proving beyond *cavil* — (a) quibble (b) certainty (e) belief (d) contradiction

5. making a *debonair* entrance — (a) badly timed (b) graceful and lighthearted (c) dejected (d) rapid

6. *doughty* Elroy Face — (a) pudgy (b) valiant (c) wealthy (d) hard-working

7. *fatuously* overplaying — (a) carelessly (b) good-naturedly (c) foolishly (d) boastfully

8. wild *hosannas* of joy — (a) celebrations (b) revels (c) exclamations (d) hand-clappings

9. the usually *imperturbable* Di Maggio — (a) faultless (b) morose (c) undemanding (d) calm

10. screaming *imprecations* at him — (a) curses (b) unintelligible sounds (c) warnings (d) instructions

11. the *indomitable* champion — (a) confident (b) unconquerable (c) undefeated (d) unknown

12. *laminated* bowling pins — (a) undersized (b) transparent (c) solid (d) made of thin layers

13. with extreme *largesse* — (a) nobility (b) courtesy (c) generosity (d) caution

14. *palpably* unfair — (a) unknowingly (b) obviously (c) extremely (d) hardly

15. the *phrenetic* details — (a) frenzied (b) gruesome (c) psychological (d) secret

16. *ramifications* of the situation — (a) consequences (b) lessons (c) branchings out (d) dangers

17. the *redoubtable* Whitey Ford — (a) formidable (b) plucky (c) confident (d) unconquerable

18. natural *repugnance* of publicity — (a) indifference (b) condemnation (c) regard (d) abhorrence

19. somewhat *reticent* in manner — (a) careful (b) solemn (c) reserved (d) ambiguous

20. encounter quick *retribution* — (a) reward (b) appreciation (c) resistance (d) punishment

21. a denial . . . so *spurious* — (a) indignant (b) speedy (c) false (d) shameless

22. the *svelte* left-hander — (a) fat (b) lithe (c) erratic (d) smooth

23. the *temerity* to approach him — (a) kindness (b) unwillingness (c) timidity (d) boldness

24. the *ubiquitous* Mr. Rickey — (a) inquisitive (b) appearing everywhere (c) stout (d) tightfisted

25. quoting him *verbatim* — (a) mockingly (b) word for word (c) though forbidden (d) unofficially

III. Genuine Sports Words

For sports aficionados who may have been disappointed because the words of this chapter were not about sports, here's a consolation round. Can you match the words on the left with the sports they belong in?

1. chancery		a.	baseball
2. crosse		b.	bowling
3. leave		c.	croquet
4. let		d.	football
5. ringer		e.	golf
6. roquet		f.	hockey
7. sacrifice		g.	lacrosse
8. safety		h.	pitching horseshoes
9. save		i.	rowing
10. scull		j.	skiing
11. slalom		k.	tennis
12. stymie		l.	wrestling

"Where's King Augeas? I'm supposed to clean his stables." *

---

17. Myths That Still Live

THE ANCIENT Greeks and Romans had no soap operas, no Superman comics, no movie romances. But they had their myths. What Hollywood heroine could be more glamorous than Helen of Troy, what soap-opera wife more faithful than Penelope, what Superman or Buck Rogers more spectacular than Hercules, son of Jupiter?

The exploits of the Greek gods and goddesses, their demi-gods and heroes run like a gold thread through the tapestry of the world's literature, music, and art, and also science. In the last-named field, some of the achievements of modern man are like myths transformed into reality. Paradoxically, but fittingly enough, man has drawn upon the myths for a great number of descriptive names in the missile, submarine, and space programs: *Apollo, Atlas, Jupiter, Mercury, Nike* (goddess of Victory), *Proteus* (who rose from the sea), *Saturn,* the Norse god *Thor* the Thunderer, *Titan, Triton* (who

* Drawing reproduced courtesy the *Saturday Review*.

blew "his wreathéd horn"), and *Zeus*. Old and new meet again in the myths, which have truly never died, for hardly a day passes without some allusion being made in our newspapers to characters and events found in the myths.

Here, for instance, is a handful of recent headlines:

Argonauts at Work

Labor of Hercules

Dan. O'Connell, Nemesis of Western Traitn Robbers

Pandora's Box

Tennessee Looks for a Sisyphus

With one exception, the stories or editorials which followed these headlines did not explain the meaning of the mythological term. Yet, the reference to a myth set the tone of the story or editorial and slanted it.

There's only one good way for us to help you fix the meaning of such words or phrases and that's to tell the story behind the word or phrase, the story that dramatizes the meaning.

ACHILLES HEEL

> Until this summer Alaska was an *Achilles Heel*. It is no longer such in like degree, but there remains much to be done that will be basically valuable in either peace or war.

By dipping the infant Achilles into the River Styx, his mother made him invulnerable except in the heel by which she held him. Therefore the heel of Achilles is a weak spot, and so it proved in the case of Achilles, who was killed before the walls of Troy when Paris shot him in the heel with a poisoned arrow.

The tendon of Achilles, which binds the muscles of the calf to the bone of the heel, receives its name from this myth. In quadrupeds this tendon is called the *hamstring*. To hamstring an animal is to lame it by cutting this tendon. So, to hamstring means to weaken, to destroy the efficiency of, to cripple.

AEGIS

> No doubt the production will grow smoother and more fluent with repetition. But there should be no improvisatory air about what we send abroad under the *aegis* of the Government.

The *aegis* (also written *egis*) was the mantle and shield of Zeus. Even the king of the gods needed protection in his wars with the Titans. Zeus lent the aegis to his daughter Athene when she went into battle on the side of the Greeks during the Trojan War. Homer describes it as a sort of cloak. It is generally associated with statues of Athene on which it appears as a short cloak covered with scales. Whether it was a shield or cloak, it certainly had protective powers since on it were serpents and the head of the Gorgon which turned men to stone if they looked at it. In modern usage the meaning of aegis as a shield or protection has been extended to mean sponsorship or auspices.

CASSANDRA

> On many aspects of policy, particularly in the foreign field, Congress and the President have falsified the *Cassandras*.

Apollo fell in love with Cassandra, a daughter of King Priam. He gave her the gift of prophecy, but when she failed

195

to carry out her promise to love him, he decreed that nobod
should believe her, although she spoke the truth. A Cassandra
is therefore a prophetess or prophet of doom. Today the
name is applied to anybody who utters warnings of troubl
to come whether the prophecy is believed or not.

CHIMERA

> However, if now military authori-
> ties approve a bridge, as they have in
> the case of the Delaware River Bridge
> seaward of the Philadelphia Navy
> Yard, it will be because they find these
> objections to be the *chimeras* Mr. Moses
> believes them to be.

The Chimera (also written *Chimaera*) was a horrible monster that breathed fire, had the head of a lion, the body of a
goat or a lion, a serpent's tail, and a goat's head on its back.
Such a combination was unusually fantastic even for the
imagination of a mythologist. So, a wild dream, an imprac-
ticable idea, a vain fancy is called a *chimera*. The adjective
is *chimerical*. In his essay "El Dorado" Robert Louis Stevenson calls the goals that men seek their *chimaeras*.

A strange picture we make on our way to our *chimaeras*,
ceaselessly marching, grudging ourselves the time for rest;
indefatigable, adventurous pioneers.

HERMETICALLY SEALED

> If one were to believe the electronists
> the day is not far distant when airmen
> will make their way about the globe
> without ever unfolding a map. Remote
> in their *hermetically* sealed cockpits,
> they will—in theory—merely follow a
> combination of meters and lines on a
> dim, phosphorescent screen.

Hermes, better known by his Roman name of Mercury,
was the patron god of magic. In the Middle Ages, alchemy,
the predecessor of chemistry, was known as a *hermetic* art.
To put the hermetic seal or the seal of Hermes on a bottle
in the laboratory meant to twist the neck with flame and

thereby seal it air-tight. The expression is often used figuratively to imply that a person's mind is shut against the infiltration of ideas or information.

HYDRA-HEADED

> But the guerrilla movement is *hydra-headed* as regards reinforcements both from within the country and from abroad.

The Hydra was a water monster (*hydr*, water, as in *hydr*ant, *hydr*aulics, *hydr*ophobia, de*hydr*ate) which had nine heads. Hercules was ordered to kill the Hydra as one of his twelve labors. The Hydra had remarkable regenerative powers, for as fast as Hercules cut off a head, two new ones replaced it. However, the heads could not grow back if fire was applied immediately to the cut. Hercules thereupon enlisted the aid of an assistant who cauterized the necks as Hercules severed the heads. *Hydra-headed* means hard to eliminate or destroy. The term is applied to an evil which, apparently put down in one place, springs up elsewhere. In biology, the hydra is a fresh-water animal of almost microscopic size which has the property of its mythological namesake. If it is cut up, each part will develop into new hydra.

IRIDESCENT

> More than fifteen years have passed since a geyser of *iridescent* vapor mushroomed 40,000 feet into the air over Hiroshima after the first atomic bomb ever launched in war exploded.

Iris was a lovely maiden who left a trail of color as she carried messages from the gods to the earth. She was the goddess of the rainbow. The word *iris* itself may mean a flower, a part of the eye, or a combination of brilliant colors, as in Tennyson's famous lines from "Locksley Hall":

> In the spring a livelier *iris* changes on the
> burnished dove,
> In the spring a young man's fancy lightly
> turns to thoughts of love.

197

Knowing the origin of the word *iridescent*, you can see why it is spelled with one *r*.

PANDORA'S BOX

> This is platoon baseball, an idea that is repugnant to the point of loathsomeness. It would open a *Pandora's box*, releasing incalculable mischief.

The first woman, according to Greek mythology, was Pandora. Milton tells us in *Paradise Lost* how she got her name:

> . . . Pandora, whom the gods
> Endowed with all their gifts.

Pan means all and *dora* means gifts. Every god and goddess contributed something to make her a perfect being. Zeus, angered at mankind, sent her down to be a curse to man. It appears that until she was created, the earth was inhabited only by man and beasts. The gods gave her a box which she was warned not to open. Unable to overcome her curiosity, she did open it one day. Trouble then came upon earth. All the ills that plague the body and mind of man flew out. Only hope remained.

This version of the myth is decidedly anti-feminist. It started the legend that woman and her curiosity are responsible for the troubles from which man suffers. A *Pandora's box* is a source of evil, a seething cauldron on which a lid must be kept.

PROMETHEAN

> It is necessary today to educate the nonscientific public to the *Promethean* nature of atomic energy and the true character of science (for example, that it contains no secrets).

Prometheus was a Titan who brought the gift of fire to mankind so that by its use man could develop his civilization. Like Prometheus the scientists of our time have wrested from Nature the secret that is no longer a secret. Once again men are turning to the symbol of Prometheus as a lesson and warning to mankind. The meaning of the new Promethean gift in all its implications is well expressed in the following item found in the science page of the New York *Times*:

> The name "prometheum" has been suggested by J. A. Marinsky and L. E. Glendenin (M.I.T.) for element 61, recently made artificially in the atomic pile at Oak Ridge. Prof. Charles D. Coryell (M.I.T. again) thinks the name appropriate.* Prometheus taught man the use of fire. By way of punishment, jealous Zeus chained him to a mountainside and set vultures to tear out his vitals. To Professor Coryell "prometheum" symbolizes the hope of scientists that man will not be punished for developing the atomic bomb by having his vitals torn out by the vultures of war.

So, the myths have never died. In the stories we have retold, we have only sampled their survival. Here is a list of useful words for which we are indebted to the myths.

English Word	Meaning	Origin
ANTAEAN:	having the power to renew one's strength.	Antaeus, a wrestler, son of Poseidon (Neptune) and Earth, was invincible as long as he was in contact with Mother Earth.
ARGONAUTS:	gold-seekers; daring adventurers.	The Argonauts were heroes who sailed with Jason on the Argo in quest of the Golden Fleece. The coinage of the name *astronauts* or *Astronauts* is clearly explained in the following sentence from an editorial in the *Herald Tribune*, "Like the Argonauts of antiquity, today's *astronauts* are venturing closer and closer to the borders of the unknown." However, the Argonauts sailed (*naut*) the seas on the *Argo*, their swift ship;

---

* At first element 61 was named *illinium* after the University of *Illinois;* finally its name was changed to *promethium.*

English Word	Meaning	Origin
		the Astronauts are being propelled in a capsule toward the *astra*, stars or outer space. On April 12, 1961, the word *cosmonaut* (*cosmos*, universe + *nautes*, sailor) became equated with *astronaut*.
ARGUS-EYED:	very watchful, keen-sighted, all observant.	Argus was a mythological monster who had a hundred eyes, some of which always remained awake.
BACCHANALIAN:	characterized by drunken revels, or by ecstatic frenzy.	Bacchus was the god of wine, and Bacchanalia were feasts or orgies in his honor.
CALLIOPE:	a series of steam whistles played from a keyboard; steam organ.	Calliope was the Muse of eloquence. Her name, meaning "beautiful voice," is humorously applied to this modern shrill, harsh-sounding instrument.
CORNUCOPIA:	"horn of plenty"; inexhaustible reserves; symbol of abundance.	The infant Zeus was nursed by a goat named Amalthea, one of whose horns had the power of being filled with whatever the owner of it desired.
CYCLOPEAN:	huge, massive, applied especially to a type of early architecture.	The Cyclopes were giants who erected structures by piling up huge stones without cementing them.
EROTIC:	pertaining to sexual desire.	Eros, Greek name of Cupid, god of love or desire.
GORGON:	an ugly person; a petrifying force.	The Gorgons were three sisters so ugly that anyone looking at their faces turned to stone. Medusa, the most famous of these sisters, was killed by the hero Perseus, who looked at her reflection in a mirror and so avoided her direct gaze.
HARPY:	a grasping, ravenous person.	The Harpies were flying female monsters that snatched the food of their victims and the souls of the dead.

English Word	Meaning	Origin
HYMENEAL:	pertaining to marriage.	Hymen, god of marriage.
JANUS-FACED:	two-faced.	Janus, god of beginnings and doors. His statues show him with two heads facing in opposite directions.
JOVIAL:	joyous; merry; inspiring mirth.	*Jovialis*, pertaining to Jupiter. Persons born under the planet Jupiter are supposed to be joyful. Ancient sculptors and poets often represented Jupiter and Zeus as smiling upon men.
MENTOR:	a teacher or wise counselor; invariably applied to athletic coaches.	Mentor was the friend of Ulysses to whom the latter entrusted the education of his son.
MERCURIAL:	swift, active; having the qualities of mercury or quicksilver; influenced by being born under the planet Mercury.	Mercury, the messenger of the gods, who flew with the aid of his winged sandals.
MYRMIDONS:	loyal followers; attendants who execute orders without question, pity or mercy.	The Myrmidons were a tribe of warriors who followed Achilles.
NARCISSISM:	self-love and admiration.	Narcissus was a handsome youth who fell in love with his own reflection and was changed into the flower of the same name.
NEMESIS:	an agent of retribution or punishment; relentless pursuer of evildoers; "jinx."	Nemesis, goddess of retribution and punishment, the upholder of the moral code.
ODYSSEY:	long voyage; dangerous journey.	Odysseus (Ulysses), hero of Homer's *Odyssey*, took ten years in which to get home

English Word	Meaning	Origin
		from the Trojan War, meeting with many strange adventures and perils.
OLYMPIAN:	majestic, awe-inspiring; detached and aloof.	Mt. Olympus was the home of the gods.
OREAD:	nymph of the hills and mountains.	Nymphs were beautiful maidens who typified the spirit of nature. *Oreads* lived in mountains, *dryads* in trees, *naiads* in streams, and *nereids* in the sea.
PAEAN:	a song of praise, triumph or thanksgiving.	From *paian*, the song of deliverance sung by Apollo after his victory over the Python.
PALLADIUM:	safeguard, as in the expression, "The Bill of Rights is the palladium of our liberties."	From Pallas Athene (Minerva). Her image or *palladium* guarded Troy and Troy could not be taken until after Ulysses had stolen the image.
PHOENIX:	a person or thing supposed to have died or to have passed into oblivion and then to have risen again; a symbol of immortality; a *rara avis* (see p. 000).	The phoenix was a fabulous bird living at least 500 years. After being consumed in fire, it rose fresh and youthful from its own ashes.
PROTEAN:	changing in shape.	Proteus was "the old man of the sea" who could change his form and appearance at will.
SATURNINE:	heavy, gloomy, serious.	Saturn (Cronus in Greek) was the father of Jupiter. Saturn himself was jovial and his period of rule was supposed to be a golden age. The feasts celebrating his worship were gay and wild, like our New Year's Eve, from which fact we get *Saturnalia* to mean a wild time. However, astrology has given *saturnine* its gloomy aspect,

		for persons born under the influence of the planet Saturn are supposed to be morose and sad.
STENTORIAN:	very loud-voiced; bellowing.	Stentor, herald of the Greeks in the Trojan War. He was their human loud speaker before microphones and public-address systems.
STYGIAN:	inky, gloomy, dark; infernal.	The River Styx flowed down into the Lower World. Spirits entering Hades had to cross it on a ferry piloted by Charon.
TERPSICHOREAN:	pertaining to dancing.	The nine Muses presided over the arts. Terpsichore was the Muse of the dance.

PHRASES THAT TELL A STORY

In your reading you will meet not only single words like these but phrases and sometimes sentences taken from mythology, phrases whose full meaning is not revealed unless you take a look behind the mythological curtain. Let's look.

SULK LIKE ACHILLES IN HIS TENT

During the siege of Troy, Achilles, the greatest of all the Greek heroes, refused to fight because of a quarrel with his leader Agamemnon who had taken away a captive girl awarded to Achilles. Achilles withdrew to his tent and didn't go out to fight until after the death of his friend Patroclus. The phrase means to refuse to participate in an important undertaking because of personal grievances.

BEWARE THE GREEKS BEARING GIFTS

The Greeks, unable to capture Troy by storm, resorted to trickery. They left a huge wooden horse filled with armed men outside the walls and pretended to sail away. The Trojans wanted to drag the horse into the town and celebrate but their priest Laocoön warned them that the horse was a ruse, with these famous words: "I fear the Greeks even when they bear gifts." The Trojans went right on with their plans, made an opening in the walls, and wheeled in the wooden horse, which, though a Greek gift, has ever since been known as the *Trojan Horse*, a symbol of treacherous infiltration.

LABORS OF HERCULES

These are superhuman labors and *herculean* is a word used to describe superhuman strength. Hercules was sentenced by Apollo to perform twelve labors of extraordinary difficulty, one of which was:

CLEANING THE AUGEAN STABLES

King Augeas owned twelve white bulls sacred to Apollo. Their stables had not been cleaned in thirty years! Hercules was called upon to do the work in one day. He diverted the course of a river, made it run through the stables, and reported his mission completed. *To clean the Augean stables* means to clear up a mess. The phrase is sometimes applied to the efforts of a reform government to undo the corruption left by its predecessors.

THE BURDEN OF SISYPHUS

This phrase has been used to describe the poor wage-earners' efforts to keep up with the rising cost of living. It's a never-ending task. Sisyphus, mythological king of Corinth, was punished for his misdeeds on earth by being forced to roll a huge boulder uphill in Hades. He never finished his assignment for no sooner had he rolled the stone near his goal than it slipped downhill, and he had to start all over again.

THE BED OF PROCRUSTES

Procrustes, "the Stretcher," was a highwayman and inn-keeper who had an ingenious method of torturing his guests and victims. He insisted that each of them must exactly fit the iron bed in his inn. To accomplish this end, he would stretch a guest if he was too short or cut his legs to size if he was too tall. A system—educational or political—in which the individual must fit a single type or pattern and conform arbitrarily is known as a *bed of Procrustes,* or *procrustean.*

A SOP TO CERBERUS

Cerberus was a three-headed dog that guarded the entrance of the Lower World and growled at newcomers. A few of the mythological heroes like Hercules, Theseus, and Aeneas wanted to visit the Lower World and return from it. They had to get by Cerberus. Aeneas did it by throwing Cerberus a drugged honey cake that put the dog to sleep. *Throwing a sop to Cerberus* means making a conciliatory offering to someone who may cause trouble.

SOWING THE DRAGON'S TEETH

Cadmus went in search of his sister, Europa, who had been abducted by Zeus. In the course of his wanderings, he killed a dragon and at the advice of Athene planted the teeth. A fierce band of warriors arose from the teeth, and again at the advice of Athene, Cadmus hurled a stone among them. Each blamed his neighbor with the result that a free-for-all took place until almost all of them were killed. (The same episode occurs in the story of Jason.) *Sowing the dragon's teeth* means planting the seeds that lead to war.

BETWEEN SCYLLA AND CHARYBDIS

This phrase is similar to "out of the frying pan into the fire," or "between the devil and the deep blue sea." Scylla and Charybdis were monsters guarding the strait between Italy and Sicily. They preyed upon vessels which tried to pass through. If the sailors gave one a wide berth, they were almost certain to come too close to the other.

I. Not a Herculean Labor

Some words that have come to us from myths do not necessarily present vocabulary difficulties. Refresh your memory of the words in the left-hand column by matching them with the terms on the right. Consult a dictionary for their origin. Answers for these tests will be found on page 366.

1.	ATLAS	a.	group of animals
2.	TITANIC	b.	marine demigod
3.	TANTALIZE	c.	lewd person
4.	TRITON	d.	very large
5.	VULCANIZE	e.	strong woman
6.	SIREN	f.	tease
7.	PANIC	g.	treat rubber by heating
8.	AMAZON	h.	book of maps
9.	FAUNA	i.	terror
10.	SATYR	j.	fascinating woman

II. Ten Small Tasks

The sentences below contain words or phrases of mythological origin. From the group of words after each sentence select the definition that comes closest to the meaning of the italicized words.

1. The recommendation that the state legalize off-track betting is quite akin to *prying the lid off the box of Pandora,* and the moralists already are mumbling in dismay.
　　(a) committing a great sin (b) winning a signal victory (c) making an irrevocable decision (d) releasing innumerable troubles

2. And so, at the very moment last fall when economic *Cassandras* were crying inflation, the curtain was already rising on the first act of an old economic drama whose title is, What Goes Up Must Come Down.
　　(a) prophets of disaster (b) experts (c) lobbyists (d) investors

3. In Washington five clemency boards are reviewing the cases of all general prisoners—a *herculean* job.
　　(a) merciful (b) time-consuming (c) difficult (d) thankless

4. Marshall and Molotov, at Moscow, warily agreed to reopen negotiations which may abolish the *hermetic* border which separates North and South Korea.
　　(a) guarded (b) ideological (c) imaginary (d) tightly sealed ·

5. They [the nations of eastern Europe] have moved beyond being a "sphere of influence" for their Russian neighbor and *mentor.*
　　(a) ruler (b) adviser (c) protector (d) supplier of weapons

6. The *mercurial* Greek reaction was immediate in the re-appearance of some scarce commodities.

    (a) quick (b) official (c) secret (d) usual

7. His fingers seem to have *the touch of Midas.*

    (a) unusual strength (b) inability to hold on to money (c) extreme sensitivity (d) ability to turn all they touch to gold

8. Mr. Priestley is a *protean* man of letters with strong moral convictions and the ability to perform equally well in different fields.

    (a) prosaic (b) versatile (c) genuine (d) prominent

9. It is not easy to be a writer, these days, but the account executives and grocery clerks are not having any *saturnalia,* either.

    (a) wild holiday (b) easy time (c) prosperity (d) public recognition

10. "The roll call is concluded," Lyndon Johnson announced in *stentorian* accents.

    (a) dignified (b) Southern (c) booming (d) weary

OH YEAH?
BOOGIE-WOOGIE
SCRAM
STINKEROO
SEZ YOU
NERTS
WISE GUY
COULD BE
HEP CAT
SNAZZY

You see, we start out by teaching them the words they'll use most frequently." *

18. Slang Is "Old Stuff"

SOME WORDS and phrases are designed for the long pull through the centuries and some serve merely to brighten the passing moment. Slang is the short, quick thrust—here today and gone tomorrow.

There are two kinds of slang—good and bad. The bad becomes feverishly popular for a while and soon dies. "So's your Aunt Tilly" and "23 skiddoo" had their brief run. Today they are amusing museum pieces, tags to identify a by-

---

* Drawing reproduced courtesy *Collier's*.

gone age. But the best slang lasts a long time because it has roots in the imagination and because it takes a vivid short-cut to our thoughts. Even our statesmen find it hard to get along without expressions like "spill the beans," "throw mud on," "go out on a limb," "left holding the bag." Such phrases will last as long as the picture they present remains true and the color vivid.

However, we are not going to deal here with slang as a special form of language. As always, we are interested in presenting words that will enrich or increase your vocabulary. We are, therefore, taking up words which are completely respectable and dignified, words which have made the long pull through the centuries but which, *when dissected, will reveal a slang or colloquial expression that is still in use.*

WHAT'S COOKING?

Many of the expressions that we regard as slang or colloquial usage today were "old stuff" to the Greeks and Romans thousands of years ago. They had words for them—single words that no longer have any slang overtones for us today. We use the word *concoct* without realizing that in one dignified word we are echoing the slang phrase "to cook up." Yet that is what *concoct* means literally (*coct* from the Latin verb meaning "to cook" + *con*, together), and the obvious question to ask someone who is concocting something is, "What's cooking?"

If we dig around among some of our respectable words, we're going to find encrusted in them the picturesque language of modern slang. For each of the expressions listed below—believe it or not—we are going to find a dignified word that says it all.

When you have finished reading the chapter come back and fill in these words. Each dot stands for a letter. You will find the answers in the reading material itself!

Slang or Colloquial Phrase	*Dignified Word*
1. a chip off the old block	. . . . .
2. close your eyes to	. . . .
3. decorate the palm	. . . . . .
4. give someone the eye	. . . .
5. going through the motions	. . . .

6. high-brow and high-hat . . . .
7. playing along with . . . .
8. sail into . . . .
9. shooting off one's mouth . . . .
10. sitting this one out . . . .
11. take a cut . . . .
12. strip the hide off . . . .
13. uppity . . . .
14. wised up . . . .

TELLING 'EM OFF

When you're not using dignified words, when instead you are abusive in your language and just "shooting off your mouth," you are unloosing a *tirade*, a volley of words. *Tirade* is from French *tirer*, to shoot.

If you "sail into" an opponent then you are *inveighing* against him; you are using *invective*. Or, perhaps, you may prefer a stronger word, one the headline writers favor when they want to describe a blistering attack:

RUSSIAN CRITICS

EXCORIATE TWO

COLUMBIA MEN

Excoriate means literally "to strip the hide off" (*ex*, off + *corium*, hide or leather). In the Middle Ages, as any reader of a best-selling historical romance knows, the well dressed knight wore a leather breast-plate called a *cuirass* (French). Also via French we get the word *scourge*, a lash or whip— something made from a strip of leather. A scourge (rhymes with *urge*) is either the means of inflicting punishment or, more often, the punishment or affliction itself.

SITTIN' PRETTY

If you don't go along with the majority point of view, you are taking a *dissident* position. You literally decide not to go along, you sit apart (*dis*, apart + *sid, sed*, sit). You are saying, "I'll sit this one out." The roots *sid* and *sed* give us many useful words that we are setting down here:

SUPERSEDE: literally "to sit above" (*super*); therefore, to displace and replace.

SEDATIVE: a drug that invites your nerves to sit down and take it easy. A peron whose personality is normall reserved, unruffled and serious is *sedate*.

INSIDIOUS: literally "sitting in" ambush, ready to pounce therefore, sly, treacherous, wily.

RESIDENCE: literally a place where (we hope) we can "sit back" and relax.

ASSIDUOUS: literally "sitting close to" one's work; therefore working diligently, devotedly, and conscientiously.

A word usually given as a synonym for *assiduous* is *sedulous*, which may well be a sitting word too but it is generally believed to come from a Latin word meaning sincerely (*se*, without + *dolo*, guile). Doing something sincerely, with complete application, is to do it assiduously. Robert Louis Stevenson attributed the development of his literary style to his assiduous study and his imitation of writers he admired, to his having "played the sedulous ape to Hazlitt, to Lamb, to Wordsworth."

But if your heart isn't in what you are doing, if you are merely "going through the motions," you are doing it in a *perfunctory* way. You're doing it just to get through with it (*per*, through + *funct*, performed). From the same root we ge the word *defunct*, having ceased to *function*, no longer performing, deceased.

PLAY BALL WITH

You "play along with" or "play ball with" those with whom you are in *collusion* (*col* for *com*, with + *lud, lus*, play). A *prelude* is something we hear before a play, an *interlude* between parts of a play, and a *postlude* after. when you *elude* someone you get away from him through quickness and cunning. An *illusion* is an appearance that plays tricks on you, not to be confused with an *allusion* which is an indirect or passing reference to something. To *delude* is to "play false," to deceive.

MAKING WITH THE EYES

The "wool is being pulled over your eyes" when you allow yourself to be *inveigled* into something. *Inveigle* comes from *aveugle*, French for blind, which goes back to *oculus*, the Latin word for eye (*ab + oculus*, without the use of your eyes).

If you "make eyes at a girl" or "give her the eye" you are *ogling* her. *Ogle* comes from the Dutch word for eye and is related both to the German word *Auge* and the Latin *oculus*. A *supercilious* person is one who arches his eyebrows and looks down his nose at you; in other words, a "high-brow" who "high-hats" you. *Supercilious* is made up of *super* (above or high) and *cilia* (eyelids or eyebrows). A person who is *haughty* (French *haut*, high) is just "uppity."

If you "close your eyes to" something that you know is going to happen you are guilty of *conniving*, the literal meaning of which is "winking along with."

CUT ME IN

Someone who has connived with another may ask for his share, and *share* is literally a "cut." *Share* goes back to an Anglo-Saxon word that also gives us *shear*, *ploughshare*, and *shard* (also *sherd* and *potsherd*), a piece of pottery that has been cut or broken off.

The Greek combining form for cut or split is *schizo*. From it we get three "cutting" words in which the *sch* sound is pronounced in three different ways! Stop, look, and listen:

1. SCHISM (pronounced sizm):	a split, a cleavage
2. SCHIST (pronounced shist):	a type of rock that splits easily into slabs or sheets
3. SCHIZOPHRENIA (pronounced skizzofreenia):	a word we use for a mental condition, popularly referred to as a split personality.

The Latin root for cut, *sec*, gives us *segment*, a *section*, a piece cut off, and probably *scion*, a descendant, "a chip off the old block."

UNDER THE COUNTER

A person who takes another kind of "cut" by means of misappropriating funds is guilty of embezzlement or *defalcation*. To *defalcate* is literally to cut down with a sickle (Latin *falx, falcis*).

Money is usually involved in the expression "decorating the palm." The person at the receiving end is being *suborned* (*sub, under, + orn,* decorate or furnish). To *suborn* means to bribe for criminal purposes, especially for perjury. The root *orn* appears in *adorn, ornament,* and *ornate,* which has come to mean over-decorated.

WISE GUYS

You're not likely to have anything put over on you if you are "wised up" or *sophisticated* (*sophos,* Greek for wise). The Sophists or Wise Men were a group of teachers who achieved great fame in Greece during the fifth century B.C. Although they had many good educational ideas, they got a bad reputation because they accepted pay—so unlike a gentleman—and because they used subtle methods of argumentation. Some of the Sophists even boasted that they could "make the worse appear the better reason." Hence the word *sophistry* has an unfavorable connotation and means arguing deceitfully, attempting to turn a poor case into a good one by means of clever but specious reasoning. And so the word *sophistry,* that contains the root for wise in it, has come to be a synonym for *evasion, fallacious reasoning, quibbling,* and *casuistry.*

SLING YOUR OWN SLANG

Can you fill in the dignified word which, when dissected, becomes a "translation" of the slang or colloquial expression? To help you, we have change or adapted the meanings of the prefixes to fit the modern slang or colloquial phrase. We are also giving you synonyms for the word to be filled in. And because you have read thus far in the book we are throwing in the suffix as lagniappe. Each dot stands for a etter. Answers will be found on page 366.

Dignified Word	Related Slang	Latin Root or Word	Synonym
1.	"burnt up"	*cens*, set on fire	enraged
2.	"a cover up"	*text*, covered	excuse
3.	"sing a different tune"	*cant*, sing	take back publicly
4.	"put something over on"	*pos*, put	deceive

Dignified Word	Related Slang	Latin Root or Word	Synonym
5. .... ate	"pile it on"	*agger*, heap	enlarge
6.	"catch on"	*prehend*, seize	understand
7. ..... ile	"fly off the handle"	*volat*, fly	unstable
8. .... ery	"cheek"	*front*, forehead	impudence
9.	"tell the world"	*vulgus*, the common people	make public
10. ..... ual	"on the dot"	*punct*, point	prompt
11.	"tied up in knots"	*plex*, interwoven, entangled	puzzled
12.	"to get around"	*vent*, come	evade, bypass

"I wonder why Damocles moved my place card to the center of the table." *

---

19. Out of the Past

PYRRHIC VICTORY

At the beginning of President Kennedy's administration the House of Representatives passed a bill enlarging the House Rules Committee. David Lawrence, no supporter of this plan, under the headline, VICTORY OVER HOUSE RULES INTERPRETED AS PYRRHIC ONE, wrote, "It was a Pyrrhic victory—the radicals won the battle over the plan to 'pack' the House Rules Committee, but it's still a question as to who will win the real war." As used here, Pyrrhic victory is a bit of wishful thinking.

A *Pyrrhic victory* costs more than it gains. This kind of hollow triumph gets its name from Pyrrhus, king of Epirus

---

* Drawing reproduced courtesy the *Saturday Review.*

in Greece, who invaded Italy in 280 B.C. and defeated the Romans at Heraclea and Asculum. However, he himself was wounded and so many of his men were killed that he was unable to follow up his victories. He won the battles but not the war. According to Plutarch, Pyrrhus remarked, "Another such victory and we are undone."

This whole story and its meaning are summarized in a single phrase—a *Pyrrhic victory*. Whenever you use this phrase or others taken from history, you are taking a short cut in language. Through this trip into the past, you are expressing in a single word or phrase an idea which saves you sentences or paragraphs of explanation.

In addition, you are making a vivid comparison which is illuminated by this flashback into the past. Stern measures become even more rigid when they are called *draconian* laws, a costly banquet appears richer when it is called a *Lucullan* feast, and cautious maneuvers are more gradual when they are termed *Fabian* tactics.

Our language is rich in terms, phrases, and expressions that recall the history of Greece and Rome. These words were once part of the everyday speech and writing of generations of students who knew Greek and Latin thoroughly and who were often more familiar with the history of Greece and Rome than with that of their own country. Thus, the phrases and words that recall events and customs of ancient times came into our language and remain a living part of it.

You will meet such phrases constantly in your reading. Expressions like the *sword of Damocles*, a *Maecenas*, *crossing the Rubicon*, words like *satrap* and *helot* will take on new meaning and broader connotation when you know their full story.

We took each of the following phrases and words from current newspapers and magazines. We are including synonyms and related words.

ACADEMIC

> It is *academic* to talk of any other expedient. And the time for *academic* theorizing is now long past.

Plato's school in Athens was called the Academy. *Academic* therefore literally means related to schools or to scholarship.

However, since what goes on in the schools is often considered remote from reality or practical life, *academic* has come to mean "without practical value." An *academic* discussion is one which does not lead to an immediate practical solution, one which is engaged in for the sake of argument only.

Synonyms of *academic* in this sense are *theoretical* and *speculative.*

AUGUR

> It is estimated there will soon be forty-five hours a week of quiz-game shows on the television networks, a prospect that *augurs* toil and moil for the network "police units" which are duty-bound to keep television antiseptic clean.

Among the Romans the *augurs* were the priests who foretold the future through the flight of birds, the weather and other signs. To *augur* well is therefore to prophesy favorably. When the augur pronounced the omens favorable, public business could begin or be *inaugurated.* The word for bird, *avis,* from which we get *aviary, aviator* and *aviation,* is contained in *augur* and *auspices,* which also is related to inspecting the flight of birds as omens.

Synonyms:

AUGUR (verb): foretell, predict, forecast, presage, portend, prognosticate, prophesy

AUGUR (noun): prophet, soothsayer, diviner, oracle

AUGURY: omen, portent, sign, symptom, prophecy (notice that *prophecy* is the noun and *prophesy* the verb)

AUSPICIOUS: favorable, propitious, benign, lucky, providential, well-omened, roseate

INAUGURATE: install, induct, initiate, commence, start, invest, institute found, establish

BREAD AND CIRCUSES

> According to the sociological theories of an ancient Roman named Juvenal there are only a couple of things needed to keep the average citizen from becoming unduly excited—*bread and circuses.*

219

As he mourned the breakdown of Roman society, the satirist Juvenal bitterly remarked that the common people desired only two things to keep them satisfied—*panem et circenses*. *Panem* is bread and *circenses* are games and entertainments. The expression "bread and circuses" is used to indicate that in times of social stress the people can be kept happy with food and entertainment at public expense, as the Roman rulers once supplied free grain and sports.

CAESAR'S WIFE

> Like *Caesar's wife*, the keeper of the British budget not only must do no wrong, but must avoid any indiscretion, however innocent or slight, that might conceivably permit any suspicion of wrongdoing.

The sentence quoted clearly explains the meaning of the phrase, "like Caesar's wife." The phrase is especially applied, as here, to public officials whose conduct must be free not only from actual misdeed but from any suspicion of wrongdoing. Plutarch tells us how the expression arose. A young nobleman Publius Clodius was accused of a religious crime in which Pompeia, the wife of Caesar, was implicated. Caesar divorced Pompeia, "but being summoned as a witness against Clodius, said the had nothing to charge him with. This looking like a paradox, the accuser asked him why he parted with his wife. Caesar replied, 'I wish my wife to be not so much as suspected.' "

CANNAE

> The enemy . . . evolved the "Sho Plan," a complicated, tortuous, . . . unworkable design for destroying American naval forces piecemeal and by a *Cannae*-like envelopment annihilating both our land and sea strength.

In 216 B.C. at Cannae in Apulia, Italy, the Carthaginian

general Hannibal achieved the classic dream of every military commander. He enveloped, encircled, and destroyed a Roman army. A defeat of this type or a total defeat is known as a *Cannae*. Von Hindenburg achieved a Cannae at the expense of the Russians near Tannenberg in 1914, and the Russians retaliated in World War II at Stalingrad for one of the decisive battles of that war. *Annihilation* and *decimation* are associated with a Cannae.

CROSSING THE RUBICON

> Two major factors have now decided the Labor party, if only by a narrow majority, to *cross* their political *Rubicon*.

To cross the Rubicon means to take a final, irrevocable step which may have dangerous consequences. The Rubicon is a small stream in northern Italy which separated the province of which Caesar was the governor from Italy proper. His political rivals at Rome had passed a law ordering him to disband his army. Caesar marched to the river and stood at the bank undecided whether to cross it and thereby precipitate civil war. Finally, according to Plutarch, "casting aside calculation, and abandoning himself to what might come, and using the proverb frequently in their mouths who enter upon dangerous and bold attempts, 'The die is cast,' he dashed across the river."

Related Expressions: to take the plunge, to burn his bridges behind him.

CUTTING THE GORDIAN KNOT

> In the modern world, however, "good government is no substitute for self-government." Strong or weak, Britons had to go from India. They solved their problem in the only possible way; they *cut the Gordian knot*.

Gordius, a legendary king of Phrygia in Asia Minor, dedicated his chariot to Zeus. The pole of the chariot was fastened to the yoke by a thong tied in an inextricable knot. The oracle declared that whoever untied the knot would rule all Asia.

221

When Alexander passed through Gordium, he did not try to untie the knot by ordinary means but cut it through with his sword. Alexander the Great was always the man for a simple, direct solution. *To cut the Gordian knot* means to attack a problem directly and solve it boldly.

CYNICAL

> An example of contemporary *cynical* thought among young German intellectuals is a poem called "Diogenes," in the latest issue of the school magazine at Heidelberg University.

The Cynics were a school of philosophers in Greece who taught the value of self-control and independence. Some of their disciples showed their independence to such an extent that they expressed contempt for ease and wealth and disbelieved any decent motives in man's actions. Diogenes, one of the most famous Cynics, is said to have despised the ordinary comforts of life to such a degree that he lived in a tub in the market place. In that same market place he went about with a lantern in broad daylight looking for a *man* or, as some say, for an honest man. Diogenes had so little faith in the honesty of mankind that once when he saw officials of a temple leading away a thief who had stolen a sacred bowl, he commented, "The big thieves have caught a little thief."

Cynic is related to the word for dog. The people of Athens called the philosophers of this sect Cynics because of their snarling manner. A *cynical* person is one who constantly finds fault, distrusts the motives of others, and has little faith in the noble aspirations of humanity.

Synonyms: sneering, captious, caviling, carping, censorious, pessimistic, disbelieving, unbelieving, misanthropic.

DRACONIAN

> Of the three measures taken against the communists, the most draconian were probably those taken by the Amalgamated Clothing Workers.

Draco was an Athentian lawgiver whose code of laws established in 621 B.C. called for the most severe penalties for the smallest offense. His laws were said to be written not in ink, but in blood.

Synonyms: severe, stern, rigid, stringent, cruel, rigorous, harsh, immitigable, drastic.

FABIAN

> . . . they meant that socialism would be achieved in all reasonable societies by gradually doing one thing after another, each in its proper turn. This faith became the cornerstone of the *Fabian* Society, of which the Webbs, George Bernard Shaw and Edward R. Pease were founding members.

Quintus Fabius Maximus was appointed dictator in 217 B.C. to lead the Romans in the war against Hannibal. Fabius, also known as *Cunctator* or the Delayer, harassed Hannibal's army, cut off his supplies, and avoided open conflict. A cautious, waiting, dilatory policy is therefore called *Fabian.*

HEDONISM

> Although "The Rubaiyat" was a poetic masterpiece, its skepticism and *hedonism* seemed deplorable to many good Victorians, as they have to many others since.

Hedonism, from a Greek word meaning sweetness or pleasure, is the name of a philosophical doctrine that pleasure is the chief aim of life. The pursuit of pleasure is associated also with the followers of Epicurus. Although the philosophy of the Epicureans embraced many other tenets, it is identified chiefly with the love of pleasure so that *epicureanism* has become a synonym for luxurious living. An *epicure* is a person who is fond of choice food and drink or has delicate tastes. In the same class are the *sybarites*—after the inhabitants of Sybaris in Southern Italy, who were noted for their love of luxury.

223

Synonyms:

EPICURE: gourmet, gourmand, glutton, bon viant, gastronome, connoisseur

EPICUREAN: sybaritic, hedonistic, voluptuous, fastidious, senuous

LUCULLAN

> The picture of overstuffed American capitalists sitting down to *Lucullan* feasts would be accepted readily by many Soviet citizens.

Lucius Licinius Lucullus, a celebrated Roman general of the first century B.C., was fond of the good things of life. After he retired from the wars, he devoted himself to a carefree life of luxury. Plutarch tells us that "his daily entertainments were ostentatiously extravagant, not only with purple coverlets, and plates set with precious stones, and dancers, and dramatic recitations, but with the greatest diversity of dishes and the most elaborate cookery." Once when he ate alone, the cook thought there was no need of display and served a simple one-course meal. Lucullus rebuked him with these famous words, "What, did you not know, then, that today Lucullus dines with Lucullus?"

Synonyms: rich, sumptuous, lavish, luxurious, magnificent, elegant, extravagant.

PHILIPPIC

> Many a *philippic* has been aimed at advertising and advertising men in our times.

When King Philip of Macedon invaded Greece, Demosthenes the Athenian, the greatest orator of ancient times, thundered at him in celebrated speeches called Philippics. A *philippic* is therefore any violent denunciation—so violent that a philippic is never uttered, it is always aimed or hurled.

Synonyms: condemnation, excoriation, tirade, invective, incrimination, vituperation, calumniation, denunciation, indictment.

ATRAP

> Mr. De Sapio lost the patronage that makes a boss strong. More of the local *satraps* turned on him, as was evidenced in the Manhattan Borough President selection. And when the political boss can't deliver, he is done for.

The viceroys or governors of the provinces of ancient Persia were called *satraps*. The ancient Greeks humorously referred to a subordinate official with power and wealth as a *satrap*. The word is used pretty nearly in the same sense today to mean "a big shot." *Nabob, pasha* or *bashaw, rajah, tycoon, mogul,* and *bigwig* are used in a similar way. A really humorous title is *panjandrum,* coined by Samuel Foote. A serious word for a governor of a province or of conquered land is *proconsul,* from the Roman title for that official.

SOLECISM

> But she [Mrs. C. P. Snow] used the word "less" in a construction in which Fowler, the Grand Panjandrum of English usage, prefers "fewer." To judge by the spate of letters in The Book Review of January 29, 1961, that *solecism* gave a number of Americans a heady feeling of upmanship.

The ancient Athenians gave to their fellow Greeks in the colony of Soli in Asia Minor the reputation which the modern Brooklynites bear without just reason: they accused them of maltreating the language. A *solecism,* from the name Soli, is an incorrect grammatical usage, a mistake in the idiom of a language, any type of error including improper use of words or a deviation from logic.

For *Panjandrum* see page 236.

STOICISM

L.I.R.R. Riders
Take Fare Rise
With Stoicism

The Stoa was a colonnade in Athens where the philosopher

Zeno founded a school about 308 B.C. His philosophy wa called Stoicism after the place where the school was estab lished. One of its principles was that the wise man should b free from passion, untouched by joy or grief, willingly sub missive to natural law. As in the case of the word *epicurean* the modern use of the words *stoic* and *stoicism* commemorate: only one aspect of the teachings of the Stoic philosophers A person who controls his emotions, who endures the hard ships of life without complaint or whimper is said to possess *stoic* resignation.

Synonyms: stolidity, impassivity, apathy, phlegm, fortitude, pluck, indifference.

SWORD OF DAMOCLES

> Nevertheless—pity the poor government worker with a *sword of Damocles* hanging over his head!

Damocles, a resident of Syracuse in Sicily, was a companion and· flatterer of Dionysius, the ruler of that city. Growing weary of his constant remarks about a king's happiness, wealth, and power, Dionysius therefore decided to teach him an object lesson. He invited Damocles to a magnificent banquet. As Damocles prepared to enjoy the first course, Dionysius asked him to look up. Directly above his head, Damocles noticed with horror than an unsheathed sword was hanging suspended by a single horse-hair. Needless to say, he lost all interest in the meal. The *sword of Damocles* has a double meaning today: It symbolizes the vanity of human wishes— "uneasy lies the head that wears a crown." More concretely, it suggests a terrible doom impending, a sense of insecurity and danger.

I. Matching

From the column on the right select the term or definition that will best explain the meaning of the words in the lefthand column. Answers for these test will be found on page 367.

1. draconian	a. love of pleasure
2. proconsul	b. favorable
3. solecism	c. theoretical

4. academic	d. governor of conquered land
5. philippic	e. mistake in grammar
6. stoicism	f. drastic
7. cynical	g. denunciation
8. epicureanism	h. cautious
9. auspicious	1. sneeringly satirical
10. Fabian	j. impassiveness

II. Treasure Hunt

You have met or probably will meet the expressions in the ft-hand column. How many can you check with the phrases d expressions on the right?

1. Croesus	a. teaching by questioning
2. Maecenas	b. spiritual love
3. solon	c. parting remarks
4. helot	d. slave
5. plebeian	e. fabulously wealthy man
6. sigh like Alexander	f. destruction of the conquered
7. Socratic method	g. wise man
8. Platonic friendship	h. lower-class
9. Parthian shot	i. long for more conquests
10. Carthaginian peace	j. patron of the arts

"Some botanist called it Scabiosa atropurpurea Linnaeus, and the name stuck." *

20. What's in a Name?

CHRISTOPHER PINCHBECK was a watchmaker and toy-maker who owned a shop on Fleet Street in London during the early part of the eighteenth century. His name lives in the English language because he invented an alloy of copper and zinc that looked like gold. He used this metal in the mak-ing of cheap toys, clocks, and watches. It became so popular that a character in one of Fielding's novels complained that

"the nobility and gentry run so much into Pinchbeck" tha
he himself "had not dispos'd of two gold watches this month."

Mr. Pinchbeck and his son, who carried on the busines
after the death of the inventor, did not attempt to fool the
public. Their advertisements plainly declared that the toy
were made of "a curious metal." However, as often happens
the word *pinchbeck* by which the metal was popularly knowr
degenerated in meaning until now the word has the connota
tion of cheap, shoddy, spurious, not genuine.

Something else happened to the word, as you've noticed. I
lost its capital letter and became a common noun. We have
hundreds of such words in English, most of them so simple
in meaning that the knowledge of their origin is a mere verbal
or historical curiosity. Everyone knows what a sandwich is
even if he doesn't know that it was named after an Earl of
Sandwich. We, therefore, are listing with their stories some
of the more useful difficult name-words.

WORDS FROM PEOPLE'S NAMES

BOWDLERIZE

Dr. Thomas Bowdler in 1818 published *The Family Shakespeare,* an edition in which "those words and expressions are
omitted which cannot with propriety be read aloud in a
family." To *bowdlerize,* therefore, means to expurgate a book
by leaving out or changing passages or words considered indelicate or offensive.

GALVANIZE

Luigi Galvani (1737-1798)), professor of physiology at
Bologna, Italy, is called the father of animal electricity. His
name has been perpetuated in many terms associated with
electricity. In everyday speech the word *galvanize* means to
electrify, to stir into action as if with an electric shock.

MACHIAVELLIAN

Niccolo Machiavelli (1469-1527) was a Florentine who
wrote a famous book called *The Prince* as a handbook of

government for the rulers of his time. He set down the principles of taking and holding power. The word *Machiavellian* is now used to mean cunning, crafty, and deceitful, although originally the book did nothing more than set down as a science what is now called power politics.

MARTINET

A *martinet* is a military taskmaster, a stickler for details of discipline. A rigid disciplinarian in any activity is called a martinet. The original was a General Martinet in the army of Louis XIV.

MASOCHISM

Leopold von Sacher-Masoch (1835-1895) was an Austrian novelist who described an abnormal mental condition in which a person derived pleasure in being abused and punished by someone he loved. The word *masochism* is often used more broadly to mean self-torture. A masochist is a person who enjoys tormenting himself.

MAUSOLEUM

Mausolus was the king of Caria, a country in Asia Minor. After his death his wife Artemisia erected an enormous and beautiful tomb which was ranked as one of the Seven Wonders of the ancient world. The word *mausoleum* is now used not only for a large tomb but for any large structure whose cheerless aspect suggests a tomb.

MAVERICK

Samuel A. Maverick was a Texan rancher of the 1840's who didn't bother to brand his calves. At first the word *maverick* was used only for unbranded calves. Then the meaning was extended to apply to one who doesn't follow the common herd. A politician who is unpredictable, who doesn't always follow the dictates of his party is called a *maverick*.

MESMERIZE

F. A. Mesmer (1734-1815) created a sensation in Vienna and Paris about 1775 by his assertion that there existed a power which he called animal magnetism. At first the name *mesmerism* was given to this power; the later term is *hypnotism*. To *mesmerize* means to hypnotize.

PASQUINADE

In the Piazza Navona in Rome stood the mutilated remains of an ancient statue. During the sixteenth century, there lived near it a tailor or a schoolmaster, a barber or shoemaker—his occupation varies according to which tradition you believe. His name was Pasquino and he possessed a biting wit and an ability to compose epigrams—short pieces of verse with a whip in their tails. On the statue he is supposed to have placed his poems satirizing the events and personages of the day. For this reason the statue was given the nickname Pasquino, and the verses were called *pasquinatas*, from which we get *pasquinade*, meaning a lampoon, or a vicious satire.

SADISTIC

The Count de Sade (1740-1814), who was infamous for his misdeeds and his writings, described a situation in which a person derived pleasure from tormenting someone he loved. Such a person is called a *sadist*. The word *sadistic* is often used more broadly today to mean abnormally cruel.

SPOONERISM

The Reverend William A. Spooner (1844-1930) was cele-brated for his habit, accidental or cultivated, of transposing the first letters of words in phrases. It is reported that in con-versation he referred to the well known two-wheeled vehicle as "a well boiled icicle" and to a friend's new cottage as a "nosey little cook." And they say that he would startle listen-ers at his sermons by referring to "tearful chidings" or assur-ing them that something was as easy as for "a camel to go through the knee of an idol."

THESPIAN

Thespian is an overworked word meaning an actor. Thespis is often called the Father of Greek tragedy. Until his time (about 535 B.C.), dramatic presentations in Greece consisted of singing by a chorus. He is supposed to have invented the role of the first actor by having a member of the chorus step out and carry on a dialogue with the rest of the chorus.

TITIAN

This adjective is formed from the name of the great Vene-tian painter Titian, or Tiziano Vecellio (1477-1576). The word *titian* describes the color of hair he liked to paint, vari-ously described as auburn, bright golden auburn, red, and reddish brown.

WORDS FROM NAMES IN BOOKS

Writers like to use words that come from books because they are verbal short cuts. For example a person who has his finger in every pie is called a *Pooh-Bah*, after W. S. Gilbert's character, who held a half dozen official posts at one time.

The words we list here are associated with the names of persons or places in books. We have selected those of moder-ate difficulty and common occurrence.

BARMECIDE FEAST

The Barmecides were a wealthy family in *The Arabian Nights*. One of them invited a begger to a banquet at which he made a pretense of serving costly food. The beggar fell in with the joke and pretended to enjoy the nonexistent dishes. Finally, Barmecide rewarded him with a real feast. A *barmecide* banquet or feast is an illusion of plenty. *Barmecidal* means unreal.

BONIFACE

This word has become the smart word for an innkeeper or hotel owner who is a genial and jolly host, as was the original Boniface, a character in George Farquhar's *The Beaux Stratgem* (1707).

CHAUVINISM

Nicholas Chauvin was supposed to have been a soldier in Napoleon's army. After the downfall of his emperor, Chauvin displayed such exaggerated loyalty and patriotism that he was held up to ridicule. In 1831 the Cogniard brothers wrote a play, *La Cocarde Tricolore*, in which a young recruit named Chauvin sang couplets expressing enthusiasm for national supremacy and military glory. The word *chauvinism* coming from the character in the play means exaggerated patriotism or jingoism, which also has an interesting story to tell.

By jingo was a magician's expression which was taken over in popular English speech to show strong affirmation. It became famous through its use in a music-hall song of 1878. In that year Disraeli sent a fleet into Turkish waters to "contain" the Russians against the Turks. The words of the song supported Disraeli's policy:

> We don't want to fight, but, by jingo
>   if we do,
> We've got the ships, we've got the men,
>   we've got the money too.

Jingoism, like *chauvinism,* is a term for strong national feeling, and a *jingoist* is a person who favors a belligerent attitude toward foreign powers.

GARGANTUA

Gargantua is the eponymous hero of the first part of *Gargantua and Pantagruel* by François Rabelais (1494-1553). He is a gigantic large-mouthed king with an appetite to match. Anything on a large scale is therefore *gargantuan.* Writers, especially Hollywood press agents, are beginning to prefer this word to *colossal* and *mammoth,* which have lost their force, especially in a climate where olives are officially graded according to these standard sizes: medium, large, larger, mammoth, giant, jumbo, colossal, and supercolossal. From Swift's *Gulliver's Travels,* we get a tongue twister to denote huge size, *brobdingnagian!* The natives of *Brobdingnag* were as tall as church steeples."

LILLIPUTIAN

The hero of *Gulliver's Travels* was wrecked on the shores of a country whose inhabitants were only six inches tall. *Lilliputian* naturally means diminutive, miniature. The tiny descendants of the hardy nation of Lilliput have been brought back to life in T. H. White's delightful fantasy, *Mistress Masham's Repose.*

MALAPROPISM

The audiences of the 1770's laughed at Mrs. Malaprop's mishandling of words in Sheridan's *The Rivals.* From her name we get the word *malapropism,* which describes what countless comedians do to English words for a laugh. A *malapropism* is a grotesque confusion of words, a verbal blunder.

It comes from the French phrase *mal à propos*, inappropriat

MRS. GRUNDY

"What will Mrs. Grundy say?" is a question often aske
when a matter of taste or conduct is being discussed. Who i
this mysterious Mrs. Grundy, the personification of soci
tyranny and conventions? Actually, she never existed even i
the play which gave us her name. In 1798, Thomas Morto
wrote *Speed the Plough*, in which a certain Dame Ashfiel
always wonders what he imaginary neighbor, Mrs. Grundy
will say: "If shame should come to the poor child, I say
Tummas, what will Mrs. Grundy say then?'

PANJANDRUM

In 1775, to test the boasted memory of Charles Macklin
who asserted that he could repeat anything he had heard o
read once, Samuel Foote made up some nonsense lines, o
which the concluding section follows:

"So he died, and she very imprudently married the barber;
and there were present the Picninnies, and the Joblillies, and
the Garyulies, and the great *Panjandrum* himself, with the
little red button at top, and they all fell to playing the game
of catch as catch can, till the gunpowder ran out at the heels
of their boots."

Samuel Foote's coinage, *panjandrum* (*pan*, Greek, meanin
all, plus a Latin-sounding ending), has proved a sturdy on
Today *panjandrum* is used humorously or mockingly of an
exalted or powerful person.

QUIXOTIC

If we refer to a person as *quixotic*, we are politely dismiss
ing him as an unrealistic visionary, one whose heart is bigg
than his head. We get the word from Cervantes' great sati
on a once-flowering knighthood that was going to seed. Do
Quixote de la Mancha, the eponymous hero, was a would-b

knight whose excited imagination turned lonely inns into castles and windmills into fearsome giants.

ROBOT

In 1923 Karel Capek, a Czech playwright, wrote a celebrated and terrifying play. Its title, *R.U.R.*, stands for Rossum's Universal Robots, the robots being a symbol of the machine age, mechanical monsters in human form who turn upon their masters. Derived from the Slavic word *robota*, meaning work, the word *robot* has become very useful in describing an automaton or a human being who has become so mechanized that he has lost his soul. (See p. 102).

RODOMONTADE

Rodomont or Rodomonte (the name means "roll a mountain" in Italian), a Moorish king in Ariosto's epic, *Orlando Furioso*, is brave but boastful. He has given his name to *rodomontade*, meaning boasting, blustering, and bragging. These qualities appear also in the word *braggadocio*, from Braggadocio, a character in Spenser's *Faerie Queene*.

THRASONICAL

The Romans had their idea of a Braggadocio and Rodomont, too. He was Thraso, a blustering soldier in Terence's play, *The Eunuch*, who was full of what Dr. Watson called "brag and bounce." In Shakespeare's *As You Like It*, Rosalind refers to "Caesar's thrasonical brag of 'I came, I saw, I overcame.' "

UTOPIAN

In 1516 Sir Thomas More wrote a book about an ideal state. Book and place bore the title *Utopia*, which means

237

No Place. (*U* is from *ou*,' a Greek negative, and *top* is from *topos*, place.) When, 250 years later, Samuel Butler wrote his novel of another utopia, he sought another disguise. He just spelled the word "nowhere" backwards and called his book *Erewhon. Utopian* is a synonym for *quixotic;* it carries the idea of impractical, unfeasible, impossible, visionary, chimerical, ideal but unattainable.

YAHOO

In *Gulliver's Travels,* the Yahoos are a tribe of brutes having the form of men and embodying all the vices of mankind. So, *yahoo* is an uncomplimentary term designating a lout, a ruffian, a brute, a degraded specimen of mankind.

WORDS OUT OF THE BIBLE

In the United States each year, about three million copies of the Bible are sold. Nevertheless, the complaint is often heard that people do not know references to the Bible when they are made. To help reduce such complaints, we are listing a few words of Biblical origin formed from names, along with the texts in which the names appear.

ANANIAS

The Ananias Club is a group of men who come together to tell tall stories. Ananias lied to Peter about his gift for the common fund.

But, Peter said, Ananias, . . . thou hast not lied unto men, but unto God. And Ananias hearing these words fell down, and gave up the ghost . . .

Acts 5: 3, 4

RMAGEDDON

And he gathered them together into a place called in the Hebrew tongue, Armageddon.

Revelation 16: 16

Armageddon is a place where the forces of good and evil met to fight a great battle. It is used to mean a final, decisive conflict.

BEHEMOTH

In Hebrew this is the word for a large animal.

Behold now behemoth, which I made with thee; he eateth grass as an ox . . . his bones are like bars of iron.

Job 40: 15, 18

Some think that the hippopotamus was referred to; at any rate, the word behemoth is used to designate a large, massive animal and is figuratively applied to a "hulk of a man."

JEHU

This word gets its meaning of coachman or driver from a line in the Bible:

. . . and the driving is like the driving of Jehu the son of Nimshi; for he driveth furiously.

II Kings 10: 20

JEHU ROUNDS UP DOBBIN

So reads the headline of a story in the *Herald Tribune*, telling of a taxi driver who caught a runaway horse. The word *jehu* is generally used humorously and ironically. O. Henry in "A Municipal Report" writes, "When the hack had ceased from rattling and the weary quadrupeds came to a rest, I handed my jehu his fifty cents with an additional quarter." And Hector Berlioz in his *Memoirs* tells about being in a "crawling coach" with "a jehu who could not speak a word of French."

JEREMIAD

A *jeremiad* is a tale of woe, a continued lament, a bitter denunciation of sorrow over a nation's sins. The word is formed from the name of the prophet Jeremiah, whose lament for Jerusalem and Zion is contained in the book of the Old Testament, the Lamentations of Jeremiah, which begins,

How doth the city sit solitary, that was full of people! how is she become as a widow! she that was great among the nations, and princess among the provinces, how is she become tributary!

JEZEBEL

A wicked abandoned woman is sometimes called a *jezebel*. The original was the wife of King Ahab of Israel. She introduced the worship of the foreign god Baal, persecuted the prophet Elijah, and instigated the murder of Naboth. She was finally slain by Jehu and her body was thrown to the dogs.

And when Jehu was come to Jezreel, Jezebel heard of it; and she painted her face, and tired her head, and looked out at a window. . . . And he said, Throw her down. So they threw her down . . .

II Kings 9: 30, 33

MAUDLIN

This word comes to us from the name of Mary Magdalene, who watched the sepulcher of Christ:

There were also women looking on afar off: among whom was Mary Magdalene . . .

Mark 15: 40

The British pronounce *Magdalen* of Magdalen College at Oxford, and *Magdalene* of Magdalene College at Cambridge as if the names were written *maudlin*. The adjective has come to mean tearfully sentimental, because Italian paintings of Mary Magdalene usually show her weeping. John Ruskin speaks of "a smooth Magdalen of Carlo Dolci with a tear in each cheek."

NIMROD

This is a term for a hunter, which, like *jehu*, is often used humorously. Nimrod was the grandson of Ham, a son of Noah:

He was a mighty hunter before the Lord: wherefore it is said, Even as Nimrod the mighty hunter before the Lord.
Genesis 10: 9

WORDS ALL OVER THE MAP

Many materials and articles are named after places associated with their manufacture or sale. The name of the town of Cambrai is found in *cambric*, Lille in *Lisle*, and Nîmes in *denim* (originally *serge de Nîmes*). Sometimes the place-name is more clearly seen as when a type of steel is called Damascus or Toledo, and a style of furniture is known as Grand Rapids. However, whether the name of the place is easy to see or not, the meanings of most words coming from place-names are fairly obvious. Again we have selected those that are a little more unusual.

ANTIMACASSAR

The harbor of Macassar on the island of Celebes is considered one of the most beautiful in the world. The English blades and dandies of the early 19th century used a hair lotion which its manufacturers advertised as containing ingredients from Macassar. In 1842 Samuel Lever, author of *Handy Andy*, wrote:

He ran his fingers through his Macassar-oiled ringlets.

However, when a well greased head leaned back against Victorian chairs or sofas, the aftereffects were not pretty. To protect their furniture women began to crochet little square coverings, which, because they were used *against* the "Macassar-oiled ringlets," were called *antimacassars*.

241

ARGOSY

The picturesque city of Dubrovnik on the Dalmatian coast was known as Ragusa before World War I. As Ragusa, centuries earlier, it had achieved a fame equal to that of Venice. The tall merchant ship of Ragusa was called at first a "ragusye" and later an argosy. *Argosy* has become a poetic word for a stately sailing vessel. Shakespeare speaks of "argosies with portly sail," and Tennyson, looking into the future, describes the merchant ships of the air as "argosies of magic sails."

BILLINGSGATE

From the poetry of *argosy*, we travel to the gutter prose and verbal slums of *billingsgate*. The Billingsgate was one of the old gates of the city of London. The fishmarket was located here and the references to the language used by the fishwives indicate that it was rough, coarse, and scurrilous. Therefore, *billingsgate* refers to foul, abusive language.

CANOSSA

To go to Canossa means to humiliate oneself. The powerful Holy Roman Emperor Henry IV once defied Pope Gregory VII. The Pope excommunicated him, and the Emperor's supporters began to abandon him. Henry IV then made a pilgrimage in January, 1077, to the village of Canossa, Italy, where the Pope was then staying. For three days the Emperor stood bareheaded and barefoot in the snow and did penance until the Pope received him. A *Canossa* is, therefore, a scene or place of humiliation and submission.

MEANDER

The Maeander (*Maiandros* in Greek) is a river in Asia Minor noted since ancient times for its winding course. *Meander*, the English word formed from its ancient Greek name, means to twist and turn, to wander aimlessly.

MECCA

Mecca in Arabia is the birthplace of Mohammed, the holy city of the Moslems. A *mecca* is a goal, an object desired by many persons. *Hegira*, from an Arabic word meaning flight, is connected with Mecca. It refers specifically to the flight made by Mohammed from Mecca in 622 A.D. because his opinions were unpopular in that city. A *hegira* is an exodus, a mass migration, a trek.

SARDONIC

This word is supposed to come from the name of a poisonous plant growing on the island of Sardinia. This plant, known to the Romans as *herba Sardonia*, contorted the face of its victim into a grim laugh (*risus sardonicus*) that became fixed at death. A *sardonic* smile or laugh, therefore, has no joy in it, only scorn and bitterness.

SERENDIPITY

Serendip is a form of the old Arabic name of the island of Ceylon. In a letter written on January 28, 1754, Horace Walpole tells that he coined the word *serendipity* from the title of a story, "The Three Princes of Serendip," the heroes of which "were always making discoveries, by accident and sagacity, of things they were not in quest of." Hence, *serendipity* is the ability to make lucky finds, the gift or faculty of making unexpected and happy discoveries by accident.

An editorial in the New York *Times* of May 24, 1961 contained some pertinent comments on serendipity in connection with Commander Shepards' suborbital flight to the edge of space:

Space and Serendipity

Dr. Bush knows very well that many of the greatest scientific discoveries were made by what is known as "serendipity," a word meaning the "finding of valuable or agreeable things not sought for"— in other words, by chance. The discovery of America is an outstanding example of serendipity. Other examples are the chance discovery of penicillin and of nuclear fission.

I. Can You Correct Mrs. Malaprop?

Here are some samples of Mrs. Malaprop's cruelty to words. The misused words are italicized. What should she have said? Each dot represents a letter. Answers for these tests will be found on page 367.

1. Now don't attempt to *extirpate* yourself from the matter

1 . . . .

2. Promise to forget this fellow—to *illiterate* him, I say, quite from your memory.

2 . . . .

3. Nay, no *delusions* to the past.

3 . . . .

4. I would by no means wish a daughter of mine to be a *progeny* of learning.

4 . . . .

5. I hope you will present her to the Captain as an object not altogether *illegible*.

5 . . . .

6. I am sorry to say, Sir Anthony, that my *affluence* over my niece is very small.

6 . . . .

7. She's as headstrong as an *allegory* on the banks of the Nile.

7 . . . .

8. I would never let her meddle with Greek or Hebrew, or Algebra, or such *inflammatory* branches of learning.

8 . . . .

9. There, Sir! an attack upon my language! What do you think of that? An aspersion upon my parts of speech! Was ever such a brute! Sure if I *reprehend* anything in this world, it is the use of my *oracular tongue*, and a nice *derangement* of *epitaphs*.

9 (a) . . . . or . . . .

9 (b) . . . .

9 (c) . . . .

9 (d) . . . .

10. Then, Sir, she should have only a *supercilious* knowledge in accounts; and as she grew up, I would have her instructed in *geometry* that she might know something of the *contagious* countries—but above all, Sir Anthony, she should be mistress of *orthodoxy*, that she might not misspell, and mispronounce words as shamefully as girls usually do.

10 (a) . . . .

10 (b) . . . .

10 (c) . . . .

10 (d) . . . .

II. A Shakespeare Gallery

The names of some characters in Shakespeare's plays are used almost as common nouns. For example, an *Ariel*, from *The Tempest*, designates an airy spirit. See whether you can match the character on the left with the description on the right.

1. Benedict (Benedick)   a. fat, jolly person

2. Dogberry   b. woman lawyer

3. Falstaff   c. blundering petty official

4. Portia   d. bridegroom

5. Puck   e. mischief-maker, impish spirit

III. How Well Do You Know Your Dickens?

The following expressions have become part of the English language. They all come from the names and characters or from phrases in Dickens' novels. Match them with the terms on the right.

1. Pickwickian sense	a. hypocrisy
2. King Charles's head	b. optimistic waiting for
3. Bumbledom	c. something to turn up
4. Micawberism	d. repeated phrase or topic
5. Pecksniffery	e. special meaning to suit the occasion

IV. The Familiar Things From the Bible

You can turn to an unabridged dictionary or better still to the pages of the Bible for the meanings of these words and phrases commonly used in English:

coat of many colors, walls of Jericho, pharisaical, mess of pottage, Gideon's army, handwriting on the wall, widow's mite, jesting Pilate, a Daniel come to judgment, the street which is called Straight, whited sepulcher, scapegoat, Philistine, Gadarene swine, a Lazarus, Goliath, good Samaritan, Babel.

V. Dictionary and Literary Treasure Hunt

You'll often meet the following real or fictitious names of persons and places and the words or phrases coming from them. How many of them can you identify or define? You'll find them in an unabridged dictionary.

Enoch Arden divorce, Tartuffian, Tommy Atkins, Slough of Despond, Delectable Mountains, simony, simon-pure, Lothario, daguerreotype, grangerize, comstockery, namby-pamby, Simon Legree, Pollyanna, Homeric laughter, lotus-eaters.

"'E pluribus unum' . . . 'E pluribus unum' . . . what's the matter . . . can't you speak English?" *

21. Translation, Please: Ancient Languages

SO MANY authors insist on using foreign words that sometimes even publications protest. In an editorial entitled "Translations, Please," appearing in *Collier's*, September 13, 1947,

---

the following complaint was made:

We will now register a loud, uncultured yawp against a habit in which some erudite authors persist in indulging, and for which we can find no justification.

What we're squawking about is the practice of ringing foreign-language words and phrases into the text of a book without furnishing translations into English in parentheses or footnotes. *

Collier's mentioned by name two authors "who have th same annoying habit."

Then the editorial continued:

We do mean annoying. Very few Americans have a working knowledge of Greek, Latin, French, and German. That is no doubt regrettable, but it is a fact. If the author thinks he is paying readers a delicate compliment by neglecting to translate his verbal jewels cut in foreign tongues, he's mistaken. Our own doubtless uncouth feeling is that he's merely trying to show us how erudite he is and how dumb we are.

Let's have translations, please, in all such cases from now on, so that all the customers can tell what the author is talking about all the time. What does a man write for, anyway, if not to get his whole meaning across to anybody who reads anything he writes?

But *Collier's* itself, in spite of its own complaint, did not follow a policy of translating foreign phrases used in its pages. A reader complained that on the same page on which this editorial appeared, another editorial writer had used the phrase *quid pro quo* without a translation. *Collier's* facetiously replied in Latin and without a translation, *"Incongrui sumus,"* or "We are not consistent."

It is not, however, a matter of consistency. The points made by the writer of the editorial, "Translations, Please," are excellent. Foreign-language quotations and phrases should not be used merely to display erudition and they should not confuse the reader. However, as the use of *quid pro quo* indicates, there are many foreign phrases and words which do useful service and which feel at home in the English language.

---

a—hat, ā—hāte, â—bâre, ä—bär, e—hen, ē—hē, i—hit, ī—hīde, o—hot, ō—hōme, ô—bôrn, u—hut, ū—hūge, û—bûrn, ōō—hood, ōō—hōōt, ou—out, oi—oil, ng—sing, ngg—finger, th—thin, th—then, zh—vision, and ə which equals a in diạl, e in model, i in pupil, o in methọd, u in circụs, or y in martyr.

---

* Reprinted by permission of *Collier's*, The National Weekly.

FOREIGN PROTESTS

It seems that in England, too, there have been protests against the increasing tendency to use Latin and other foreign expressions. A member of the London County Council, F. Griffiths Woollard, complained to the chairman, J. R. Oldfield, about this tendency.

The latter, an old Etonian, replied with a straight face: "I am not aware of any such increasing tendency but I will be pleased to examine the matter *de novo*. That reports should be readily intelligible is a *sine qua non*. It should not, however, be assumed that every Latin phrase is, *ipso facto*, unintelligible. Many such phrases are in common use and have indeed become the *lingua franca* of local government. They can be used *pari passu* with an English equivalent."

Mr. Woollard, not to be outdone, replied with equal gravity:

"In order to clarify the matter, will you, *inter alia*, form an *ad hoc* subcommittee, or would this be *ultra vires?*"

The New York *Times* appropriately headed this story:

AEDILES JEST IN LATIN

The *aediles* were Roman municipal authorities. Actually most of the foreign phrases used by the modern aediles are in fairly common use. All of them are Latin except *lingua franca* which is Italian. How many of them did you know? You can check with the translations given by the London *Daily Express* which carried the original story.

de novo	anew
sine qua non	something indispensable
ipso facto	by the fact itself

a—hat, ā—hāte, â—bâre, ä—bär, e—hen, ē—hē, i—hit, ī—hīde, o—hot, ō—hōme, ô—bôrn, u—hut, ū—hūge, û—bûrn, ŏŏ—hood, ōō—hōōt, ou—out, oi—oil, ng—sing, ngg—finger, th—thin, th—then, zh—vision, and ə which equals a in dial, e in model, i in pupil, o in method, u in circus, or y in martyr.

lingua franca	common language
pari passu	side by side
inter alia	among others
ad hoc	for this special purpose
últra vires	beyond the powers possessed

In spite of objections, writers and speakers will continue to use these phrases and many others like them. English has always been hospitable to words and phrases from other languages.

LATIN

Latin was an international language of diplomacy, science, medicine, law, and literature until the end of the 16th century. Its influence on our language has never died and many of its phrases and expressions are used without change to this very day. From the hundreds we have found in newspapers and magazines, we have selected those we thought most useful.

A word about the pronunciation. If you know Latin and the Anglicized pronunciations given here don't go down easily, go right on pronouncing them the Latin way. We have starred those words in which the Anglicized pronunciation has not completely taken over, and in which the Latin pronunciation or a mixed Latin and English pronunciation is often heard.

*A FORTIORI (ā fôrshiŏ'rī)
    For the more compelling reason; all the more.

---

a—hat, ā—hāte, â—bâre, ä—bär, e—hen, ē—hē, i—hit, ī—hīde, o—hot, ō—hōme, ô—bôrn, u—hut, ū—hūge, û—bûrn, ōo—hood, ōō—hōōt, ou—out, oi—oil, ng—sing, ngg—finger, th—thin, th—then, zh—vision, and ə which equals a in dial, e in model, i in pupil, o in method, u in circus, or y in martyr.

AD NAUSEAM (ad nô′shēəm *or* nô′zeəm)

To a sickening or disgusting degree. *Nausea* originally meant seasickness.

ALTER EGO (al′tər ēgō)

a second self; a bosom friend.

*__AMICUS CURIAE__ (əmi′kəs kyoor′iē)

"A friend of the court"; a person who voluntarily or at the request of a judge gives advice or presents a brief in a case in which he is not legally involved.

ANNUS MIRABILIS (an′nəs mirab′əlis)

"A wonderful year"; a year in which great events take place.

ANTE BELLUM (an′tē bel′əm)

"Before the war"; applied especially to the period before the American Civil War.

*__A POSTERIORI__ (ā postēriō′rī)

Reasoning based on observed facts; applied to conclusions arrived at after (*post*) the study of the facts; inductive reasoning; opposed to *a priori.*

*__A PRIORI__ (ā prīō′rī)

Reasoning based on general principles, not supported by factual study.

*__ARS GRATIA ARTIS__ (ärz grā′shiə är′tis)

"Art for art's sake"; motto of MGM Films, seen when Leo the Lion roars. Bernard Shaw must have believed that this motto typifies the spirit of the movie industry. A magnate who asked him for permission to film *Pygmalion* asserted, "I don't care if the picture does lose money. I'm thinking only of its service to art."

---

a—hat, ā—hāte, â—bâre, ä—bär, e—hen, ē—hē, i—hit, ī—hīde, o—hot, ō—hōme, ô—bôrn, u—hut, ū—hūge, û—bûrn, ŏŏ—hood, ōō—hōŏt, ou—out, oi—oil, ng—sing, ngg—finger, th—thin, th—then, zh—vision, and ə which equals a in dial, e in model, i in pupil, o in method, u in circus, or y in martyr.

shaw answered, "That's the difference between us. You think of nothing but art, and I think of nothing but money."

ARGUMENTUM AD HOMINEM   (ärgumen'təm ad hom'inem)

"An argument to a man (or person)"; an appeal to emotion rather than to facts. "In the 'Provincial Letters' Pascal used the *argumentum ad hominem*— which means that he called his opponents everything but horse thieves." (HTB)

BONA FIDE   (bō'nə fī dē)

"In good faith"; without fraud. *Bona fides* means good faith; honesty; freedom from fraud or deceit.

*CASUS BELLI   (kā'səs be'lī)

Event or situation used as a pretext for going to war; a cause of war.

*CAVEAT EMPTOR   (kā'vēat emp'tôr)

"Let the buyer beware"; a legal phrase implying that the purchaser buys at his own risk.

*CORPUS DELICTI   (kôr'pəs dēlik'tī)

"The body of the crime." A legal phrase meaning evidence to prove that a crime has been committed. Often the phrase is mistakenly understood to mean the body of a murdered victim.

CUI BONO?   (kī *or* kwē bō'nō)

"For whose good?" First used by a Roman magistrate to indicate that in every crime one must look for the person who stands to gain by it. Although "For what good?" is an erroneous translation, the Latin phrase is popularly used in that sense.

---

a—hat, ā—hāte, â—bâre, ä—bär, e—hen, ē—hē, i—hit, ī—hīde, o—hot, ō—hōme, ô—bôrn, u—hut, ū—hūge, û—bûrn, ŏŏ—hood, ōō—hōōt, ou—out, oi—oil, ng—sing, ngg—finger, th—thin, th—then, zh—vision, and ə which equals a in dial, e in model, i in pupil, o in method, u in circus, or y in martyr.

*DE FACTO   (dē fac'tō)

Functioning; in fact; in reality. A *de facto* government is one which is set up and exists in fact although it is not yet recognized *de jure,* or legally.

DE PROFUNDIS   (dē prōfun' dis)

"Out of the the depths" of sorrow and despair, from the opening of Psalm 130; title of work by Oscar Wilde.

*DEUS EX MACHINA   (dē'əs eks mak'inə)

A god (or goddess) appearing in a Greek tragedy was brought into view by a crane or derrick. His special duty was to ordain the ritual of the tragedy or to bring the action to a quiet close. The appearance (epiphany) of the god was interpreted by some critics, like the Roman poet Horace, as proof that the dramatist (notably Euripides) had so piled up complications that he needed divine intervention to untangle the situation. Hence, a thing or person who solves a difficulty artificially and abruptly is called a *deus ex machina,* as in the following item about the promotion of a Bowl game:

> In the long history of promotion this has been the most botched job on record and only a *deus ex machina* can save the game now.

*DRAMATIS PERSONAE   (dram'ətis persō'nē)

Characters in a play; chief actors in a dramatic series of events.

*EMERITUS   (ē mer' i tus *or* i mer'ə təs)

An *emeritus* was a Roman veteran, a soldier who had completed his term of service and had obtained his discharge (*emereor,* "obtain by service"). The term *emeritus* is today applied to a clergyman, professor,

---

a—hat, ā—hāte, â—bâre, ä—bär, e—hen, ē—hē, i—hit, ī—hīde, o—hot, ō—hōme, ô—bôrn, u—hut, ū—hūge, û—bûrn, o͝o—hood, o͞o—ho͞ot, ou—out, oi—oil, ng—sing, ngg—finger, th—thin, th—then, zh—vision, and ə which equals a in dial, e in model, i in pupil, o in method, u in circus, or y in martyr.

college president or any other official who has been retired from service because of age, but who still retains his rank or title in a nonofficial capacity.

*ERGO (ûr'gō)
Therefore; hence.

EX CATHEDRA (eks kəthē'drə *or* kath'ədrə)
"From the chair"; by the authority of one's position.

EX OFFICIO (eks əffish'io)
"By virtue of one's office." When an officer of an organization is on a committee *ex officio,* it means that his office automatically includes his being a member of a committee.

EX POST FACTO (eks pōst fac'tō)
"From a thing done after" the event or deed; retroactive; generally applied to a law passed after the offense with which it is concerned has been committed.

FLAGRANTE DELICTO (fləgran'tē dēlik'tō)
"While the crime is blazing"; in the very act; red-handed.

*HIC JACET (hik jās'ət)
"Here lies"; an epitaph.

HOMO SAPIENS (hō'mō sā'pienz)
Man as a thinking animal; the genus or division of mankind as distinct from other forms of life.

IN EXTENSO (in eksten'sō)
At full length.
IN EXTREMIS (in ekstrē'mis)
In the last extremity; near death.

---

a—hat, ā—hāte, â—bâre, ä—bär, e—hen, ē—hē, i—hit, ī—hīde, o—hot, ō—hōme, ô—bôrn, u—hut, ū—hūge, û—bûrn, ŏŏ—hood, ōō—hōōt, ou—out, oi—oil, ng—sing, ngg—finger, th—thin, th—then, zh—vision, and ə which equals a in dial, e in model, i in pupil, o in method, u in circus, or y in martyr.

*INFRA DIGNITATEM   (in'frə dignitā'təm)

Beneath one's dignity; colloquially shortened to *infra dig.*

IN LOCO PARENTIS   (in lōkō pəren'tis)

"In the place of a parent"; acting as guardian.

*IN MEDIAS RES   (in mē'diàs rēz)

"Into the middle of things"; starting in the middle of a story; without preliminaries.

IN RE *or* RE   (in rē)

In the matter of; concerning; in reference to.

*IN SITU   (in sī tū)

"In place"; in its original place; a term used in geology and archaeology.

IN TOTO   (in tō'tō)

Entirely; in full.

IN VACUO   (in vak'ūō)

"In a vacuum"; without reference to surroundings; without regard for reality.

IPSE DIXIT   (ip'sē dik'sit)

"He himself said it"; an assertion to be taken on authority.

*LAPSUS LINGUAE   (lap'səs ling'gwē)

A slip of the tongue.

MAGNUM OPUS   (mag'nəm ōp'əs)

"A great work"; masterpiece; *chef d'oeuvre;* crowning achievement.

---

a—hat, ā—hāte, â—bâre, ä—bär, e—hen, ē—hē, i—hit, ī—hīde, o—hot, ō—hōme, ô—bôrn, u—hut, ū—hūge, û—bûrn, o͞o—hood, o͞o—ho͞ot, ou—out, oi—oil, ng—sing, ngg—finger, th—thin, th—then, zh—vision, and ə which equals a in diạl, e in modẹl, i in pupịl, o in methọd, u in circụs, or y in martỵr.

*MARE NOSTRUM (mä′rē no′strəm)

"Our Sea." The Romans looked upon the Mediterranean as their private lake and therefore called it, "Mare Nostrum."

*MIRABILE DICTU (mirab′ilē dik′tōō)

"Wonderful to tell"; "believe it or not."

*MODUS OPERANDI (mō′dəs opəran′dī)

"Manner or way of working"; a working agreement.

*MODUS VIVENDI (mōdəs-viven′dī)

"Manner of living"; temporary agreement; a way of getting along with another person or nation despite basic differences.

*NE PLUS ULTRA (nē plus ul′trə)

"Not more beyond"; the highest point of perfection.

NON COMPOS MENTIS (non kom′pos men′tis)

"Not in control of one's mind"; not of sound mind. Samuel Johnson suggested that *nincompoop*, a fool, simpleton, blockhead, or ninny, was derived from the Latin phrase, but modern etymologists reject this idea and believe that *nincompoop* is a nonsense word of fanciful formation.

NON SEQUITUR (non sek′witər)

"It does not follow." Applied to remarks or conclusions which don't have a logical connection with what has gone before.

---

a—hat, ā—hāte, â—bâre, ä—bär, e—hen, ē—hē, i—hit, ī—hīde, o—hot, ō—hōme, ô—bôrn, u—hut, ū—hūge, û—bûrn, ŏŏ—hood, ōō—hōōt, ou—out, oi—oil, ng—sing, ngg—finger, th—thin, th—then, zh—vision, and ə which equals a in dial, e in model, i in pupil, o in method, u in circus, or y in martyr.

OBITER DICTUM   (ōb'itər dik'təm)

An incidental opinion by a judge, not binding on the final decision; a side remark or digression. The plural is *obiter dicta.*

O TEMPORA! O MORES!   (ō tem'pərə, ō mō'rēz) mō'rēz)

"O the times! O the customs!" An interjection first used by Cicero in the First Oration against Catiline as a complaint against the manners and morals of the times.

*PACE   (pā'si)

By leave of; with apologies to; showing polite disagreement. Do not confuse it with Italian *pace,* "peace."

PASSIM   (pas'im)

"Here and there"; applied to a word or phrase used many times in a piece of writing.

PAX   (paks)

"Peace"; *pax vobiscum,* "Peace be with you"; *Pax Romana,* a peace imposed by the Romans through conquest.

*PER SE   (pûr sē)

By one's self; by itself; essentially; intrinsically.

*PERSONA GRATA   (pərsō'nə grā'tə)

An acceptable person; often applied to an ambassador or representative who is agreeable to the country to which he is sent. An unacceptable person is *persona non grata.*

POST FACTUM   (pōst fak'təm)

After the fact, event, or deed.

---

a—hat, ā—hāte, â—bâre, ä—bär, e—hen, ē—hē, i—hit, ī—hīde, o—hot, ō—hōme, ô—bôrn, u—hut, ū—hūge, û—bûrn, ōo—hood, ōō—hōot, ou—out, oi—oil, ng—sing, ngg—finger, th—thin, th—then, zh—vision, and ə which equals a in dial, e in model, i in pupil, o in method, u in circus, or y in martyr.

PRIMA FACIE (prī'mə fā'shiē)
At first view; on first appearance; on the surface.

PRO BONO PUBLICO (prō bō' nō pub'likō)
"For the public good"; a favorite signature of writers of letters to the editor.

PRO TEMPORE (prō tem'pōrē)
For the time being; temporary; often shortened to *pro tem*.

QUA (kwā *or* kwä)
As; considered as.

QUID NUNC (kwid nungk)
"What now?" One who is always asking the question, "What now?"; a *quidnunc* is, therefore, a gossip.

QUID PRO QUO (kwid prō kwō)
"Something for something"; tit for tat; an equivalent exchange.

QUONDAM (kwon'dam)
Former.

*****RARA AVIS** (rä'rə āv'is)
"A rare bird"; an unusual specimen; an extraordinary person.

*****REDUCTIO AD ABSURDUM** (rēduk'shiō ad absûr'dəm)
"A reduction to the absurd"; a train of reasoning in which a proposition is proved false by arguing it to an obviously false, ridiculous, or absurd conclusion; carrying an argument to logical extremes.

---

a—hat, ā—hāte, â—bâre, ä—bär, e—hen, ē—hē, i—hit, ī—hīde, o—hot, ō—hōme, ô—bôrn, u—hut, ū—hūge, û—bûrn, ŏŏ—hood, ōō—hōot, ou—out, oi—oil, ng—sing, ngg—finger, th—thin, th—then, zh—vision, and ə which equals a in dial, e in model, i in pupil, o in method, u in circus, or y in martyr.

SANCTUM SANCTORUM (sangk'təm sangktōr'əm)

"Holy of holies"; humorously, the office of an awesome person like the editor or boss.

*SINE DIE (sī'nē dī'ē)

"Without a day" being set for meeting again.

SINE QUA NON (sī'nē kwā non)

An indispensable condition; a prerequisite.

STATUS QUO (stā'təs kwō)

The condition in which anything is; present conditions. An upholder of the *status quo* is one who wishes to keep things as they are.

SUB ROSA (sub rō'zə)

"Under the rose"; secretly; confidentially; privately. The connection between roses and secrecy is hidden unless one believes a story to the effect that a statue of the Egyptian god Horus shows him carrying a rose and holding his fingers to his lips and that in this way the rose became a symbol of secrecy.

*SUI GENERIS (sōō'ī jen'əris)

"Of his, her, its own kind"; unique; in a class by itself.

TERRA INCOGNITA (ter'rə in kog'ni tə)

"unknown land"; an unexplored country or field of knowledge.

*TU QUOQUE (tū kwō'kwē)

"You too" or "You're another"; a charge accusing an opponent of doing the same thing he's charging you with.

---

a—hat, ā—hate, â—bâre, ä—bär, e—hen, ē—hē, i—hit, ī—hīde, o—hot, ō—hōme, ô—bôrn, u—hut, ū—hūge, û—bûrn, ŏŏ—hood, ōō—hōōt, ou—out, oi—oil, ng—sing, ngg—finger, th—thin, th—then, zh—vision, and ə which equals a in dial, e in model, i in pupil, o in method, u in circus, or y in martyr.

*VADE MECUM (vā'dē mĕ'kəm)

"Go with me"; a handbook or manual; a book carried as a constant companion.

*VOX POPULI (voks pop'ulī)

One half of the expression, *Vox populi, vox Dei,* "The voice of the people is the voice of God," which is further shortened to *vox pop.* Like *pro bono publico* it is a favorite signature of writers of letters to the editor.

ABBREVIATIONS FROM LATIN

Many abbreviations of Latin words and phrases have become established in English. We are listing some of the most common ones which offer vocabulary difficulties.

AD LIB for *ad libitum:*

At will; at pleasure; to improvise; to add numbers to a program extemporaneously. On stage, radio, and TV, it means interpolating words not appearing in the script, but radio comedians will readily admit that their ad libs are often written in for them. Once Milton Berle was throwing in a couple of thoughts of his own when to the radio audience was a genuine ad lib. "I wanted he began to stumble badly over his words. His apology to ad lib," he explained, "but it wasn't written on the paper."

C. *or* CA. for *circa:*

About: approximately: as ca. 1800.

CF. for *confer:*

Compare: check with.

E.G. for *exempli gratia:*

For example.

---

a—hat, ā—hāte, â—bâre, ä—bär, e—hen, ē—hē, i—hit, ī—hīde, o—hot, ō—hōme, ô—bôrn, u—hut, ū—hūge, û—bûrn, o͝o—hood, o͞o—ho͞ot, ou—out, oi—oil, ng—sing, ngg—finger, th—thin, th—then, zh—vision, and ə which equals a in dial, e in model, i in pupil, o in method, u in circus, or y in martyr.

ET AL.   for   *et alii* or *alia:*
>   And others.

ETC.   for   *et cetera:*
>   And the rest; and so forth; never write or say "and et cetera."

ET SEQ.   for   *et sequens, et sequentes, et sequentia:*
>   And the following.

F.V.   for   *folio verso:*
>   On the back of the page.

IB., IBID.   for   *ibidem:*
>   In the same place, passage, or book.

ID.   for   *idem:*
>   The same; the same author.

I.E.   for   *id est:*
>   That is.

INF.   for   *infra:*
>   Below.

IN LOC. CIT.   for   *in loco citato:*
>   In the place cited or mentioned.

IN OP. CIT.   for   *in opere citato:*

>   In the work cited.

L.S.   for   *locus sigilli:*

>   The place of the seal. L.S. is still printed on many legal forms next to the place for the signature as a carry-over from the days when a seal in wax or an impression was placed on the document to give it full legal force.

---

a—hat, ā—hāte, â—bâre, ä—bär, e—hen, ē—hē, i—hit, ī—hīde, o—hot, ō—hōme, ô—bôrn, u—hut, ū—hūge, û—bûrn, o͝o—hood, o͞o—ho͞ot, ou—out, oi—oil, ng—sing, ngg—finger, th—thin, th—then, zh—vision, and ə which equals a in dial, e in model, i in pupil, o in method, u in circus, or y in martyr.

N.B. for *nota bene:*
Note well; pay special attention.

NOL. PROS. for *nolle prosequi:*
To be unwilling to prosecute. *Nol-pros* is an English word formed from this phrase. "The case was nol-prossed."

OP. for *opus:*
A work; a term usually applied to a musical composition.

OP. CIT. for *opus citatum:*
The work cited or mentioned before.

PROX. for *proximo (mense):*
In or of the next month.

Q.V. for *quod vide:*
Which see; look this up.

℞ for *recipe:*
Take: an order at the head of a prescription. The symbol ℞ is also believed to come from ♃, the sign of Jupiter, whose favor was once asked to bring about an effective cure.

S.C. for *scilicet:*
It is permitted to know; to wit; understood.

ST. for *stet:*
Let it stand; do not change or take out. The opposite is *d.* or *dele*, written δ: destroy or take out.

SUP. for *supra:*
Above.

---

a—hat, ā—hāte, â—bâre, ä—bär, e—hen, ē—hē, i—hit, ī—hīde, o—hot, ō—hōme, ô—bôrn, u—hut, ū—hūge, û—bûrn, o͝o—hood, o͞o—ho͞ot, ou—out, oi—oil, ng—sing, ngg—finger, th—thin, th—then, zh—vision, and ə which equals a in dial, e in model, i in pupil, o in method, u in circus, or y in martyr.

T.I.D.   for *ter in die:*
Three times a day, a term found in prescriptions.

ULT.   for *ultimo (mense):*
In or of the last month.

VIZ.   for *videlicet:*
It is permitted to see; namely; to wit. The z is a type
of shorthand used by scribes of former centuries to
show an abbreviation like the z of oz. for ounce(s).

VS.   for *versus:*
Against.

GREEK

Thousands of words used in the sciences, especially in
medicine, are borrowed directly from Greek or are formed
by adding together Greek roots and words. The process is
still going on, and these words are fully naturalized even if
they are as new as the daily paper. You'll find such words
treated elsewhere in the book. Here we are stopping for only
two expressions which you'll frequently encounter in English.

EUREKA (urē'kə)
"I have found it!" Archimedes, the ancient scientist of
Syracuse, Sicily, is supposed to have run through the
streets shouting, "Eureka," after he had discovered a
method of finding the exact amount of gold in a crown.
This discovery led to the formulation of the principles
of flotation. *Eureka* is a cry of triumph. Appropriately,
it is the motto of California where gold was once found
in a different way.

HOI POLLOI (hoi pəloi')
"The many"; applied to the masses, the people. It is
not considered good form to put "the" in front of *hoi
polloi*, since *hoi* already means "the" in Greek.

We are not going to give you cause to complain about the
use of foreign words. We'll give you the translations of the

I. Translation, Please

italicized words and expressions used in the sentences below. However, you'll have to pick out the correct translation from the group below each sentence. Answers for these tests will be found on page 367.

1. Spec [Sanders] does everything with a football but swallow it. And he has a great *alter ego* in Buddy Young, who blocks almost as well as he runs.
   (a) rival (b) substitute (c) double (d) helper

2. By their refusals they have *ipso facto* stigmatized themselves as recalcitrant oppositionists.
   (a) without doubt (b) by the very act (c) obstinately (d) forever

3. For by this, it is reasoned that the *magnum opus* of the Roosevelt era, the Wagner Act, was in effect revoked.
   (a) masterpiece (b) injustice (c) early work (d) compromise

4. The United States declined to work on this basis and the commission was adjourned *sine die*.
   (a) immediately (b) without setting a day (c) without dissent (d) by voice vote

5. Book reviews do tend to be cluttered up with *obiter dicta*.
   (a) side remarks (b) prejudices (c) dull writing (d) small details

II. These Are Familiar

The expressions in the left-hand column are among the most frequently met Latin phrases or words in English. Match them with the definitions on the right.

1. DE JURE   a. here and there

2. IN TOTO   b. unique

3. PER SE	c. it doesn't follow
4. PASSIM	d. in good fatih
5. PRIMA FACIE	e. entirely
6. SINE QUA NON	f. legally
7. STATUS QUO	g. in itself
8. SUI GENERIS	h. indispensable condition
9. BONA FIDE	i. present condition
10. NON SEQUITUR	j. at first glance

III. Latin Shorthand

From the expression after the letters, select the one which best completes the statement after the numbers.

1. The abbreviation *N.B.* means (a) not good (b) take out (c) note carefully (d) new books.

2. *Prox.* is most generally read as an abbreviation for (a) approximately (b) next month (c) proxy (d) last month.

3. The abbreviation *e.g.* means (a) in regard to (b) namely (c) for example (d) English goods.

4. The abbreviation *i.e.* means (a) that is (b) look up (c) in reference to (d) always.

5. *Cf.* instructs you (a) to look on the reverse side (b) to compare (c) to cross out (d) to be careful.

IV. So You're Speaking Latin!

Hundreds of Latin words have been borrowed directly with little or no change of spelling, or new Latin words have been formed in English on ancient examples. Sometimes the meaning has been changed to fit modern times. You're speaking Latin every time you use any of the words in the left-hand column. Match them with the meanings in the right-hand column.

A

1. amanuensis   a. small quantity

2. acumen   b. beginnings

3. desideratum   c. without preparation

4. factotum   d. gap

5. impedimenta   e. secretary

6. impromptu   f. something wanted

7. incunabula   g. customs

8. lacuna   h. man of all work

9. modicum   i. hindrances

10. mores   j. mental keenness

B.

1. cadaver   a. favorite remedy
2. congeries   b. puzzle

3. conspectus   c. period between change of governments

4. credo   d. moving force

5. interregnum   e. heap

6. nonplus   f. tiny particle

7. impetus   g. corpse

8. nostrum   h. general survey

9. optimum   i. belief

10. scintilla   j. most favorable point

V. And You're Speaking Greek Too!

What we said about Latin words is true of many Greek words in English. Match the words in the left-hand column with the definitions in the right-hand column.

A

1. ACME   a. end; used with *alpha* to mean the

2. AEON   b. beginning and end

3. ANTITHESIS   c. glory

4. APOTHEOSIS   d. mark of disgrace

5. DIAPASON   e. riddle

6. ENIGMA   f. highest point

7. EPITOME   g. idealization

8. KUDOS   h. complete range of tones

9. OMEGA   i. long period of time

10. STIGMA   j. summary

                k. complete opposite

B

1. BASIS   a. culmination

2. CANON   b. injury

3. CHAOS   c. soul, mind

4. CLIMAX   d. gravestone

5. HUBRIS   e. rule, criterion

6. LEXICON   f. foundation

7. PSYCHE   g. long scarf

8. STELE   h. arrogance

9. STOLE   i. utter confusion

10. TRAUMA   j. dictionary

*"Of course it loses something in the translation." ***

22. Translation, Please: Modern Languages

IN A STORY in the *Saturday Evening Post*, a writer used the phrase "effulgent brouhaha." A reader unable to find it in his unabridged dictionary, wrote to ask the editor for the meaning. The editor replied, *"Brouhaha* is French for 'uproar'; the phrase 'effulgent brouhaha' means, roughly, 'glowing applause.' We recommended using an English equivalent, but the author insisted on his French word."

There is also the story of a young British reporter who was overfond of using French words in his news stories. One day when he was writing a short piece for a Paris journal, he burst into the editorial office of his paper and demanded, "What's the bloomin' French word for 'débâcle'?"

In this chapter we're going to take up a number of French, Italian, Spanish, German, and other foreign words which are blooming in our newspapers and finding permanent roots in our language.

FRENCH

French was for many centuries the language of diplomacy and of international society and culture. It was a second language for educated people all over Europe. English is now replacing French in this respect, but in English there are hundreds of currently used words and phrases which have been borrowed from French.

Strictly speaking there are no accented syllables in French words. The last pronounced syllable in a word gets a slight upward swing which we translate as an accent. You will, therefore, notice that almost all the French words listed here are accented on the last pronounced syllable.

A final *n* or *m* after a vowel is usually not pronounced. The word *bon*, for instance, is neither bô nor bôn. The same is true about *m* or *n* inside a word, if they are not doubled and are followed by a consonant. Examples: *entendre, accompli*. The *n* becomes nothing more than a slight explosive nasal sound after the vowel. We shall indicate this nasal sound by an italicized *n*, thus: bô*n*. The French *u* also gives difficulties. You can make this *u* sound properly by pursing your mouth for a *u* sound and saying ē. We shall indicate this sound thus: ü. There is one comforting thought. We Americans do not pronounce French words the way the French do; we merely approximate their sounds.

AGENT PROVOCATEUR (äzhän′ prôvôkətûr′)
> A person who joins an organization like a trade union or political group, pretends sympathy with their aims and incites them to commit an act for which they can be punished. This lengthy explanation shows why it is sometimes necessary to use foreign phrases in the interest of economy of expression.

---

a—hat, ā—hāte, â—bâre, ä—bär, e—hen, ē—hē, i—hit, ī—hīde, o—hot, ō—hōme, ô—bôrn, u—hut, ū—hūge, û—bûrn, ŏŏ—hood, ōō—hōōt, ou—out, oi—oil, ng—sing, ngg—finger, th—thin, th—then, zh—vision, and ə which equals a in dial, e in model, i in pupil, o in method, u in circus, or y in martyr.

AIDE-MÉMOIRE (ād māmwär′)

A memorandum; in diplomacy, an outline or summary of items of an agreement; literally, something that helps or jogs the memory.

AMOUR-PROPRE (əmōōr′ prōpr′)

Self-love; self-esteem; vanity.

AU COURANT (ō kōōrän′)

Well up in; well informed; up to date; in touch with.

AVANT-GARDE (avän gärd′)

Advance guard; vanguard; pioneers; offbeat.

BÊTE NOIRE (bet nwär′)

"a black beast"; a bugbear; a pet aversion; a person who is hated and detested.

BISTRO (bēstrō)

Small wine shop; tavern; used in this country to mean saloon or bar.

BOITE (bwat)

Short for *boîte de nuit*, literally "night box." The circumflex accent may be dropped in English. A boite may be a little more elegant than a bistro. In Paris it refers to a small dancing club or a *café chantant*. Establishments like the Cafe Espresso places in Greenwich Village are often referred to as *boites*.

BON VIVANT (bôn vēvän′)

A lover of good living; epicure; gourmet.

CANARD (kənärd′ *or* kanar′)

"Duck." A canard is a silly or absurd story circulated to impose on people's credulity; a hoax; a sensational

a—hat, ā—hāte, â—bâre, ä—bär, e—hen, ē—hē, i—hit, ī—hīde, o—hot, ō—hōme, ô—bôrn, u—hut, ū—hūge, û—bûrn, ŏŏ—hood, ōō—hōŏt, ou—out, oi—oil, ng—sing, ngg—finger, th—thin, th—then, zh—vision, and ə which equals a in dial, e in model, i in pupil, o in method, u in circus, or y in martyr.

manufactured story. One explanation of its origin is that it is taken from the French expression *vendre un canard a moitié*, "to half-sell a duck." For, if one half-sells a duck, one does not sell it at all but takes somebody in or imposes upon him. Another explanation is that *canard* refers to a duck-story, a silly tale that was spread in many newspapers about the voracity of ducks, and that fooled many readers. The following headline (above a stock-market story) interestingly links neswspapers and *canards*:

NEWSPAPERS TAKE STEP
TO REFUTE A CANARD

CARTE BLANCHE   (kärt blänsh)
"A white paper"; blank paper containing only a signature giving another person permission to write his own terms; blank check; unlimited authority; blanket permission.

CAUSE CÉLÈBRE   (kōz säleb'r)
Celebrated legal case; criminal case that arouses wide interest.

CHEF D'OEUVRE   (she'dû'vr')
Masterpiece; a *magnum opus*.

COMME IL FAUT   (kômēlfō')
As it should be; proper; in good form.

CONTRETEMPS   (kûntrətän')
Mishap; embarrassing moment.

COUP DE GRÂCE   (kōō də gräs')
"A blow of mercy"; a final, decisive stroke; the death blow given by an executioner to end the victim's suffering; the blow with which a knight despatched his beaten

a—hat, ā—hāte, â—bâre, ä—bär, e—hen, ē—hē, i—hit, ī—hīde, o—hot, ō—hōme, ô—bôrn, u—hut, ū—hūge, û—bûrn, ōō—hood, ōō—hōōt, ou—out, oi—oil, ng—sing, ngg—finger, th—thin, th—then, zh—vision, and ə which equals a in dial, e in model, i in pupil, o in method, u in circus, or y in martyr.

opponent or with which a bull-fighter finally ends the bull's agony.

COUP D' ÉTAT   (kōō dätä')
A sudden stroke of state policy; a sudden decisive stroke by which a government is overthrown.

CUL-DE-SAC   (kool or kul də sak', Fr. küd'sak')
Blind alley; dead-end street.

DÉJÀ VU   (dāzhä'vü)
"Already seen"; a feeling that one has been to a place or has lived through an experience before; the technical name for this experience is *paramnesia.*

DÉMARCHE   (dämärsh')
A step or course of action, especially in diplomacy, often marking a change of policy.

DE RIGUEUR   (də rēgûr')
According to strict etiquette; very formal; in good form or taste.

DERNIER CRI   (dârnyā'krē')
The last word; the latest, newest fashion.

DESHABILLE   (dezəbēl')
Undressed; partly dressed; in negligee; the word is also written *déshabillé, dishabille,* and *en deshabille.*

DÉTENTE   (dätänt')
Diplomatic word referring to a slackening or relaxation of strained relations between governments.

DE TROP   (də trō')
Superfluous; in excess; in the way.

---

a—hat, ā—hāte, â—bâre, ä—bär, e—hen, ē—hē, i—hit, ī—hīde, o—hot, ō—hōme, ô—bôrn, u—hut, ū—hūge, û—bûrn, ŏŏ—hood, ōō—hōōt, ou—out, oi—oil, ng—sing, ngg—finger, th—thin, th—then, zh—vision, and ə which equals a in dial, e in model, i in pupil, o in method, u in circus, or y in martyr.

DOUBLE-ENTENDRE (dōō′bländänd′r)

A word or phrase allowing two interpretations, one of which may be off-color; indelicate; *risqué.*

ECHELON (esh′əlon)

This is the French word *échelon,* which has lost its French accent and pronunciation in English. Its original French meaning is a step, rung of a ladder (*échelle,* from Latin *scala, scalae,* flight of steps, ladder), and, figuratively, a steplike formation of troops, ships, aircraft, or a subdivision of a military command. Formerly used almost exclusively in its military sense in English, the word *echelon* is now being used more and more extensively by writers to denote a grade, level, rank, or an order of importance or standing, as in these expressions taken from newspapers: second-*echelon* American advisers: a three-team *echelon;* dipping several *echelons* in the leagues of organized baseball.

ENFANT TERRIBLE (änfän′ tərē′bl)

"A bad child" who speaks out of turn; a child whose remarks cause embarrassment; a person who puts his party on the spot with inopportune remarks.

EN RAPPORT (än rapôr′)

In harmony; with mutual understanding and sympathy.

ESPRIT DE CORPS (esprē də kôr′)

A common spirit of pride in a group; a spirit of devotion and loyalty to an organization.

FAIT ACCOMPLI (fetakônplē′)

A thing that is accomplished and irrevocable; an action finished and over with and then presented to a debating body; a program decided upon and presented without warning.

---

a—hat, ā—hāte, â—bâre, ä—bär, e—hen, ē—hē, i—hit, ī—hīde, o—hot, ō—hōme, ô—bôrn, u—hut, ū—hūge, û—bûrn, ōō—hood, ōō—hōōt, ou—out, oi—oil, ng—sing, ngg—finger, th—thin, th—then, zh—vision, and ə which equals a in diạl, e in model, i in pupịl, o in methọd, u in circụs, or y in martyr.

FAUTE ED MIEUX   (fōt də myû)
    For want of something better.

FAUX PAS   (fō pä′)
    "False step"; mistake; social error.

FEMME FATALE   (fam fətal′)
    A woman who leads men to destruction; a Mata Hari;
    cf. Circe and the Sirens of the myths.

FIN DE SIECLE   (fan də sye′kl)
    "End of (the) century"; now generally used to indicate
    decadence; first applied to the end of the nineteeth cen-
    tury, the fabulous 1890's.

FLÂNEUR   (flänûr′)
    Idler; an aimless stroller along the Parisian bouevards;
    therefore, an intellectual trifler; a dilettante; a *boule-
    vardier*.

FORCE MAJEURE   (fôrs mäzhûr′)
    Superior or irresistible force; act of God.

GAFFE   (gaf, rhymes with *calf*)
    A clumsy mistake; a bloomer; a howler; a faux pas.

HORS DE COMBAT   (ôr də kônbä′)
    "Out of the combat"; disabled; incapacitated.

IDÉE FIXE   (ēdā fēks′)
    Fixed idea; obsession.

INSOUCIANCE   (insōō′siəns; Fr. ans ōōsyäns′)
    Indifference; lack of concern.

JOIE DE VIVRE   (zhwä də vēvr)
    "Joy of living"; a zest for life.

---

a—hat, ā—hāte, â—bâre, ä—bär, e—hen, ē—hē, i—hit, ī—hīde,
o—hot, ō—hōme, ô—bôrn, u—hut, ū—hūge, û—bûrn, o͝o—hood,
o͞o—ho͞ot, ou—out, oi—oil, ng—sing, ngg—finger, th—thin,
th—then, zh—vision, and ə which equals a in diạl, e in modẹl,
i in pupịl, o in methọd, u in circụs, or y in martỵr.

LAISSEZ-FAIRE (lesāfâr´)

"Let [the people] do [what they choose]"; a policy of non-interference; letting things drift; the economic doctrine that the government should allow business to proceed with a minimum of regulation. The opposite is *dirigisme* or full government direction.

LÈSE-MAJESTÉ (lēz mahzhəstā´ *or* lēz´ majís ti)

A crime against a sovereign or a sovereign power; an insult to a ruler or superior; treason.

MÉLANGE (mālä*n*zh´)

Mixture; blending; medley; macédoine.

MÉNAGE (mānäzh´)

Household; domestic establishment; family.

MISEENSCÈNE (mēzä*n*sen´)

Scenery and property needed for a play; setting; background; milieu.

NOBLESSE OBLIGE (nōbles´ ōblēzh´)

"Nobility obligates." A code of behavior associated with persons of high rank; graciousness that is supposed to spring from noble birth.

NOM DE PLUME (no*n* də plōōm´, Fr. no*n*´ də plüm´)

Pen name; the expression *nom de guerre* is used by the French to mean any pseudonym.

NOUVEAUX RICHES (nōōv ō rēsh´)

People who are newly-rich, who have suddenly come up in the world; upstarts. Other terms for the same idea are *nouveaux arrivés* and *parvenus.*

---

a—hat, ā—hāte, â—bâre, ä—bär, e—hen, ē—hē, i—hit, ī—hīde, o—hot, ō—hōme, ô—bôrn, u—hut, ū—hūge, û—bûrn, ōō—hood, ōō—hōōt, ou—out, oi—oil, ng—sing, ngg—finger, th—thin, th—then, zh—vision, and ə which equals a in dial, e in model, i in pupil, o in method, u in circus, or y in martyr.

OUTRÉ (ōōtrā' *or* ōō'trā)
Exaggerated; out of the ordinary; extravagant; *bizarre*.

PETIT BOURGEOIS (pətē' boorzhwä')
"The little man"; a member of the lower middle class.

PIÈCE DE RÉSISTANCE (pyes də räzistäns')
The main dish or course; the chief article of a collection; the major work on a program.

POTPOURRI (pōp ōōrē' *or* potpoor'ī)
Medley; mishmash; mixture; olio; *olla podrida;* farrago; *pasticcio; mélange;* miscellany. How many ways there are of saying this!

QUI VIVE (kē vēv')
A sentry's challenge equivalent to "Who goes there?" To be on the *qui vive* means to be alert.

RAISON D' ÊTRE (räzôn' dâ'tr', Fr. de'tr')
"Reason for being"; justification.

RAPPROCHEMENT (raprôshmän')
Drawing closer together; diplomatic term for the establishment of cordial relations between nations; cf. *détente.*

RÉCLAME (räclam')
Publicity; press-agent stunt.

RIPOSTE (rēpōst')
Repartee; a quick answer; a fencing term meaning a quick return thrust after a parry.

---

a—hat, ā—hāte, â—bâre, ä—bär, e—hen, ē—hē, i—hit, ī—hīde, o—hot, ō—hōme, ô—bôrn, u—hut, ū—hūge, û—bûrn, ŏŏ—hood, ōō—hōŏt, ou—out, oi—oil, ng—sing, ngg—finger, th—thin, th—then, zh—vision, and ə which equals a in diál, e in model, i in pupil, o in method, u in circus, or y in martyr.

277

ROMAN À CLEF *or* **CLÉ** (rô män nä klä)

"Novel with a key"; a novel, which despite its author's disclaimers about "any similarity," has real people and places in it, identifiable if you have the *key*.

This novel is in many of its aspects a *roman à clef*: Paris is here the city of Sybaris, the German conquerors are the Armagnacs; atomic scientists, poets, dancers, and political figures are easy enough to recognize.

SANG-FROID (sän frwä')

"Cold blood"; coolness under fire; self-possession; composure.

SANS (sanz *or* Fr. sän)
Without; deprived of.

SAVOIR-FAIRE (savwärfâr')

"To know how to do"; tact; poise, polish; experienced cleverness. However, our *know-how* implies "savvy," technical knowledge, or mechanical ability.

SOUPÇON (sōōpsôn')

"Suspicion"; a dash of; small portion.

SUCCÈS D'ESTIME (sükse' destēm')

Success achieved by a play which gets the reviews but not the customers; an artistic success but a financial failure; also applied to a favorable review given out of respect to the author's known ability or sincerity.

SUCCÈS FOU (sükse' fōō')

"A wild success"; a smash hit.

---

a—hat, ä—hāte, â—bâre, ä—bär, e—hen, ē—hē, i—hit, ī—hīde, o—hot, ō—hōme, ô—bôrn, u—hut, ū—hūge, û—bûrn, ŏŏ—hood, ōō—hōŏt, ou—out, oi—oil, ng—sing, ngg—finger, th—thin, th—then, zh—vision, and ə which equals a in dial, e in model, i in pupil, o in method, u in circus, or y in martyr.

TÊE-À-TÊTE   (tātətāt, Fr. tet′atêt′)

"Head to head"; a face-to-face conversation; confidential chat.

TOUCHÉ   (tōōshā′)

"Touched," a term used in fencing. "A hit, a very palpable hit!" says Osric during the fencing match in *Hamlet. Touché* is generally used as an exclamation to acknowledge the scoring of a successful point in argument or a witty retort.

TOUR ED FORCE   (tōōr də fôrs′)

A feat of strength or skill; a literary or dramatic trick; a work done to exhibit the mechanical ability of an author in a field not his own—just to show he can do it.

VIS-À-VIS *or* VIS A VIS   (vēzəvē′)

Directly opposite to; facing; in regard to; over against; in reference to.

VOLTE-FACE   (vôltfäs′)

A complete turnabout; a reversal of policy, opinion, or attitude; an about-face.

SPANISH

Out West and along the Rio Grande, in those regions once settled by the Spaniards, many words coming from Spain or Mexico have settled down in the daily speech of the cowboys and other inhabitants of the West. Words of Spanish origin are also common in terms relating to art and the dance. Here, however, we have room for only a few borrowings of a general nature.

AFICIONADO   (äfisiōnä′dō)

A fan; amateur; devoted follower of a sport.

---

a—hat, ā—hāte, â—bâre, ä—bär, e—hen, ē—hē, i—hit, ī—hīde, o—hot, ō—hōme, ô—bôrn, u—hut, ū—hūge, û—bûrn, ŏŏ—hood, ōō—hōōt, ou—out, oi—oil, ng—sing, ngg—finger, th—thin, th—then, zh—vision, and ə which equals a in dial, e in model, i in pupil, o in method, u in circus, or y in martyr.

BONANZA (bŏnan′zə)

Originally a mine with a rich yield of silver or gold; a gold mine; a rich return on an investment or a source of large income; a stroke of good luck.

CANTINA (kantēn′ä)

Canteen; a combination saloon and supply store where entertainment is also provided.

HIDALGO (hidal′gō)

A second-degree nobleman; a "somebody" since *hidalgo* is formed from two words meaning son of somebody.

JUNTA (jun′tə or Spanish hōōn′ta)

A council or committee; a secret council; a group of plotters; a cabal, clique, faction, or *junto.*

OLLAPODRIDA (ōlə pōdrĕ′də)

A mixture; miscellany; hodgepodge. Like *potpourri, olla podrida* means a rotten pot, a stew of meat and vegetables. *Olio,* coming from olla, is used in the theater to mean a number of short pieces as in vaudeville.

VAQUERO (väkâr′ō)

Cowboy. The cowboys corrupted this word to *buckaroo.*

PORTUGUESE

AUTO-DA-FÉ (ôtōdəfā′)

"Act of the faith"; the ceremony accompanying the pronouncement of judgment by the Inquisition, which was followed by the execution of the guilty by secular authorities; an execution; used figuratively to denote the punishment of an unorthodox person.

---

a—hat, ā—hāte, â—bâre, ä—bär, e—hen, ē—hē, i—hit, ī—hīde, o—hot, ō—hōme, ô—bôrn, u—hut, ū—hūge, û—bûrn, ōō—hood, ōō—hōōt, ou—out, oi—oil, ng—sing, ngg—finger, th—thin, th—then, zh—vision, and ə which equals a in dial, e in model, i in pupil, o in method, u in circus, or y in martyr.

ITALIAN

From Italy, land of art and music, we have borrowed many words pertaining to the arts. The musical terms you'll find on your concert-hall program are almost all Italian. We shall not list the special musical vocabulary of Italian origin; we shall limit ourselves to a few common words and phrases.

A CAPPELLA (ä käppel′lä)
> Unaccompanied choral music "in chapel style."

AL FRESCO (al fres′ḳō)
> "In the fresh air"; out of doors.

BRAVURA (brəvū′rə or brəvōōrə)
> "Bravery"; a show of dash and spirit; florid.

CHIAROSCURO (kiärōskūr′ō)
> *Chiaro*, clear or light + *oscuro*, dark or shadowy; a sketch in black and white; a sharp contrast.

CICERONE (chēchərō′nā *or* sisərō′nē)
> A guide to a museum or other sights. The word comes from the name of Rome's greatest orator, Cicero. Silent guides are rare, as any tourist will tell you.

COMMEDIA DELL'ARTE (kômme′diä del lär′tä)
> A type of comedy as played by a guild of Italian artists who improvised from a written plot. Brooks Atkinson once called a production of *Volpone* "a noisy stage circus which scholars might .describe as commedia dell'arte and theatergoers would call burlesque."

CON AMORE (kōn ämō′rä)
> Tenderly; with love and devotion.

---

a—hat, ā—hāte, â—bâre, ä—bär, e—hen, ē—hē, i—hit, ī—hīde, o—hot, ō—hōme, ô—bôrn, u—hut, ū—hūge, û—bûrn, o͝o—hood, o͞o—ho͞ot, ou—out, oi—oil, ng—sing, ngg—finger, th—thin, th—then, zh—vision, and ə which equals a in dial, e in model, i in pupil, o in method, u in circus, or y in martyr.

DILETTANTE   (dilətan′ti)

A lover of the fine arts whose interest is amateurish or superficial; a dabbler.

DOLCE FAR NIENTE   (dôl′che fär nyen′te)

"Sweet to do nothing"; delightful idleness.

PRESTO   (pres′tō)

Quickly; rapidly, a musical direction calling for quick tempo; a magician's command, as in "Presto, chango!" A prestidigitator is a "quick-change" artist, a magician who is nimble and quick with the hands (*digit*, finger). His art is *prestidigitation* or *legerdemain* which is French for *sleight-of-hand*.

PUNCTILIO   (pungktil′io)

From the same Latin root which gives us *point, punctual, punctuation,* and *pungent.* Originally a fine point; now it means a nice point of etiquette or behavior; exactness; fastidiousness; attention to the niceties; meticulousness.

RISORGIMENTO   (risôrjimen′tō)

A revival; a resurrection; applied especially to the awakening of national feeling in Italy in the 19th century and the movement for unity.

SOTTO VOCE   (sŏt′tō vō′chā)
                          vō′chā)

"Under the voice"; privately; aside; in an undertone or whisper.

VENDETTA   (vendet′ə)

A *vendetta* is a blood-feud, originally applied to the feuding families of Corsica who avenged the deaths of relatives.

---

a—hat, ā—hāte, â—bâre, ä—bär, e—hen, ē—hē, i—hit, ī—hīde, o—hot, ō—hōme, ô—bôrn, u—hut, ū—hūge, û—bûrn, ŏŏ—hood, ōō—hōōt, ou—out, oi—oil, ng—sing, ngg—finger, th—thin, th—then, zh—vision, and ə which equals a in dial, e in model, i in pupil, o in method, u in circus, or y in martyr.

VIRTUOSO (vûrchōō ō'sō)

> One who excels in the practice of an art; applied especially to pianists and violinists; an expert.

GERMAN

Once, words borrowed from German were reminiscent of the famed German *Gemütlichkeit,* suggestive of comfort, good living, easygoing kindness, and graciousness. These words were related to music, food, and the arts. Later, German words of war and politics came into our language.

The *ch* in German is not *tsh* but is the guttural or back-of-the-throat sound heard in *loch,* the Scottish word for *lake.*

DOPPELGÄNGER (dôpəlgeng'ər)

> A double; a spiritual, ghostly, or actual counterpart of a living person; also written as an English word *double-ganger.*

ERSATZ (erzäts')

> Substitute material; shoddy; inferior; hollow.

GESTALT (ge shtält' or gə shtält')

> "Form, shape, configuration"; generally found in the expression *Gestalt psychology,* of which the basic principle is that the response of an organism to a situation is a complete whole rather than the sum of responses to separate elements in the situation; that in perception the mind does not build up wholes out of specific elements but grasps *Gestalten,* configurations, which may then be analyzed into simpler elements.

GÖTTERDÄMMERUNG (gûtərdem'əroong)

> *Twilight of the Gods;* the last opera in Richard Wagner's tetralogy, *The Ring of the Nibelung;* a word used to denote a final breakdown and crash amid thunder and lightning; a supremely tragic end.

---

a—hat, ā—hāte, â—bâre, ä—bär, e—hen, ē—hē, i—hit, ī—hīde, o—hot, ō—hōme, ô—bôrn, u—hut, ū—hūge, û—bûrn, ŏŏ—hood, ōō—hōōt, ou—out, oi—oil, ng—sing, ngg—finger, th—thin, th—then, zh—vision, and ə which equals a in dial, e in model, i in pupil, o in method, u in circus, or y in martyr.

HINTERLAND (hin'tərland)

Back regions; frontiers; borderlands; regions remote from towns; originally, the land beyond a strip of sea-coast or *littoral*.

POLTERGEIST (pōl'tərgīst)

A noisy spirit or ghost.

PUTSCH (pootsh)

A petty rebellion or popular uprising; if successful it may result in a *coup d'état*.

REALPOLITIK (rääl'pōlətēk)

Practical or realistic politics and diplomacy; a cynical interpretation of political policy as power politics.

VERBOTEN (ferbōt'ən)

Forbidden.

WELTANSCHAUUNG (veltänshou'oong)

A world view; a philosophic view of the universe in relation to the purpose of actions and events.

WELTSCHMERZ (velt'shmerts)

Sorrow over the state of the world; sentimental pessimism.

ZEITGEIST (tsīt'gīst')

Spirit of the times.

OUR OWN FOREIGN DEPARTMENT

Because of the rapid coverage of events in all parts of the world through lightning-quick means of communication, foreign words appear in the newspapers daily. All of the follow-

a—hat, ā—hāte, â—bâre, ä—bär, e—hen, ē—hē, i—hit, ī—hīde, o—hot, ō—hōme, ô—bôrn, u—hut, ū—hūge, û—bûrn, o͝o—hood, o͞o—ho͞ot, ou—out, oi—oil, ng—sing, ngg—finger, th—thin, th—then, zh—vision, and ə which equals a in dial, e in model, i in pupil, o in method, u in circus, or y in martyr.

ing foreign words listed below have been used in reporting news from abroad.

APARTHEID (əpärt′hīt) [Dutch, Afrikaans]
A word used in the Union of South Africa to denote a policy of segregation.

BAKSHEESH (bak′shēsh [Persian]
Tip; gratuity; money given as a bribe for a favor. The German word *Trinkgeld* and the French word *pourboire* meaning tip indicate that the money is given for a drink. It's interesting to note that *baksheesh* is related to the Greek root *phag*, eat, as in .eso*phag*us, *phag*ocyte, *and* sarco*phag*us.

BANZAI (bän′zī′) [Japanese]
A shout meaning forever, or at least for ten thousand years; a loud greeting similar to *Viva!*

CUMSHAW (küm′shô) [Chinese]
Tip; present; like *baksheesh*.

GHAT (gôt) [Hindustani]
Steps leading down to a river. A burning *ghat* (or *ghaut*) is a wide space on the steps where the Hindus place funeral pyres and cremate the bodies of the dead.

HIBACHI (hi bä′chē) [Japanese]
A combination portable grill and heater using coal, wood, or charcoal.

JIHAD (jēhäd′) [Arabic]
Religious war; war for a principle.

---

a—hat, ā—hāte, â—bâre, ä—bär, ᵊ—hen, ē—hē, i—hit, ī—hīde, o—hot, ō—hōme, ô—bôrn, u—hut, ū—hūge, û—bûrn, o͞o—hood, o͞o—ho͞ot, ou—out, oi—oil, ng—sing, ngg—finger, th—thin, th—then, zh—vision, and ə which equals a in dial, e in model, i in pupil, o in method, u in circus, or y in martyr.

KIBBUTZ (kiboots') [Hebrew]
From a Hebrew root meaning to gather; a community or colony; refers specifically to a communal settlement in Israel.

NISEI (nē'sā') [Japanese]
Native-born citizens of the United States and Canada of Japanese descent whose parents were immigrants and non-citizens.

PURDAH (pûr'də) [Hindustani and Persian]
A *purdah* is a veil. Purdah is the name given to the covering or curtain used to screen women in India from public view. Figuratively, it is applied to the retirement of women from public life and may mean a secluded, sheltered, cloistered existence for women.

SABRA (sä'brə) [Aramaic and Arabic]
The name of a cactus growing in Israel that is hard and tough on the outside but soft and sweet inside; an affectionate, descriptive name applied to native-born Israelis.

SAMURAI (sam'oorī) [Japanese]
Originally the titles of feudal military retainers; now applied to military officers as a class.

SHALOM (shälōm' *or* shô'lōm) [Hebrew]
"Well-being, peace."

SHINTO (Shin'tō) [Japanese]
Literally "the way of the gods." A religion of reverence to the spirits of imperial ancestors and historical personages.

---

a—hat, ā—hāte, â—bâre, ä—bär, e—hen, ē—hē, i—hit, ī—hīde, o—hot, ō—hōme, ô—bôrn, u—hut, ū—hūge, û—bûrn, oo—hood, ōō—hōot, ou—out, oi—oil, ng—sing, ngg—finger, th—thin, th—then, zh—vision, and ə which equals a in dial, e in model, i in pupil, o in method, u in circus, or y in martyr.

SHOGUN (shō′ gōōn) [Japanese]

Literally, "leader of an army"; originally the title of military governors. Associated with this word is *tycoon*, from a Japanese word meaning great lord. *Tycoon* has passed into English to describe an industrial magnate, a man of great power and wealth in the world of business.

SPOOR (spoor *or* spōr) [Dutch-South African]

Track or trace; trail of an animal.

SPUTNIK (sput nik) [Russian]

On October 4, 1957, an artificial satellite was shot into space by the Russians, who called it Sputnik, "fellow traveler." Etymologically the name consists of three parts: prefix *s together*, root *put*, travel, suffix *nik*, one who or that which.

SUTTEE (sutĕ′ *or* sut′ē) [Hindustani]

The custom of self-sacrifice once common in ancient times and more recently in India. A faithful wife cremated herself on her husband's funeral pyre as an act of devotion.

TARBOOSH (tärbōōsh′) [Arabic]

Fez or turban; red cap formerly worn by the Turks.

ZAIBATSU (zī′bätsōō′) [Japanese]

Families holding control over large business corporations; monopolies and interlocking directorates.

---

a—hat, ā—hāte, â—bâre, ä—bär, e—hen, ĕ—hē, i—hit, ī—hīde, o—hot, ō—hōme, ô—bôrn, u—hut, ū—hūge, û—bûrn, ŏŏ—hood, ōō—hōŏt, ou—out, oi—oil, ng—sing, ngg—finger, th—thin, th—then, zh—vision, and ə which equals a in dial, e in model, i in pupil, o in method, u in circus, or y in martyr.

I. Parlez-vous Français?

Each of the incomplete statements below can be completed by a French expression. Choose the correct one from the four given at the end of each statement.

Answers for these tests will be found on page 367.

1. A sudden act of force by which a government is changed is called (a) *coup d'état* (b) *tour de force* (c) *coup de grâce* (d) *succès fou.*

2. A feeling of pride in the common interests of an organization is often referred to as (a) *beau monde* (b) *en rapport* (c) *esprit de corps* (d) *élan.*

3. The justification for the existence of a condition or an event is its (a) *savoir-faire* (b) *raison d'être* (c) *cause célèbre* (d) *rapprochement.*

4. Calmness under trying circumstances is an example of (a) *volte-face* (b) *qui vive* (c) *force majeure* (d) *sang-froid.*

5. A school subject which a pupil dislikes and has great difficulty in passing may become his (a) *faux pas* (b) *dernier cri* (c) *cul-de-sac* (d) *bête noire.*

6. A matter presented for discussion after it has already been acted upon is called (a) *fait accompli* (b) *apropos* (c) *fin de siècle* (d) *au courant.*

7. An idle stroller is known as (a) *hors de combat* (b) *outré* (c) *rococo* (d) *flâneur.*

8. To give a person unlimited permission is to give him (a) *démarche* (b) *double entendre* (c) *carte blanche* (d) *feuilleton*.

9. A relaxation of tensions between two countries is called (a) *entente* (b) *impasse* (c) *détente* (d) *laissez-faire*.

10. The main dish or course is called (a) *hors d'oeuvre* (a) *potpourri* (c) *réclame* (d) *pièce de résistance*.

II. An Easy French Lesson

In the left-hand column are ten English words which were borrowed from French. Match these naturalized words with their definitions in the right-hand column.

1. sangfroid	a. file
2. argot	b. background
3. badinage	c. contractor
4. cadre	d. class, kind
5. confrère	e. teasing small talk
6. dossier	f. self-possession
7. entrepreneur	g. ghost
8. genre	h. slang
9. milieu	i. colleague
10. revenant	j. framework

III. Encore! Bis!

And here are ten more words of the same kind.

1. abattoir		a. paid applauders
2. canard		b. nursery
3. claque		c. nickname
4. concierge		d. uneasiness
5. crèche		e. small pleasing sketch
6. embonpoint		f. slaughterhouse
7. malaise		g. doorkeeper
8. persiflage		h. hoax, false report
9. sobriquet		i. pamphlet
10. vignette		j. plumpness
		k. communication, link
		l. small talk

IV. Polyglot

The left-hand column is multilingual containing a variety of words taken from Spanish, Italian, and German. Match them with their meanings in the right-hand column.

1. aficionado		a. noisy spirit
2. bonanza		b. commerce, clique
3. crescendo		c. fine point
4. dilettante		d. stroke of good luck
5. ersatz		e. feud
6. junta		f. enthusiast
7. poltergeist		g. expert performer
8. punctilio		h. dabbler
9. vendetta		i. shoddy
10. virtuoso		j. rising in volume

IV. PASS THAT TEST!

Ralph Newman

"I saw you with Mary Smith last night! I think you are untrustworthy, disloyal, unhelpful, unfriendly, discourteous, unkind, disobedient, uncheerful, unthrifty, cowardly, unclean, and irreverent!" *

---

23. What Do They Ask?

FOR THOSE who are preparing for a test these chapters are for immediate use; for those who are interested in building their vocabularies in a leisurely way these chapters are a long-term project.

If a position comes under civil service and a test is given, that test is sure to contain a considerable number of vocabulary questions. Job-placement and personnel tests, aptitude and intelligence tests, scholarship and comprehensive examinations in English—all include an important section on vocabulary. Therefore, to help you pass that test, we are devoting the two final chapters to the types of questions you are likely to meet and in our examples and tests words that have appeared or are likely to appear on such tests.

TYPES OF TESTS

There are about twenty different types of vocabulary questions. The type most frequently used in this book and found on most examinations is the one offering a multiple choice of definitions. The next chapter contains multple-choice tests of words. In this chapter we shall take up with examples most of the other types of questions found on examinations. Answers for tests in this chapter will be found on page 000.

I. Matching

You are given two columns of words and phrases or expressions. You are asked to match the terms in one column with their corresponding definitions in the other column.

Note that one column may contain more entries than the other column. Don't be alarmed if you can't find a place for some of the definitions in the longer column. It was planned that way to cut down guessing. Also note that the columns contain a mixed assortment of nouns, adjectives, verbs, and other parts of speech. Let this fact help you. Match nouns with nouns, etc.

Below is a matching exercise. Take each word in Column A in order and find the expression or word in Column B that is nearest to it in meaning.

Example: Suppose that *saffron* were in Column A as Number 11. You look down Column B until you come across *yellow-orange*. Then you write 11n as the correct answer.

Column A	Column B
1. buttress	a. sully
2. distend	b. climb a mountain
3. edification	c. urging
4. excrescence	d. sidetrack
5. habiliments	e. make a temporary stay
6. purview	f. superfluous growth

7. shunt	g. contentment
8. sojourn	h. power
9. solicitation	i. support
10. tarnish	j. full scope
	k. instruction
	l. newspaper
	m. swell
	n. yellow-orange
	o. clothing

II. Group Choice

This is a variation of the multiple-choice type. You are given a list of numbered words in one column and groups of four words each in another column. Each group is designated by a letter. You must take each numbered word in order and in one of the groups on the right find the word closest in meaning. Then you write down the number of the word and the letter of the group in which its synonym is found.

Example: Suppose that *propensity* were Number 11 in the left-hand column below. Its synonym in the groups to the right is *tendency* in Group B. The answer would be 11-B.

1. descry	**GROUP A**
2. extant	batter shameful risen exclaim
3. jocund	**GROUP B**
4. opprobrious	tendency error detect wordy
5. oriented	**GROUP C**
6. proclivity	odd desire existing adjusted
7. ramification	**GROUP D**
8. remiss	substitute branch attachment clownish
9. verbose	**GROUP E**
10. vicarious	negligent laudable merry starry

III. A Pair of Synonyms

In this type of question you are asked to select from a group of four words the two words that are synonyms or that are closely related in meaning.

Example: (a) choleric (b) demented (c) angry (d) imperturbable.

The correct answer is: (a) and (c).

1. (a) demeanor (b) enjoyment (c) behest (d) command
2. (a) aberrant (b) evanescent (c) lucid (d) fleeting
3. (a) gullible (b) spirited (c) craven (d) pusillanimous
4. (a) changeable (b) perverse (c) learned (d) obdurate
5. (a) impair (b) rival (c) damage (d) judge
6. (a) thin out (b) excuse (c) extenuate (d) condemn
7. (a) dissolute (b) easy (c) melted (d) immoral
8. (a) slimness (b) lenity (c) bias (d) mildness
9. (a) languor (b) beauty (c) lassitude (d) heat
10. (a) scruple (b) qualm (c) devotion (d) complaint

IV. A Pair of Antonyms

This is the opposite of the previous type. You must pair off words with opposite meanings, *antonyms*. We'll make it a little harder by asking you to pick two out of five choices.

Example: (a) interminable (b) vague (c) coincidental (d) finished (e) unbearable

The correct answer is: (a) and (d).

1. (a) sincere (b) bigoted (c) contrite (d) tolerant (e) deep
2. (a) valid (b) concise (c) dignified (d) written (e) fallacious
3. (a) long (b) prosaic (c) sanguine (d) believable (e) inspired
4. (a) contemplating (b) complete (c) scathing (d) laudatory (e) eminent
5. (a) unite (b) compare (c) despair (d) believe (e) sunder
6. (a) guard (b) persuade (c) vouchsafe (d) teach (e) deny
7. (a) representative (b) thrifty (c) honest (d) atypical (e) notable
8. (a) furry (b) covert (c) convinced (d) open (e) agreed
9. (a) quiescent (b) friendly (c) joking (d) turbulent (e) faithful
10. (a) prevail on (b) pamper (c) continue (d) discipline (e) convert

V. Finding an Opposite

In this type of question you are asked to find in a group of four words a word that is opposite in meaning to a given word.

Example: adamant: (a) thick (b) complaint (c) stubborn (d) precious

The correct answer is (b).

1. affable   (a) pleasant (b) surly (c) weak (d) unknown
2. bizarre   (a) normal (b) enormous (c) occupied (d) eccentric
3. clemency   (a) necessity (b) good health (c) sternness (d) aid
4. denegate   (a) belittle (b) refuse (c) affirm (d) defer
5. enhance   (a) widen (b) risk (c) sell (d) decrease
6. niggardly   (a) generous (b) parsimonious (c) fitfully (d) comprehensive
7. occult   (a) open (b) hidden (c) respectful (d) regional
8. palliate   (a) gloss over (b) spread thickly (c) extenuate (d) aggravate
9. sobriety   (a) moderation (b) drunkenness (c) darkness (d) sincerity
10. untenable   (a) defensible (b) immeasurable (c) incorrigible (d) difficult

VI. Eliminate the Impostor

In this type of question you are given a group of four words, three of which are closely related or similar in meaning. You are asked to pick the word that does not belong in the group.

Example: (a) false (b) deceitful (c) untruthful (d) authentic

The correct answer is (d).

1. (a) quandary (b) scrape (c) predicament (d) subterfuge
2. (a) atrocious (b) heinous (c) sanguinary (d) nefarious
3. (a) affirm (b) refute (c) disprove (d) rebut
4. (a) august (b) warm (c) majestic (d) superb
5. (a) altruistic (b) charitable (c) gaudy (d) benevolent
6. (a) evince (b) exhibit (c) display (d) contest
7. (a) glacial (b) gelid (c) glaring (d) icy
8. (a) hermit (b) cenobite (c) anchorite (d) recluse
9. (a) eldritch (b) weird (c) horrifying (d) drawn-out
10. (a) curse (b) objurgate (c) extol (d) execrate

VII. One-Word Completions

In this type you are asked to complete a sentence by choosing one of four words necessary to make the statement true or to complete it most satisfactorily.

Example:

If you want to look up the meaning of a word you consult (a) a lexicon (b) a concordance (c) an encyclopedia (d) a rubric.

The correct answer is (a).

Now try the following:

1. If a person cannot be easily handled or dealt with he will not be complimented for his (a) domesticity (b) knowledge (c) tractability (d) eulogy.

2. The science of words and language is known as (a) philology (b) paleontology (c) bibliography (d) entomology.

3. The junction of the Missouri and the Mississippi can be called a (a) crisis (b) confluence (c) conference (d) levee.

4. The order to stay in one's own bailiwick means that a person should remain in his own (a) room (b) district (c) country (d) bed.

5. Because the orator's speech was high-flown and pretentious, the reporters termed it (a) bombastic (b) austere (c) untruthful (d) vituperative.

6. When the courtier had advanced to the highest position attainable he was said to have reached the (a) vigil (b) precipice (c) threshold (d) pinnacle.

7. Accepting his fate with calmness, the camel driver said, "It is (a) growing late (b) kismet (c) kiosk (e) suttee."

8. Nations that do not trust each other look upon each other (a) calmly (b) hopefully (c) askance (d) retrospectively.

9. A person who constantly thinks he is sick is a (a) hypo-hondriac (b) misogynist (c) misanthrope (d) hyperpituitary.

10. But a person who is really sickly and is unduly solici-ous about his health is a (a) valedictorian (b) vegetarian c) valetudinarian (d) dialectician.

Another type of one-word completion follows:

11. One of the time-tested ways of remembering a series f items is known as a_____ device. (a) intellectual b) recollected (c) schematic (d) mnemonic (e) ingenious

12. As the waves rose and the ship tossed, many of the assengers felt _____. (a) lethargic (b) subdued c) tremulous (d) homesick (e) queasy

13. More than fourteen years have passed since Jackie Robinson broke the color line in major league baseball, but _____ problems keep troubling the sport. (a) per-sonnel (b) segregation (c) financial (d) expansion (e) ex-clusion

14. The basic structure of the living cell is a problem whose _____ can be judged by reference to the diffi-cult exploration of the structure of the atom. (a) importance (b) universality (c) antiquity (d) need (e) complexity

15. Cyprus is still not economically viable and, though _____ important, it is militarily weak in its own right. (a) necessarily (b) strategically (c) scarcely (d) inde-pendently (e) technically

VIII. Two-Word Completion

A

Each question in this group consists of a sentence from which two words have been omitted. Below each incomplete sentence are five pairs of words. You must choose one of these groups to complete the sentence and make it a true statement. Try each pair and choose the one that makes the most sense.
Example:
A _____ response is one that is made with _____.
(a) stupid, fear (b) speedy, alacrity (c) sure, slowness (d) harmful, grimaces (e) pleasant, surmise
The correct answer is (b).

1. —— persons are inclined to ——.
   (a) obese, corpulence (b) generous, leanness (c) domineering, temperance (d) vacillating, determination (e) cowering, effrontery

2. A large —— center is an ——.
   (a) district, affliction (b) transport, automobile (c) civic autarchy (d) shopping, emporium (e) educational, indignity

3. A —— is a temporary ——.
   (a) deviation, rest (b) shambles, journey (c) respite, relief (d) paradox, quietus (e) feint, spell

4. A —— is a ——.
   (a) norm, standard (b) criterion, mistake (c) disciple, school (d) doctrine, follower (e) thesis, superstition

5. A —— shade of distinction is a ——.
   (a) fine, vindication (b) crass, profanity (c) subtle, nuance (d) thorough, prejudice (e) complete, paradox

6. A —— of small stones is called a ——.
   (a) collection, numismatist (b) collar, tiara (c) seller, connoisseur (d) mound, lithograph (e) pattern, mosaic

7. At some private schools pupils are under the —— of a ——.
   (a) guidance, palladium (b) tutelage, preceptor (c) coaching, verity (d) assiduity, library (e) consensus, mentor

8. —— praise is known as ——.
   (a) continuous, maturity (b) indiscriminate, encomium (c) servile, adulation (d) unasked for, gratitude (e) cowardly, temerity

9. Suzerainty is —— control over a —— state.
   (a) complete, democratic (b) native, backward (c) central, unified (d) political, dependent (e) economic, federated

10. —— language may also be termed ——.
    (a) eloquent, exiguous (b) frenzied, placid (c) abusive, scurrilous (d) contumelious, flattering (e) denunciatory, peripatetic

B

These two-word completion exercises are designed to find out (1) whether you can comprehend through clue words the meaning of a sentence still incomplete (2) whether your vocabulary is not only precise but discriminating and (3) whether you possess some sense of style.

1. Though the Oxford English Dictionary is undoubtedly the greatest dictionary ever _____, it is designed for scholars and research workers rather than for the _____ dictionary user.

(a) assembled, assiduous (b) demonstrated, amateur (c) compiled, casual (d) published, professional (e) projected, omniscient

2. Hence the word sophistry has an unfavorable _____ and means arguing deceitfully, attempting to turn a poor case into a good one by means of clever but _____ reasoning.

(a) denotation, ingenuous (b) meaning, ingenious (c) significance, vague (d) connotation, specious (e) impact, cogent

3. He warned the workers against supporting these antisocial policies, which he declared would _____ rather than _____ the plight of the common people.

(a) rescue, destroy (b) aggravate, alleviate (c) impair, improving (d) protract, inhibit (e) encourage, defy

4. Into the limited space given him a headline writer must compress the _____ of the news and he must do it without _____.

(a) bias, apology (b) magnitude, distortion (c) totality, hedging (d) synopsis, suggestions (e) gist, ambiguity

5. To cross the Rubicon means to take a final _____ step which may have dangerous _____.

(a) irrevocable, consequences (b) well-considered, implications (c) unnecessary, potentialities (d) inconsequential, concomitants (e) hazardous, antecedents

6. We have criticized our university students for preferring the security of political silence and the safety of _____ to the excitement of social _____ and humanitarian action.

(a) concealment, revolution (b) acquiescence, dissent (c) tolerance, antagonism (d) college, adventure (e) security, insecurity

7. Among the younger people there are complaints tha the sight of ex-Nazis flourishing recommends _____ to youth that it instills, instead of needed moral values, the dubious precept that _____ is the best policy.

(a) emulation, honesty (b) desperation, dishonesty (c) selfishness, indifference (d) cynicism, expediency (e) dishonesty, intolerance

8. Although there were _____ circumstances in this particular violation of the law, the judge ruled that there had to be strict _____ or there would be no law at all.

(a) extraordinary, complaisance (b) specific, obedience (c) questionable, observation (d) extenuating, compliance (e) tantalizing, adherence

9. Oddly enough _____ the prestige of the United States in such countries as Britain, France, and Italy is considered important here, Congress has been _____ about supplying funds to the U.S. Information Agency in these countries.

(a) since, dilatory (b) whereas, wasteful (c) when generous (d) inasmuch as, indigenous (e) although, niggardly

10. Like the _____ part of an iceberg, much of what is really interesting in the capital is not _____.

(a) greater, dangerous (b) submerged, visible (c) upper, viable (d) lower, penetrable (e) inner, known

11. In diplomatic _____, the _____ sought by one government from another to the name of a proposed ambassador is known as an "agreement."

(a) circles, permission (b) channels, condition (c) language interpretation (d) parlance, assent (e) dealings, understanding

12. For some years past, Franch governments have been _____ and divided, and French parliaments have been incoherent and _____.

(a) weak, inchoate (b) unstable, domineering (c) vacillating, irresponsible (d) many, few (e) inarticulate, responsive

13. The increasing revival of dramatic classics is, to one critic, _____; it seems to him a sign of the _____ of the modern theater.

(a) deplorable, anemia (b) astounding, vitality (c) auspicious, resurgence (d) incomprehensible, paradox (e) understandable, prosperity

14. But even Mr. Moses, one of the most _____ public servants of our time, is at a loss to convey in words the size, the imaginative engineering _____ that built this contribution to the welfare of family and industry.
(a) public spirited, skill (b) dedicated, cogitated (c) unappreciated, technique (d) articulate, ingenuity (e) tongue-tied, miracle

15. If it were true that enduring lessons are learned from _____ errors, Broadway would be the repository of _____ theatrical wisdom.
(a) dubious, profound (b) egregious, sublime (c) dramatic, lasting (d) stupid, tenuous (e) accidental, occult

16. In architecture, much more than in any of the other arts, there is a marked timelag between the _____ of ideas and their _____ in the shape of completed buildings.
(a) dawn, practicability (b) settlement, fruition (c) emergence, application (d) tradition, modernization (e) burgeoning, welcoming

17. Scientific imagination is a specific intellectual power that is _____ in every population that has learned to be _____ about the mechanisms governing the physical world.
(a) latent, curious (b) teeming, diffident (c) growing, self-possessed (d) encouraged, wary (e) evoked, self-depreciatory

18. The westerlies normally cross the United States at altitudes from 10,000 to 50,000 feet along the Canadian border, acting as a _____ to Arctic winds and giving the Middle Atlantic States relatively _____ winters.
(a) catalyst, unsettled (b) deterrent, cold (c) counterpart, predictable (d) buffer, temperate (e) propellent, mild

19. The practice of painting slogans on rock faces, once a thriving industry in Britain, has fallen into _____, but there has recently been a(n) _____ in County Antrim.
(a) disfavor, upheaval (b) disuse, recrudescence (c) oblivion, demand (d) misuse, artisan (e) mediocrity, renascence

20. Athletes have so perfected their techniques in track and field events that the _____ becomes _____ before record books can be published.
(a) meet, official (b) time, authentic (c) fantastic, commonplace (d) result, obsolete (e) announcement, public

IX. Analogies

A

This type of question involves more than merely a knowledge of the meanings of words—it tests your ability to see relationships, your power to reason, and your knowledge of subject matter and everyday affairs. Often the words themselves are very simple, but you must be careful to distinguish fine shades of meaning.

The more usual form of questions involving analogies consists of two words or phrases (generally printed in CAPITAL letters) that are related to each other in a specific way followed by five pairs of words or phrases. Of these five pairs you are asked to select the *one* pair that *best* or *most closely* expresses a relationship *similar* to or the *same* as that expressed in the original pair. The symbols used are those used in ratio and proportion:

2 : 4 :: 3 : 6.

The sign : means *is to* or *are to*, and :: means *as*. An example of a simple verbal analogy is:

APPLE : FRUIT :: carrot : vegetable.

It is, of course, impossible to list all the relationships existing among persons, places, things, words, and ideas, but we are putting down a list of most of the types that have been used on scholarship and aptitude examinations. In each case we are giving you an example to fix the idea firmly in your mind.

Please note that the relationships may be expressed vice versa.

EXAMPLES OF TYPES OF ANALOGIES

1. Like is to like, such as synonyms, and including similarity between persons, objects, concepts, as well as degree of similariy.

(a) DECLARE :: ASSERT :: impugn : attack verbally.
(b) APPLE : PEAR :: carrot : turnip.
(c) SADNESS : DEPRESSION :: happiness : exhilaration.

2. Like is to unlike, such as antonyms, and including dissimilarity between persons, objects, concepts, as well as degree of dissimilarity.

INEPT : CLEVER :: languid : active.

3. One is to many or part is to the whole, such as the individual or special member as part of a group, class, political division, or general concept.

(a) SOLDIER : ARMY :: sailor : navy.
(b) CHIEF : TRIBE :: governor : state.
(c) BEAD : NECKLACE :: link : chain.

4. User is to object, tool, or implement that he uses.

(a) WOODSMAN : AX :: farmer : scythe.

5. Material is to its product

WOOL : BLANKET :: leather : shoes.

6. Collector or scholar or professional man is to a specialty.

PHILOLOGIST : WORDS :: podiatrist : feet.

7. One geometric figure or body is to another.

SPHERE : CUBE :: circle : square.

8. Units of number and quantity are to other units.

(a) TEN : DECADE :: 1,000 : millenium.
(b) PINT : QUART :: nickel : dime.

9. Special article of dress is to the wearer.

LIVERY : DOORMAN :: uniform : soldier.

10. Person, animal, or object is to a characteristic activity or trait (expressed by verbs, nouns or adjectives).

(a) HEN : CLUCKS :: goose : quacks.
(b) LAMB : MILDNESS :: leopard : ferocity.
(c) LAMB : GENTLE :: leopard : fierce.

11. Noun is to its corresponding adjective.

BULL : TAURINE :: sheep : ovine.

12. Adjective is to its abstract noun.

AMICABLE : FRIENDSHIP :: inimical : unfriendliness.

13. Noun is to a verb showing what is being done to the noun.

GRAIN : SOW :: ideas : spread.

14. Thing or idea is to what it ordinarily does.

SCISSORS : CUT :: pen : write.

15. Cause is to effect.

GRIEF : TEARS :: joy : laughter.

16. Symbol is to what it stands for, including insignia and the person or group the insignia are associated with.

(a) TRYLON AND PERISPHERE : 1939 WORLD'S FAIR :: Unisphere : 1964 World's Fair.

(b) CHEVRONS : SERGEANT :: eagle : colonel.

17. Young is to old.

COLT : HORSE :: cub : lion.

18. Singular is to plural.

GOOSE : GEESE :: passerby : passersby.

19. Grammatical case form is to another form.

I : ME :: who : whom.

20. Masculine is to feminine.

BULL : COW :: fox : vixen.

21. One form of a verb is to another of the same verb.

DO : DID :: sing : sang.

22. Implied relationships and comparisons, such as metaphors.

(a) PREDJUDICE : JUSTICE :: clouds : sun.

(b) IGNORANCE : DARKNESS :: knowledge : light.

(c) SKELETON : BODY :: laws : society.

AND MANY MORE!

Before we put you on your own, we shall work out two questions together. Here is the first:

HAMMER : CARPENTER ::

    (a) reins : horse
    (b) brush : painter
    (c) shaves : barber
    (d) anchor : sailor
    (e) blueprint : architect

FIRST STEP! Examine the relationship in the first pair from all possible angles. Express the relationship not "as this is to that," but in more specific terms. *Example:* "A hammer is used by a carpenter as an essential tool."

SECOND STEP! Repeat the formula for each of the choices. Discard those that obviously do not fit, such as (a) and (c). THIRD STEP! Weigh the arguments for each of the choices that appear to fit: (b), (d), and (e), then make the final decision. Where two or more seem to fit because of general agreement with the original pair, you must find additional specific agreement to narrow the choice to only one pair. In the above question, the sailor and the architect make use of an anchor or blueprint, respectively. However, the sailor does not handle the anchor or make anything with it, as a carpenter does with a hammer. The architect constructs but does not wield a blueprint. Therefore, the remaining choice (b) is correct, because the correspondence with the original choice is the closest.

Of course, you might have made this choice at first glance, but remember that about 230 years ago, Alexander Pope wrote, "For fools rush in where angels fear to tread." Be an angel! Test all possibilities; beware of traps.

Now let us try the second example, which is more difficult:

AFFECTION : INFATUATION ::

    (a) frankness : candor
    (b) boasting : braggart
    (c) large : gigantic
    (d) timidity : cowardice
    (e) lenient : forgive

Taking the first step again, you discover that the original pair consists of synonyms.

Taking the second step, you eliminate (b) and (e).

Taking the third step, you weigh the arguments. What specific relationship can be established in addition to the general relationship that holds for (a), (c), and (d), that will narrow the choice to only one of the five pairs? *Affection* and *infatuation* are extremes. Hence (a) is eliminated because *frankness* and *candor* express practically the same degree. However, *large* and *gigantic* are also extremes. So are *timidity* and *cowardice*. There is therefore still another specific detail to be considered. *Large* and *gigantic* refer to size; *timidity* and *cowardice* refer to mental or emotional states, as do the words in the original pair. Therefore the correc answer is (d).

NOTE. In both examples given for analysis, the origina pair of words consist of two nouns. Most frequently, the correct choice will consist of the same kind of words as in the original pair. However, it is possible for a pair of nouns to be compared with two verbs or two adjectives. You may also find a noun and an adjective in the original pair. In such instances, the correct choice will also contain two unlike parts of speech. What you must see clearly is that the relationship of the parts of speech in the original pair must be maintained in the correct choice. Within each pair there must be exact correspondence as if:

NOUN : NOUN :: noun : noun : verb : verb : adjective : adjective.

Now you are ready to try the questions below. Answers will be found on p. 368.

1. DOUGH : BREAD ::

    (a) sugar   : cake
    (b) words   : speech
    (c) ink   : pen
    (d) paper   : author
    (e) skates : ice

2. SCALP : HAIR ::

    (a) curtain : window
    (b) cloth   : table
    (c) earth   : grass
    (d) shoe   : foot
    (e) house : roof

3. FAÇADE : BUILDING ::

    (a) dial   : watch
    (b) fence   : garden
    (c) neck   : bottle
    (d) page   : book
    (e) drawer : desk

4. SLEEK : GLOSSY ::

    (a) rapid   : tepid
    (b) vapid   : complete
    (c) dejected : jubilant
    (d) contrite : unrepentant
    (e) credible : believable

5. COGENT : CONVINCING ::
- (a) banal : inane
- (b) nonchalant : disturbed
- (c) insular : continental
- (d) cunning : ingenuous
- (e) dubious : certain

6. MORASS : SWAMP ::
- (a) forest : tree
- (b) steppe : plain
- (c) desert : oasis
- (d) sea : gulf
- (e) peak : mountain

7. INCONGRUOUS : HARMONIOUS ::
- (a) laughable : ludicrous
- (b) tedious : wearisome
- (c) nonplussed : distracted
- (d) tall : short
- (e) fickle : rebellious

8. PULSATE : THROB ::
- (a) abate : increase
- (b) expropriate : deprive
- (c) accede : disagree
- (d) condone : condemn
- (e) disperse : collect

9. LOBSTER : CRUSTACEAN ::
- (a) lion : horse
- (b) tiger : cat
- (c) dolphin : whale
- (d) eagle : sparrow
- (e) reason : man

10. ZEALOT : FANATICISM ::
- (a) parasite : food
- (b) umpire : team
- (c) vagabond : nostalgia
- (d) orator : frenzy
- (e) impostor : sham

11. ISLANDS : ARCHIPELAGO ::
> (a) stars : constellation
> (b) hors d'oeuvre : banquet
> (c) nickels : dollar bill
> (d) birds : apiary
> (e) stamps : philately

12. ASTRONOMY : ASTROLOGY ::
> (a) geology : geography
> (b) magic : science
> (c) science : folklore
> (d) chemistry : alchemy
> (e) symbolism : superstition

13. PAIN : ANODYNE ::
> (a) harshness : leniency
> (b) accident : insurance
> (c) trifle : enormity
> (d) grief : solace
> (e) savagery : music

14. MULE : BURDEN ::
> (a) scholar : books
> (b) musician : violin
> (c) house : tenants
> (d) ship : cargo
> (e) animal : oppression

15. FORGERY : SIGNATURE ::
> (a) carbon copy : original
> (b) faked : genuine
> (c) false : truth
> (d) proxy : delegate
> (e) amateur : professional

16. PHILATELIST : STAMPS ::
> (a) thesaurus : pictures
> (b) dilettante : music
> (c) numismatist : coins
> (d) connoisseur : dining
> (e) philologist : books

17. ENERVATE : STRENGTHEN ::
> (a) invigorate : brighten
> (b) aver : attribute
> (c) divert : turn
> (d) apprise : obfuscate
> (e) stultify : enliven

18. FLAMBOYANT : ROCOCO ::
    (a) florid   : fragrant
    (b) ornate   : baroque
    (c) flagrant   : flagitious
    (d) debased   : invaluable
    (e) inflammable   : restrained

19. PREDATORY : HAWK ::
    (a) ugly   : vulture
    (b) speedy   : vessel
    (c) tawny   : lion
    (d) contortion   : grimace
    (e) voracious   : glutton

20. GUTTURAL : THROAT ::
    (a) palmar   : fist
    (b) hair   : hirsute
    (c) manual   : hand
    (d) mantle   : cloak
    (e) venal   : wine

21. ENGINEER : CAB ::
    (a) aviator   : cockpit
    (b) sailor   : compass
    (c) driver   : wheel
    (d) passenger   : taxi
    (e) shepherd   : flock

22. ISTHMUS : LAND ::
    (a) neck   : head
    (b) strait   : water
    (c) channel   : stream
    (d) wire   : pole
    (e) tunnel   : mandolin

23. STRINGS : VIOLIN ::
    (a) plectrum   : madolin
    (b) air   : flute
    (c) membrane   : drum
    (d) pedal   : organ
    (e) wind   : leaves

24. I : MY ::
    (a) him   : his
    (b) you   : you're
    (c) it   : it's
    (d) they   : there
    (e) who   : whose

25. ALTHOUGH : NEVERTHELESS ::
    (a) since   : therefore
    (b) in spite of   : consequently
    (c) notwithstanding : if
    (d) when   : simultaneously
    (e) because   : therefore

26. LAUREL : VICTOR ::
    (a) power   : glory
    (b) chevrons   : army
    (c) rabbit's foot : luck
    (d) caduceus   : medical profession
    (e) plant   : drugs

27. CARELESSNESS : JEOPARDIZE ::
    (a) carefulness : security
    (b) crowding   : discomfort
    (c) neglect   : endanger
    (d) failure   : discouragement
    (e) penalty   : chastise

28. MENDACITY : DISTRUST ::
    (a) begging   : charity
    (b) integrity   : confidence
    (c) truth   : falsehood
    (d) stupidity   : failure
    (e) untruth   : doubtful

29. FRIGHT : STAMPEDE ::
    (a) clouds   : tornado
    (b) rain   : snow
    (c) haste   : crowds
    (d) wildness   : cattle
    (e) flow of water : erosion

30. PRECEDENT : JUSTIFICATION ::
    (a) tradition   : novelty
    (b) authority   : sanction
    (c) orthodoxy : heresy
    (d) kindness   : obedience
    (e) usage   : submission

B

In the second type of question involving analogies, one term of the analogy is omitted, and you are asked to select the missing term from five given choices. Apply the same principles of selection as you did in answering part A, above. *Example:*

SEAL : (a) flippers (b) tusk (c) tail (d) fin (e) tentacle :: SWIMMER : HANDS.

The seal *uses* flippers to aid its swimming as a swimmer *uses* his hands. The correct choice is therefore (a).

1. SYLVAN : WOODS :: TERRESTRIAL : (a) stars (b) planets (c) earth (d) fear (e) urban.

2. PEDIATRICIAN : (a) children (b) hair (c) feet (d) plants (e) philosophy :: DERMATOLOGIST : SKIN.

3. SNAKE : REPTILIAN :: LION :: (a) bovine (b) feline (c) lemurine (d) vulpine (e) leotard.

4. NEPTUNE : (a) scepter (b) smile (c) trident (d) spear (e) thunderbolt :: CUPID : ARROW.

5. ACTOR : STAGE :: (a) acrobat (b) pilot (c) orator (d) soldier (e) rider : ROSTRUM.

6. (a) colors (b) small stones (c) bricks (d) straw (e) papyrus : MOSAICS :: WORDS : SENTENCES.

7. SANCHO PANZA : DON QUIXOTE :: (a) Nero Wolfe (b) Zorro (c) Don Ameche (d) Perry Mason (e) John H. Watson : SHERLOCK HOLMES.

8. ASTRONAUTS : SPACE :: ARGONAUTS : (a) treasure (b) fire (c) ship (d) birds (e) sea.

9. CYGNET : SWAN :: (a) stallion (b) mule (c) hoof (d) colt (e) bridle : HORSE.

10. (a) Lerner (b) Bellini (c) Gilbert (d) Mozart (e) Kern : SULLIVAN :: HAMMERSTEIN : RODGERS.

11. MAXIM : PITHY :: CLAPTRAP : (a) simple (b) pretentious (c) sincere (d) accidental (e) thoughtless.

12. DONKEY : BRAYS :: WOLF : (a) roars (b) whimpers (c) whines (d) howls (e) bellows.

13. GENUINE : SIMULATED :: BOMBASTIC : (a) dynamic (b) elevated (c) destructive (d) unaffected (e) magniloquent.

14. INVEIGLE : CAJOLE :: MALIGN : (a) slander (b) enlighten (c) eulogize (d) compile (e) acclaim.

15. URANIUM (U-235) : FISSIONABLE :: (a) diamond (b) atoms (c) ideas (d) nucleus (e) gold : MALLEABLE.

X. Peculiar Adjectives

There are some English nouns whose adjectives are very queer. For example, how would you express in one word the idea of *pertaining to a shore?* The adjective for *shore* (unless you use *shore* itself) is *littoral;* for a riverbank it is *riparian.*

Some of our most common words have to use learned words derived from Latin or Greek as their adjectives. This is especially true of parts of the body. For example, *aural, auricular,* and *otic* are all adjectives that refer to *ear!*

Match the words on the left with their corresponding adjectives on the right.

1. arm	a. umbilical
2. finger	b. digital
3. hair	c. cardiac
4. head	d. cervical
5. heart	e. labial
6. lips	f. capillary
7. navel	g. cephalic
8. neck	h. lingual
9. teeth	i. dental
10. tongue	j. brachial

XI. Forming Adjectives

In this type of question you are asked to write an adjective derived from a given word. Forms ending in ED, ING, and FUL are not accepted. Watch your spelling!

Example: climax, *climactic.*

1. admonish	5. author	9. conifer
2. apostle	6. axis	10. context
3. arbor	7. Cambridge	11. delta
4. Aristotle	8. coma	12. deride

13. Descartes	26. governor	39. periphrasis
14. doubt	27. homily	40. recede
15. encomium	28. Jupiter	41. reveal
16. enemy	29. labyrinth	42. sect
17. enigma	30. libido	43. sepsis
18. epistle	31. lion	44. Shaw
19. equinox	32. litigate	45. solstice
20. eulogy	33. menace	46. therapy
21. example	34. money	47. Thomas Aquinas
22. exegesis	35. nitrogen	48. title
23. forum	36. oracle	49. usury
24. fragment	37. orgy	50. viceroy
25. geodesy	38. Oxford	

XII. Forming Nouns

In this type of test you are asked to write a generally accepted noun form of a given word. Forms ending in ING, ER, OR are not accepted. Watch your spelling!

Example: collide, *collision.*

1. absolve	11. disburse	21. rarefy
2. absorb	12. discern	22. rescind
3. anonymous	13. liquefy	23. resent
4. banal	14. manumit	24. retrograde
5. compel	15. osmotic	25. scan
6. constrain	16. periodic	26. scorbutic
7. contend	17. prodigal	27. senile
8. contingent	18. pungent	28. spatulate
9. decrepit	19. pusillanimous	29. temerarious
10. deify	20. rachitic	30. virulent

XIII. Singular or Plural

DIRECTIONS: If the plural is given, write P next to the word and give the singular.

If the singular is given, write S and give the plural.

Examples:

analysis	S	analyses
opus	S	opera
cherubim	P	cherub
insignia	P	insigne
bacteria	P	bacterium

1. amanuensis
2. attorney general
3. automata
4. axis
5. bacilli
6. candelabra
7. chateau
8. court-martial
9. crisis
10. criteria
11. data
12. erratum
13. fungi
14. genus
15. handful
16. larva
17. phenomenon
18. species
19. stigmata
20. thesis

XIV. Male and Female

DIRECTIONS: If the masculine is given, write M and give the feminine form.

If the feminine is given, write F and give the masculine:

Example: bachelor M spinster.

1. abbot
2. dam
3. doe
4. drake
5. earl
6. equestrian
7. executor
8. filly
9. goose
10. hart
11. heifer
12. marchioness
13. peacock
14. ram
15. sow
16. testator
17. tragedian
18. traitor
19. vixen
20. witch

XV. Getting at the Roots

(WARNING: These questions are extremely difficult and require a background of etymological study. Although such questions appear rarely, we include them for those who may want to trace word origins.)

Each of the following groups contains either three or four words derived from the same root.

If three of the words are derived from the same root, write down the letter found before the word which does *not* come from that root.

If all four words are derived from the same root, write the letter *e.*

Example 1:

(a) amorous (b) amateur (c) amity (d) amiable

316

Since all four come from the root AM meaning *love*, the correct answer is (e).

Example 2:
   (a) regent (b) direct (c) dirigible (d) record
   The first three are derived from the root REG meaning *guide; record* comes from CORD, heart. The correct answer is therefore (d).

1. (a) lucid (b) ineluctable (c) elucidate (d) lucubrate
2. (a) enthusiasm (b) apotheosis (c) theocracy (d) anathema
3. (a) deviate (b) viable (c) impervious (d) obvious
4. (a) conclave (b) clef (c) clavichord (d) clavicle
5. (a) vivid (b) convivial (c) victual (d) evict
6. (a) captain (b) capitol (c) precipitate (d) achieve
7. (a) emancipate (b) maneuver (c) maintain (d) mansion
8. (a) fragile (b) refractory (c) frail (d) fragrant
9. (a) logistics (b) logic (c) epilogue (d) eulogy
10. (a) confident (b) affidavit (c) defy (d) fiancé
11. (a) podium (b) chiropodist (c) antipodes (d) platypus
12. (a) relish (b) relinquish (c) derelict (d) relic
13. (a) attain (b) maintain (c) retain (d) tenement
14. (a) core (b) coronet (c) encourag (d) concord
15. (a) corpulent (b) corpse (c) excoriate (d) corporation
16. (a) ditto (b) interdict (c) indite (d) addict
17. (a) conduit (b) aqueduct (c) duchess (d) conducive
18. (a) debit (b) debilitate (c) indebt (d) debenture
19. (a) polemics (b) cosmopolite (c) metropolitan (d) political
20. (a) perceive (b) receptive (c) capitulate (d) captive

XVI. The Story Behind the Word

In this type of question your knowledge of etymology is tested. Next to each word you are given four expressions. You are to select the one that most clearly indicates the origin or etymology of the word. The correct answer is not necessarily the best definition.

Example 1:
   egregious   (a) remarkable (b) flagrant (c) outside the
                          herd (d) extraordinary
   Although all four choices are correct, the correct answer as you know from Chapter 4, "Deep Are the Roots," (See page 51) is (c).

Example 2:

tantalize

based on the story of: (a) a goddess who was fond of teasing (b) a difficult labor by Hercules (c) the quest of a treasure (d) the punishment of a demigod suffering from hunger and thirst

Correct answer is (d) from the myth of Tantalus.

1. accost — (a) address (b) rub elbows (c) tap on shoulder (d) touch ribs

2. anthology — (a) collection of flowers (b) collection of poems (c) golden treasury (d) collection of essays

3. cadence — (a) falling (b) rhythm (c) grieving (d) cutting

4. candidate — (a) self-seeker (b) clothed in white (c) person of tested integrity (d) competitor

5. cardinal — (a) important (b) colorful (c) hinging (d) chosen

6. colossal — (a) like an obelisg (b) like a large ancient statue (c) gigantic (d) like a god

7. cursory — (a) swearing (b) running (c) hasty (d) superficial

8. dilapidated — (a) ruined (b) with framework collapsing (c) stones falling apart (d) clothes in pieces

9. disastrous — (a) unlucky (b) thoughtless (c) sinister (d) ill-starred

10. divest — (a) take off clothing (b) disgrace publicly (c) remove from office (d) deprive

11. eliminate — (a) put out of sight (b) remove a barrier (c) put out of mind (d) put outside the threshold

12. endorsement — (a) approval (b) backing (c) financial aid (d) getting the inside track

13. eradicate — (a) eliminate (b) abolish (c) root out (d) rub out

14. galactic — (a) eye-filling (b) festive (c) astronomical (d) pertaining to the Milky Way

15. inexorable — (a) not deserving pardon (b) unchangeable (c) incapable of pity (d) unable to plead one's way out

318

6. investigate   (a) look into (b) spend time on (c) spend money on (d) follow footprints

7. mellifluous   (a) full of song (b) singing like a bird (c) flowing with honey (d) sweet and gentle

8. precarious   (a) calling for prayer (b) dangerous (c) tottering (d) costly

19. precocious   (a) obnoxiously clover (b) above normal (c) cooked in advance (d) immature

20. sarcophagus   (a) flesh-consuming (b) memorial (c) stone monument (d) heavy casket

319

"Boy, did I learn a new word today—wow!" *

24. Words, Words, Words

ONCE MORE from *The Child Buyer* by John Hersey:

SENATOR MANSFIELD. You really love words, don't you?

BARRY RUDD. Oh, yes! Kismet, hieratic, mellific, nuncupative, sempiternal, mansuetude, jeremiad, austral, diaphanous, hegemony, exculpatory, homunculus, melanistic, cenobite, prolepsis, platykurtic, mephitic, ceraceous, inspissation, lanate—

* Drawing reproduced courtesy the *Saturday Evening Post.*

Since for the most part we are not including words already discussed in the body of this book or those used in previous exercises, it would be advisable—if you are taking a test—to review the exercises at ends of chapters.

In this type of test you are asked to select the definition *closest* in meaning. The correct answer is not necessarily an exact equivalent or even a very good definition. But it is the one choice that comes *closest* in meaning to the word to be defined. In our own tests which follow we have tried as far as possible to give you clear and simple definitions. The words to be defined are arranged in groups of progressive difficulty. Added to the words in Chapter 23, they make about 1500 words to help you pass that test (at least four times that many—if you study the choices also). Answers will be found on page 372.

I. Preliminary

1. abash — (a) squash (b) embarrass (c) amaze (d) refuse
2. abate — (a) aid (b) remove (c) lessen (d) howl
3. abominable — (a) unfortunate (b) loathsome (c) cheap (d) stormy
4. acclaim — (a) demand (b) applaud (c) surpass (d) elect
5. addicted — (a) strongly disposed to (b) mad (c) increased (d) sentenced
6. affront — (a) insult (b) projection (c) invasion (d) success
7. altercation — (a) drastic change (b) angry dispute (c) noisy dialogue (d) loud explosion
8. anomaly — (a) abnormality (b) ignorance (c) accident (d) rarity
9. arboreal — (a) holiday (b) bower (c) treelike (d) shady
10. askew — (a) turned to one side (b) direct (c) doubtful (d) wide open
11. avowal — (a) sacred oath (b) open declaration (c) harsh sound (d) stern denial
12. berate — (a) deny (b) downgrade (c) scold (d) judge
13. bicameral — (a) meeting twice a year (b) having two legislative branches (c) having twin lenses (d) published every two years
14. blatant — (a) tardy (b) futile (c) depressed (d) noisy
15. capitulate — (a) summarize (b) execute (c) withdraw (d) surrender
16. careen — (a) secure (b) sway (c) decay (d) fondle
17. cauterize — (a) sear (b) warn (c) cut away (d) bind
18. cherubic — (a) mischievous (b) expensive (c) rustic (d) angelic

19. compliance — (a) flexibility (b) spite (c) obedience (d) weakness

20. compunction — (a) remorse (b) conscience (c) piercing blow (d) satisfaction

21. consternation — (a) group of stars (b) humble service (c) large display (d) great amazement

22. corrosive — (a) polishing (b) acid-forming (c) hiding (d) eating away

23. covert — (a) patent (b) secret (c) ditch (d) greedy

24. covetous — (a) sheltered (b) hidden (c) grasping (d) thrifty

25. cumbersome — (a) heavy (b) sorrowful (c) unwieldy (d) laborious

26. debility — (a) debit (b) instability (c) pain (d) weakness

27. decor — (a) dramatic presentation (b) showpiece (c) ornamental setting (d) rich furniture

28. derisive — (a) mocking (b) copied (c) limited (d) borrowed

29. derogatory — (a) questionable (b) inquisitive (c) humble (d) depreciating

30. devious — (a) multitudinous (b) guessing (c) circuitous (d) premature

31. dilatory — (a) expanded (b) casual (c) slow (d) amateurish

32. discursive — (a) profane (b) rambling (c) detailed (d) extraneous

33. disparage — (a) separate (b) discourage (c) compare (d) belittle

34. diurnal — (a) news account (b) solar (c) daily (d) everlasting

35. dolorous — (a) sorrowful (b) financial (c) sacred (d) parsimonious

36. dowdy — (a) corpulent (b) rakish (c) elegant (d) unstylish

37. dulcet — (a) melodious (b) zither (c) pastry (d) twofold

38. echelon — (a) level of command (b) squadron leader (c) summit (d) battleground

39. edify — (a) amuse (b) satisfy (c) consume (d) instruct

40. engender — (a) maneuver (b) cause (c) fertilize (d) incite

41. epithet — (a) inscription (b) shoulder piece (c) descriptive term (d) honorary award

42. expedient — (a) advantageous (b) free (c) fatigued (d) rapid

43. expiate — (a) expire (b) sanctify (c) demolish

(d) atone

44. exude — (a) evaporate (b) overflow (c) wither away (d) ooze out

45. facet — (a) gem (b) aspect (c) spout (d) trait

46. filial — pertaining to a: (a) parent (b) son (c) duty (d) wise man

47. fillip — (a) beverage (b) acrobatic trick (c) large dose (d) stimulus

48. flippancy — (a) levity (b) dexterity (c) heaviness (d) clumsiness

49. germane — (a) bacterial (b) Teutonic (c) relevant (d) miscroscopic

50. gratuitous — (a) thankful (b) reproachful (c) satisfactory (d) uncalled for

51. guise — (a) deceit (b) malice (c) protection (d) appearance

52. heterogeneous — composed of: (a) similar parts (b) unlike elements (c) smooth surfaces (d) complex problems

53. idiosyncrasy — (a) personality (b) lack of intelligence (c) absolute rule (d) distinctive characteristic

54. impinge — (a) paint (b) constrict (c) steal (d) encroach

55. incisive — (a) penetrating (b) short (c) compendious (d) assured

56. incongruous — (a) unofficial (b) incompatible (c) poorly timed (d) uneven

57. incumbent — (a) obligatory (b) dutiful (c) weak (d) slanting

58. ineptitude — (a) dullness (b) vacillation (c) awkwardness (d) inexperience

59. insinuate — (a) spy upon (b) suggest slyly (c) set free (d) cause injury

60. insipid — (a) tasteless (b) animated (c) interminable (d) unplanned

61. interloper — (a) acrobat (b) intruder (c) slanderer (d) malingerer

62. jocose — (a) trite (b) playful (c) useless (d) illusory

63. malign — (a) disapprove (b) mistreat (c) curse (d) slander

64. manifesto — (a) cargo list (b) secret treaty (c) revolutionary plot (d) public declaration

65. maudlin — (a) overwrought (b) weakly sentimental (c) exceedingly sad (d) dispirited

66. morose — (a) quick-tempered (b) miserly (c) ill-humored (d) despondent

67. mutation — (a) silence (b) severance (c) display (d) variation

324

68. obviate — to make: (a) unnecessary (b) clear (c) sure (d) difficult

69. ostentatious — (a) modest (b) flagrant (c) showy (d) diligent

70. perfunctory — (a) lazy (b) official (c) mechanical (d) impromptu

71. plaudit — (a) expression of approval (b) consent (c) detonation (d) pleasure

72. prevaricate — (a) authenticate (b) delay (c) lie (d) anticipate

73. pristine — (a) meritorious (b) original (c) expensive (d) traditional

74. privation — (a) seclusion (b) sloop (c) security (d) hardship

75. proton — (a) tribal leader (b) meat substitute (c) food element (d) positive particle

76. protrude — (a) stick out (b) insult (c) act discourteously (d) emigrate

77. raffish — (a) made of straw (b) ludicrous (c) disreputable (d) due to chance

78. rampant — (a) forbidding (b) lionlike (c) protective (d) raging unchecked

79. reiterate — (a) stutter (b) repeat (c) rewrite (d) reassess

80. replica — (a) mythical creature (b) answer (c) copy (d) public building

81. retrospect — (a) brief summary (b) survey of the past (c) close examination (d) full payment

82. rhapsodic — (a) ecstatic (b) bombastic (c) tightly knit (d) fervent

83. roster — (a) nesting place (b) professional team (c) speaker's platform (d) list of persons

84. ruminate — (a) slander (b) digest (c) meditate (d) remove

85. salacious — (a) briny (b) purchasable (c) obscene (d) flavored

86. savant — (a) cleansing agent (b) learned person (c) young student (d) French courtier

87. scrutinize — (a) erase completely (b) turn aside (c) examine closely (d) read aloud

88. silo — (a) sandy surface (b) water tower (c) structure for storage (d) musical notes

89. subsidy — (a) replacement (b) financial aid (c) public funds (d) depth charge

90. torpid — (a) stormy (b) hibernating (c) warm (d) inactive

91. travesty — (a) garment (b) long journey (c) parody (d) deterioration

325

92. tussock   (a) soft cushion (b) low hammock (c) bunch of grass (d) small hill
93. tycoon   (a) labor leader (b) autocratic ruler (c) mystic prophet (d) industrial magnate
94. upbraid   (a) plait (b) reproach (c) elevate (d) foster
95. vapid   (a) spiritless (b) foggy (c) accelerated (d) shapeless
96. venerable   (a) antique (b) retired (c) inimitable (d) worthy of respect
97. vernacular   (a) native speech (b) slang (c) local custom (d) uneducated group
98. vituperation   (a) wordy abuse (b) poisonous liquid (c) bombast (d) violent action
99. winnow   (a) blow (b) fish (c) separate (d) minimize
100. wry   (a) sad (b) smiling (c) undeserved (d) twisted

II. Setting-up Exercises

1. amulet   (a) turban (b) small village (c) charm (d) large bottle
2. arroyo   (a) cliff (b) plain (c) ranch (d) gully
3. assuage   (a) ease (b) enlarge (c) prohibit (d) rub out
4. atelier   (a) hat shop (b) workshop (c) tea room (d) jeweler
5. bellicose   (a) pugnacious (b) graceful (c) threatening (d) horrifying
6. carrion   (a) large bell (b) wild animal (c) decaying flesh (d) mechanical belt
7. comely   (a) plain (b) tall (c) long-haired (d) handsome
8. contiguous   (a) infectious (b) adjacent (c) accidental (d) simultaneous
9. cynosure   (a) guiding star (b) safe position (c) minor office (d) self-reliant person
10. deference   (a) postponement (b) respect (c) pride (d) obligation
11. denouement   (a) negation (b) intricacy (c) condemnation (d) outcome
12. ebullient   (a) enthusiastic (b) arrogant (c) luscious (d) gilt-edged
13. éclat   (a) fine pastry (b) command (c) brilliance (d) suddenness
14. embryonic   (a) hereditary (b) developed (c) functioning (d) rudimentary
15. euphemism   (a) inoffensive expression (b) accurate information (c) affected speech
16. evince   (a) provoke (b) reveal (c) conquer (d) drive out

17. excision — (a) deletion (b) determination (c) example (d) migration

18. extirpate — (a) plant (b) make excuses (c) eradicate (d) clear of charges

19. extrinsic — (a) external (b) high-priced (c) strange (d) romantic

20. furtive — (a) baffling (b) fleeing (c) hasty (d) stealthy

21. gastronomy — (a) stomach distress (b) fortunetelling (c) art of good eating (d) study of minerals

22. grisly — (a) tough (b) horrifying (c) white-haired (d) shaggy

23. gustatory — (a) pertaining to taste (b) fitful (c) loathsome (d) pertaining to wind currents

24. immure — (a) ripen (b) shut in (c) exempt (d) betray

25. immutable — (a) debatable (b) unalterable (c) impractical (d) not susceptible

26. impute — (a) slander (b) disagree (c) attribute (d) rely on

27. incantation — (a) pouring liquids into casks (b) repentance (c) magic formula (d) long operatic aria

28. incarcerate — (a) imperil (b) torture (c) imprison (d) behead

29. inscrutable — (a) mad (b) malicious (c) misleading (d) unfathomable

30. inured — (a) opposed (b) hardened ((c) impoverished (d) degraded

31. levity — (a) forgetfulness (b) gentleness (c) increase (d) flippancy

32. livid — (a) discolored (b) sensational (c) bilious (d) smarting

33. mastodon — (a) gigantic hound (b) extinct elephant (c) threat (d) disease of the ear

34. motley — (a) of various colors (b) undistinguished (c) dirty (d) abundant

35. odium — (a) hatred (b) rest (c) taste (d) concern (d) obvious

36. palpable — (a) subtle (b) persuasive (c) excited (d) obvious

37. pariah — (a) prophet (b) skin disease (c) tribal head (d) outcast

38. parsimonious — (a) stingy (b) hypocritical (c) stiff (d) poverty-stricken

39. pragmatic — (a) perplexing (b) ideal (c) practical (d) experienced

40. profligacy — (a) forward motion (b) wickedness (c) productivity (d) ability to foretell the future

41. prophylactic — (a) curative (b) toxic (c) preventive (d) sterile

42. proselyte — (a) falsifier (b) convert (c) essayist (d) distinguished person

43. quizzical — (a) puzzling (b) queer (c) ill-tempered (d) antiquated

44. recluse — (a) miser (b) aged person (c) woman-hater (d) hermit

45. recrimination — (a) double jeopardy (b) flattery (c) needless repetition (d) counter-accusation

46. reproof — (a) demonstration (b) censure (c) check (d) strengthening

47. sanguinary — (a) hopeful (b) unlimited (c) unnecessary (d) bloody

48. squalid — (a) stormy (b) enclosed (c) filthy (d) humble

49. truncate — (a) end swiftly (b) cut off (c) act cruelly (d) cancel

50. urbane — (a) surly (b) congested (c) shrewd (d) polished

III. Warming Up

1. adjunct — (a) adaptation (b) addition (c) decree (d) solemn oath

2. aphorism — (a) wise saying (b) digression (c) casual remark (d) repetition

3. arbiter — (a) leader of a team (b) party to a dispute (c) judge (d) shop worker

4. arraign — (a) call to court (b) convict (c) serve on jury (d) put in order

5. arrant — (a) knightly (b) boastful (c) downright (d) cowardly

6. asperity — (a) harshness (b) slander (c) sour taste (d) lost hope

7. asteroid — (a) canine tooth (b) disease (c) flowerlike (d) star-shaped

8. astringent — (a) styptic (b) flexible (c) thin (d) powerful

9. attenuate — (a) listen carefully (b) make thin (c) achieve (d) imply

10. attrition — (a) wearing down (b) charm (c) brashness (d) severance

11. bastion — (a) part of a fortification (b) column (c) coat of mail (d) stitching

12. brindled — (a) cowlike (b) having dark streaks on gray background (c) held by a tether (d) pickled

328

13. buffet — (a) cold meat (b) blow (c) clown (d) noise deadener

14. bumptious — (a) ill-tempered (b) colliding (c) brashly self-assertive (d) illiterate

15. censer — (a) pendulum (b) container for burning incense (c) balance (d) guardian of public morals

16. choler — (a) hunger (b) typhus (c) sadness (d) anger

17. concordat — (a) agreement (b) document (c) indrosement (d) liaison

18. conglomeration — (a) fit of insanity (b) cluster (c) folly (d) brilliant thought

19. construe — (a) confuse (b) unite (c) scatter (d) interpret

20. contingent — (a) contractual (b) conditional (c) expeditionary (d) universal

21. corollary — (a) consequence (b) artery of the heart (c) enclosure for cattle (d) part of a flower

22. crass — (a) brittle (b) established (c) gross (d) sure

23. cubicle — (a) geometric figure (b) small bedroom (c) measure of length (d) sailing craft

24. curmudgeon — (a) churlish fellow (b) buffoon (c) high anger (d) tropical fish

25. debauch — (a) corrupt (b) open a bottle (c) branch off (d) cheapen

26. debilitate — (a) attack (b) weaken (c) become accustomed (d) overwhelm

27. decadent — (a) aristocratic (b) subtle (c) occurring every ten years (d) deteriorating

28. demise — (a) false statement (b) death (c) message (d) stage set

29. depredation — (a) disapproval (b) decrease in value (c) warding off (d) plundering

30. duenna — (a) governess (b) royal lady (c) bullfighter's assistant (d) jail-keeper

31. effigy — (a) image (b) fireplace (c) scaffold (a) attachment

32. expatiate — (a) go into exile (b) expand (c) pardon (d) watch out for

33. figment — (a) pure invention (b) small part (c) art of the novelist (d) worthlessness

34. foible — (a) animal story (b) frailty (c) deceptive scheme (d) decoration

35. foment — (a) instigate (b) drive insane (c) cherish (d) whip into a froth

36. foray — (a) food for cattle (b) campaign hat (c) hullabaloo (d) raid

37. furbelow — (a) decorative trimming (b) weak trait

38. gainsay — (c) continued trill (d) small stove / (a) assure (b) sing (c) deny (d) profit
39. garrulity — (a) untamable nature (b) talkativeness (c) simple-mindedness (d) cheapness
40. hybrid — (a) of mixed origin (b) spirited (c) well mannered (d) poor
41. imbue — (a) sprinkle (b) dress (c) inspire d) pardon
42. imponderable — (a) incapable of being weighed (b) very small (c) unthinkable (d) of tremendous importance
43. inadvertence — (a) oversight (b) inflexibility (c) lack of accuracy (d) hatred
44. incidence — (a) uprising (b) number of cases (c) similar event (d) cutting into
45. incontinent — (a) not happy (b) completed surrounded (c) innumerable (d) unrestrained
46. ineffable — (a) speechless (b) feminine (c) rude (d) unspeakable
47. iniquitous — (a) wicked (b) biased (c) excessively curious (d) unequal
48. innuendo — (a) investigation (b) foul language (c) injustice (d) hinting
49. insensate — (a) aromatic (b) angered (c) without feeling (d) easily stirred
50. instanter — (a) in haste (b) during this month (c) at once (d) pleadingly
51. interlocutory — pertaining to: (a) minstrel show (b) provisional legal decision (c) long sermon (d) cross-examination
52. jowl — (a) jaw b) fiesta (c) bellowing (d) small jar
53. lintel — (a) flax thread (b) small vegetable (c) bar above a door (d) bitter spice
54. lissome — (a) dainty (b) thin (c) supple (d) inactive
55. litany — (a) legal altercation (b) popular choice (c) series of similar responses (d) deep moan
56. lugubrious — (a) mournful (b) sleek (c) deceitful (d) consolatory
57. matutinal — (a) musical (b) ripe (c) devotional (d) early
58. mayhem — (a) deep sigh (b) act of chance (c) criminal mutilation (d) murder
59. meticulous — (a) lying (b) extremely painstaking (c) irascible (d) tawdry
60. minaret — (a) oriental bazar (b) slender tower (c) prayer rug (d) tyrant
61. mollification — (a) washing with soap (b) softening ruffled feelings (c) dressing expensively (d) slight change

330

2. mote — (a) beam (b) scar (c) water-filled ditch (d) speck

3. obeisance — (a) justification (b) conduct c) deference (d) forethought

4. oscillate — (a) kiss (b) vibrate (c) tell time (d) seal a document

5. pachyderm — (a) thick-skinned animal (b) skin eruption (c) heavy cloth (d) leather traveling bag

56. palliate — (a) cast gloom over (b) relieve without curing (c) make a mattress (d) dislike

57. perfidy — (a) confidence (b) treachery (c) obstinacy (d) insolence

68. peruse — (a) exhaust (b) change (c) read through (d) condense

69. piscatorial — relating to: (a) fortunetelling (b) fishing (c) letter-writing (d) portraiture

70. platitudinous — (a) trite (b) level (c) boastful (d) oratorical

71. premonitory — (a) ill-fated (b) warning in advance (c) peninsular (d) financial

72. probity — (a) honesty (b) nearness (c) definite proof (d) investigation

73. propinquity — (a) absolute proof (b) searching quality (c) nearness (d) stinginess

74. prosody — (a) art of versification (b) convert (c) treachery (d) unimaginative writing

75. pundit — (a) martyr (b) scholar (c) vain person (d) gag-writer

76. querulous — (a) habitually complaining (b) questioning (c) seeking anxiously (d) whimsical

77. rancor — (a) bitter resentment (b) pride (c) attainment (d) superciliousness

78. raucous — (a) pugnacious (b) harsh-sounding (c) immature (d) despairing

79. redolent — (a) grieving (b) fragrant (c) needy (d) lazy

80. regimen — (a) systematic diet (b) royal attendant (c) conquered province (d) distinction

81. requite — (a) punish (b) favor (c) repay (d) spare

82. revulsion — (a) backward motion (b) change of government (c) degradation (d) sudden change of feeling

83. runnel — (a) small stream (b) grainstalk (c) race track (d) underground passage

84. sapient — (a) juicy (b) flavorful (c) wise (d) dried up

85. sartorial — (a) well-dressed (b) relating to a tailor (c) costly (d) flashy

86. simulated — (a) pretended (b) mocked (c) compared (d) done at same time

87. sluice   (a) period between wars (b) artificial water channel (c) a great number (d) microscopic section

88. soporific   (a) adolescent (b) indiscreet (c) inducing sleep (d) trouble-making

89. spate   (a) handful (b) flood (c) spade-shaped (d) rubber hose

90. supernumerary   (a) beyond belief (b) additional (c) countless (d) petty officer

91. tactile   (a) discreet (b) capable of being touched (c) of a quiet disposition (d) attached to a wall

92. talon   (a) buzzard (b) card game (c) claw (d) hunting horn

93. tantamount   (a) equivalent (b) gigantic (c) superior (d) far-removed

94. terrapin   (a) defensive earthwork (b) small diamond (c) canvas covering (d) turtle

95. truckle   (a) domineer (b) huckster (c) seek special favor (d) show servility

96. truculent   (a) juicy (b) ferocious (c) trashy (d) servile

97. tundra   (a) small cart (b) hooded jacket (c) treeless arctic plain (d) mossy growth

98. virulent   (a) overpowering (b) venomous (c) manly (d) sudden

99. vitiate   (a) clear up (b) corrupt (c) act as umpire (d) put life into

100. welter   (a) turmoil (b) heat (c) limpness (d) secretion

IV. Getting Tough

1. ablution   (a) innocence (b) difficult problem (c) washing (d) flight

2. abrade   (a) twist (b) wear off (c) attach (d) scold

3. abstruse   (a) missing (b) sprawling (c) obscure (d) stupid

4. abut   (a) collide with (b) touch (c) deny (d) make excuses for

5. agronomist   (a) scientific farmer (b) aggressive nation (c) field hand (d) historian

6. amenities   (a) prayers (b) pageantries (c) courtesies (d) social functions

7. amortization   (a) sudden death (b) long delay (c) liquidation (d) small refund

8. animus   (a) keen wit (b) hostile feeling (c) great courage (d) friendship

9. apiary   (a) bird cage (b) high flying (c) set of beehives (d) house for primates

10. arable — (a) willing to agree (b) dehydrated (c) scientifically practical (d) suitable for cultivation

11. arbitrament — (a) acidity (b) conciliation (c) final judgment (d) superhuman task

12. atrophy — (a) sudden change (b) lack of sunlight (c) wasting away (d) affinity

13. baleful — (a) overflowing (b) pernicious (c) unethical (d) envious

14. ballistics — (a) study of bullets (b) art of balancing (c) art of juggling (d) study of weights

15. barouche — (a) jeweled clip (b) veranda (c) carriage (d) fancy headdress

16. bemused — (a) enchanted (b) entertained (c) lost in thought (d) ridiculous

17. bespeak — (a) engage for in advance (b) be critical of (c) praise (d) promise

18. bifurcated — (a) forked (b) ploughed (c) stabbed (d) reduced

19. blatant — (a) senseless (b) sheepish (c) boastful (d) noisy

20. calumny — (a) warmth (b) slander (c) retribution (d) relaxation

21. capillary — pertaining to: (a) head (b) chapter (c) thin tube (d) climax

22. cartographer — (a) licensed peddler (b) league secretary (c) explorer (d) mapmaker

23. catapult — (a) hurl (b) dive (c) struggle (d) cause violent change

24. cavil — (a) haggle (b) prance (c) conspire (d) pick flaws

25. celibate — (a) unmarried (b) leafy (c) wild (d) heavenly

26. centrifugal — (a) symmetrical (b) flying from a center (c) divisive (d) fearful

27. ceramics — (a) old stamps (b) rocks (c) pottery (d) food

28. codicil — (a) unwritten code (b) small item (c) addition to a will (d) remainder

29. cognate — (a) known (b) of common origin (c) wheel-shaped (d) substantial

30. colander — (a) Eastern prince (b) container (c) strainer (d) grinder

31. comatose — (a) unconscious (b) disheveled (c) obstinate (d) punctual

32. compendium — (a) notebook (b) full explanation (c) reprint (d) comprehensive summary

33. complicity — (a) deceit (b) variety (c) partnership in crime (d) relief from debt

34. concomitant — (a) acompanying (b) reserved (c) unnec essary (d) half-asleep

35. crotchety — (a) eccentric (b) boring (c) knitted bad] (d) broken down

36. cruet — (a) bottle (b) cake (c) napkin (d) oil

37. deleterious — (a) considerate (b) eliminating (c) harm ful (d) informative

38. dipsomaniac — (a) given to changing moods (b) unhapp person (c) confirmed drunkard (d) vampire

39. disparity — (a) partiality (b) stinginess (c) injustic (d) unlikeness

40. disputatious — (a) insistent (b) argumentative (c) insin cere (d) contradictory

41. dissimulate — (a) refuse to imitate (b) spread about (c) pretend (d) hasten

42. distrait — (a) absent-minded (b) afflicted (c) sepa rated (d) inconvenienced

43. doggerel — (a) short slogan (b) trivial verse (c) small pet (d) snapshot

44. effulgent — (a) bursting (b) sacred (c) emergency (d) radiant

45. emblazon — (a) decorate magnificently (b) set fire to (c) persevere (d) set an example

46. eviscerate — (a) disembowel (b) bring out into view (c) extract (d) make less sticky

47. exacerbate — (a) scold (b) make more bitter (c) etch out (d) hurl insults

48. execrate — (a) reveal (b) eliminate (c) detest (d) develop

49. expostulation — (a) afterthought (b) earnest appeal (c) il lustration (d) violent threat

50. extant — (a) still in existence (b) no longer in ex istence (c) outstanding (d) valueless

51. febrile — (a) nervous (b) feverish (c) slight (d) moody

52. fluted — (a) fretted (b) arched (c) thinned-out (d) grooved

53. frieze — (a) pedestal (b) ornamental strip (c) top section (d) niche

54. frond — (a) superstrutcure (b) stem (c) bending tree (d) leaf

55. hibernal — (a) Irish (b) Spanish (c) wintry (d) vegetative

56. histrionic — (a) theatrical (b) informed (c) famous (d) microscopic

57. impecunious — (a) moral (b) niggardly (c) begging (d) poor

58. importunate — (a) sinful (b) unyielding (c) insistent (d) valuable

59. lachrymose — (a) delicate (b) milky (c) tearful (d) sugary

60. lexicographer — (a) shorthand expert (b) dictionary maker (c) typesetter (d) forger

61. limpid — (a) transparent (b) crustacean (c) obscure (d) crippled

62. macerate — (a) strike (b) disfigure (c) cut up (d) soften by soaking

63. malleable — (a) permeable (b) pliant (c) stringy (d) punctureproof

64. metaphoric — (a) renowned (b) figurative (c) unintelligible (d) undergoing changes

65. miasma — (a) deep swamp (b) potent drug (c) dizzy spell (d) poisonous exhalation

66. misogynist — (a) masseur (b) ne'er-do-well (c) woman-hater (d) sadist

67. mordant — (a) depressed (b) festering (c) sarcastic (d) mild

68. myopic — (a) obscure (b) shortsighted (c) big-hearted (d) negligent

69. olfactory — pertaining to: (a) sense of smell (b) manufacture of perfume (c) gasoline (d) design

70. parious — (a) dangerous (b) talkative (c) agreeable (d) uncertain

71. paroxysm — (a) suffocation (b) speechlessness (c) continuation (d) fit

72. peremptory — (a) unusual (b) decisive (c) abrupt (d) warning

73. pertinacious — (a) stubbornly persistent (b) related (c) bold (d) unabashed

74. polemic — (a) eloquent (b) awkward (c) controversial (d) disparaging

75. predatory — (a) plundering (b) anticipating (c) powerful (d) carnivorous

76. predilection — (a) forecast (b) preference (c) earliest remembrance (d) gratification

77. preempt — (a) vacate (b) substitute (c) establish prior claim (d) place a bet

78. progenitor — (a) supporter (b) descendant (c) forefather (d) director

79. prolixity — (a) tedious length (b) lack of firmness (c) nearness (d) tension

80. propitiate — (a) approach (b) influence (c) conform (d) appease

81. proscenium — (a) front part of a stage (b) first act of a play (c) box-office receipts (d) act of censorship

82. protagonist   (a) opponent (b) chief participant (c) rebel (d) wrestler

83. provender   (a) thriftiness (b) dry food for animals (c) hawker (d) careful person

84. refractory   (a) disobedient (b) easily broken (c) telescopic (d) faultfinding

85. relegate   (a) relieve (b) banish (c) put in order (d) tie together

86. sacerdotal   (a) hallowed (b) priestly (c) sweet-tasting (d) immersed

87. sanguine   (a) modest (b) hopeful (c) proud (d) clever

88. serried   (a) scattered (b) notched (c) pursued (d) crowded together

89. spoliation   (a) act of plundering (b) decay (c) gambling (d) act of coddling

90. surreptitious   (a) wicked (b) clandestine (c) cautious (d) cowardly

91. talisman   (a) charm (b) juror (c) informer (d) lecturer

92. termagant   (a) unreliable (b) shrewish (c) desperate (d) fishy

93. terminology   (a) technicality (b) finality (c) explanation (d) nomenclature

94. testily   (a) irritably (b) professionally (c) experimentally (d) weakly

95. timbre   (a) percussion instrument (b) warning (c) quality of tone (d) musical string

96. transcend   (a) move about freely (b) degrade (c) go beyond (d) delay

97. unmitigated   (a) impure (b) absolute (c) dishonest (d) impudent

98. vernal   (a) mercenary (b) surprising (c) sensitive (d) related to spring

99. virago   (a) mixture (b) shrew (c) clown (d) strong wind

100. votary   (a) elector (b) legal partner (c) cavity (d) worshiper

V. Tough

1. abnegation   (a) association (b) renunciation (c) affirmation (d) indignation

2. absolution   (a) positiveness (b) forgiveness (c) punishment (d) religious explanation

3. accoutrements   (a) sealed orders (b) equipment (c) correspondence (d) financial records

4. acerb — (a) foreign (b) dangerous (c) harsh (d) unwilling

5. agglomeration — (a) vagueness (b) shimmering (c) enumeration (d) confused mass

6. analgesic — (a) counterirritant (b) chemical compound (c) pain-soother (d) medicine

7. anomalous — (a) similar (b) abnormal (c) unexplainable (d) shapeless

8. aphasia — (a) formlessness (b) loss of memory (c) loss of speech (d) loss of dignity

9. apposite — (a) extreme (b) inimical (c) appointive (d) appropriate

10. apprise — (a) evaluate (b) inform (c) award (d) draw close

11. appurtenance — (a) countenance (b) insistence (c) substitute (d) accessory

12. arrogate — (a) belittle (b) assume presumptuously (c) show pride (d) question harshly

13. articulation — (a) accent (b) dialect (c) enunciation (d) impediment

14. ascetic — (a) unprejudiced (b) pale (c) sterile (d) self-denying

15. aseptic — (a) surgically clean (b) poisonous (c) seven-sided (d) star-shaped

16. asperse — (a) rout (b) deflate (c) deny (d) slander

17. asseveration — (a) separation (b) indignation (c) assertion (d) retention

18. astral — (a) unreal (b) flowerlike (c) stellar (d) geometric

19. auroral — pertaining to: (a) cataracts (b) ear (c) dawn (d) gold

20. baroque — (a) extravagantly ornamented (b) baronial (c) medieval (d) made of small chips

21. beleaguered — (a) worried (b) bedridden (c) surrounded (d) joined together

22. bosky — (a) wooded (b) vague (c) shy (d) stout

23. brackish — (a) salty (b) muddy (c) swampy (d) slightly acid

24. burnoose — (a) long rope (b) hooded cloak (c) Indian headdress (d) Oriental food

25. categorically — (a) purposefully (b) introductorily (c) without qualification (d) relatively

26. collate — (a) demonstrate clearly (b) comprehend (c) dine together (d) arrange correctly

27. colloquy — (a) directive (b) altercation (c) conversation (d) difference of opinion

28. comestibles — (a) odds and ends (b) superior products (c) spices (d) foodstuffs

337

29. commensurate   (a) punctual (b) proportionate (c) acquainted with (d) certain

30. confabulate   (a) embroider on (b) chat (c) muddle (d) put an end to

31. contentious   (a) quarrelsome (b) keeping pace with (c) happy (d) ambitious

32. culvert   (a) firearm (b) crossing (c) tillage (d) drain

33. debenture   (a) account rendered (b) bond (c) stronghold (d) servitude

34. deciduous   (a) critical (b) not evergreen (c) trifling (d) downcast

35. decrepitude   (a) horror (b) slow pace (c) cowardice (d) enfeeblement

36. deliquescent   (a) glittering (b) liquefying (c) attractive (d) motionless

37. demonic   (a) degrading (b) popular (c) frenzied (d) deserted

38. depilate   (a) bow to (b) unpack (c) remove hair (d) put off

39. didactic   (a) boring (b) vehement (c) educative (d) miserly

40. dross   (a) laziness (b) thin thread (c) Chinese temple (d) waste matter

41. effete   (a) worn out (b) effeminate (c) unrealistic (d) malodorous

42. emendation   (a) elimination (b) legislative proposal (c) correction (d) praise

43. enervate   (a) calm down (b) weaken (c) pep up (d) lure on

44. enjoin   (a) commit (b) please (c) unite (d) prohibit

45. fatuity   (a) foolishness (b) smugness (c) luck (d) casualty

46. fecundity   (a) validity (b) poverty (c) fertility (d) depth

47. fetid   (a) stinking (b) exhausted (c) festive (d) medicinal

48. fugacious   (a) rapid (b) transitory (c) irresponsible (d) fanciful

49. gambit   (a) opening move (b) frolic (c) hazard (d) cut of meat

50. germinate   (a) end suddenly (b) inoculate (c) spread disease (d) sprout

51. grandiloquent   (a) generous (b) domineering (c) pompous (d) genuine

52. haft   (a) weight (b) leather pouch (c) handle (d) weapon

53. homily — (a) sermon (b) porridge (c) recipe (d) scolding

54. hoyden — (a) unpleasant sound (b) tomboy (c) small animal (d) old coin

55. implacable — (a) fussy (b) unappeasable (c) dissatisfied (d) well hidden

56. imprimatur — (a) censorship (b) official approval (c) movable type (d) significant event

57. inanition — (a) silliness (b) strictness (c) emptiness (d) passivity

58. invidious — (a) subtle (b) unconquerable (c) giving offense (d) apt

59. laity — (a) religious chant (b) responsibility (c) covering (d) laymen

60. licentious — (a) sanctioned (b) wanton (c) self-seeking (d) dramatic

61. ligneous — (a) explosive (b) woodlike (c) related (d) reclining

62. limbo — (a) embarrassing situation (b) catch-phrase (c) a place of forgotten things (d) identification

63. marmoreal — pertaining to: (a) a tomb (b) lower order of monkeys (c) coat-of-mail (d) marble

64. minion — (a) hanger-on (b) wing (c) small measure (d) power

65. minuscule — (a) terrifying (b) deficient (c) small (d) colorless

66. mores — (a) idols (b) sins (c) fixed customs (d) dignity

67. moribund — (a) superfluous (b) dying (c) gloomy (d) stagnant

68. offal — (a) tendency (b) sacrifice (c) refuse (d) poison

69. orotund — (a) stout (b) hoarse (c) resonant (d) gilded

70. paucity — (a) costliness (b) short rest (c) scantiness (d) misuse

71. pendulous — (a) tawdry (b) hanging down loosely (c) making an arc (d) contrite

72. pluvial — (a) deadly (b) wealthy (c) rainy (d) jolly

73. preclude — (a) raise the curtain (b) make sure (c) prevent (d) foretell

74. predicate — (a) base upon (b) follow (c) prejudge (d) speak boldly

75. prehensile — (a) before recorded history (b) without written record (c) capable of grasping (d) forewarning

76. privy — (a) doing without (b) sharing secret knowledge (c) underprivileged (d) unconcerned

339

77. prodigality — (a) lavishness (b) stimulus (c) sinfulness (d) negligence

78. pterodactyl — (a) poetic foot (b) irregular petals (c) flying reptile (d) prehistoric rodent

79. quagmire — (a) large clam (b) bog (c) underbrush (d) gradual rise

80. queasy — (a) jealous (b) peculiar (c) out of tune (d) squeamish

81. recherché — (a) old-fashioned (b) modest (c) startling (d) choice

82. risible — (a) likely (b) climbable (c) inducing laughter (d) shimmering

83. salubrious — (a) flavored (b) healthful (c) lewd (d) pathetic

84. sanctimonious — (a) hypercritical (b) upright (c) cowardly (d) hypocritically devout

85. semantic — (a) Eastern (b) pertaining to meaning (c) hairsplitting (d) emotional

86. senescence — (a) rebirth (b) belief in hereafter (c) beginning of old age (d) growing

87. septic — (a) infected (b) heavy (c) rusted (d) sterilized

88. sequacious — (a) preceding (b) isolated (c) always questioning (d) following

89. simian — (a) Malayan (b) resembling (c) apelike (d) foolish

90. specious — (a) monetary (b) silent (c) plausible (d) qualified

91. sporadic — (a) momentary (b) occurring at irregular intervals (c) drawn-out (d) enclosed

92. spume — (a) scorn (b) foam (c) decoration (d) venom

93. supervene — (a) precede (b) displace (c) interfere (d) ensue

94. surcease — (a) survival (b) end (c) relief (d) onslaught

95. suture — (a) dressing (b) wound (c) surgical stitch (d) decay

96. touchstone — (a) crumbly rock (b) lucky charm (c) pedestal (d) criterion

97. ukase — (a) unconfirmed report (b) official edict (c) Russian hut (d) secret order

98. umbrage — (a) resentment (b) humility (c) delight (d) meditation

99. unconscionable — (a) unmindful (b) excessive (c) unmangeable (d) distasteful

100. wraith — (a) uncontrolled anger (b) mist (c) deep concern (d) specter

VI. Tougher

1. **actuarially** — (a) normally (b) realistically (c) by virtue of office (d) according to insurance statistics

2. **alembic** — (a) chemical formula (b) distilling vessel (c) rhythmic foot (d) drinking mug

3. **ambergris** — (a) semiprecious jewel (b) healing ointment (c) forever oily (d) perfume base

4. **anathema** — (a) curse (b) pun (c) musical subject (d) religious chant

5. **ancillary** — (a) hooked-on (b) pertaining to the ankle (c) auxiliary (d) self-evident

6. **apothegm** — (a) parallel story (b) high point (c) glandular secretion (d) pithy saying

7. **apotheosis** — (a) glorification (b) religious controversy (c) conclusion (d) relaxation

8. **archetype** — (a) model (b) diabolic nature (c) mansion (d) pointed arch

9. **astrolabe** — (a) planetary body (b) ship's rigging (c) sunspot (d) astronomical instrument

10. **atavism** — (a) disbelief (b) sinfulness (c) reversion (d) prevention

11. **baize** — (a) Indian corn (b) transparent cotton (c) imported corn (d) feltlike fabric

12. **beatific** — (a) orderly (b) beautiful (c) blissful (d) morose

13. **bedizen** — (a) blind (b) dress gaudily (c) undernourish (d) confuse

14. **bittern** — (a) northern tree (b) marsh bird (c) condiment (d) part of a harness

15. **breviary** — (a) last words (b) prayer book (c) short journal (d) authority

16. **burgeon** — (a) leaven (b) batter (c) sprout (d) beg

17. **cabal** — (a) intrigue (b) mystical doctrine (c) insurrection (d) ruthlessness

18. **cadge** — (a) imprison (b) bicker (c) hide (d) beg

19. **calligraphy** — (a) mathematical measurement (b) dance composition (c) handwriting (d) musical pipe

20. **centripetal** — (a) attracted to the center (b) leaf-shaped (c) circular in design (d) tending to deceive

21. **cheetah** — (a) multicolored bird (b) catlike animal (c) Chinese sailing vessel (d) small prayer rug

22. **conch** — (a) spiral shell (b) heavy blow (c) woolen blanket (d) thick strap

23. convoluted — (a) transformed (b) knotted (c) accompanied (d) coiled

24. countervailing — (a) hiding (b) compensating for (c) bargaining (d) winning

25. demesne — (a) vileness (b) region of activity (c) good behavior (d) resignation

26. demotic — (a) fanatical (b) crazed (c) pertaining to language d) belonging to the people

27. dialectics — (a) socialism (b) elocution (c) logical argument (d) reading

28. disquisition — (a) uneasiness (b) formal request (c) itemized list (d) elaborate treatise

29. dissemble — (a) conceal one's motives (b) break up (c) disagree (d) overlook

30. dudgeon — (a) resentment (b) small fish (c) underground cell (d) pride

31. elegiacal — (a) laudatory (b) sorrowful (c) fastidious (d) desirable

32. empyreal — (a) celestial (b) ruling absolutely (c) imaginary (d) based on experience

33. encomium — (a) friendship (b) embrace (c) panegyric (d) revenue

34. endemic — (a) suffering from loss of blood (b) perpetual (c) related to internal medicine (d) peculiar to a locality

35. enfilade — (a) rake with gunfire (b) slip inside of (c) cut into strips (d) stack in a heap

36. esculent — (a) edible (b) hungry (c) thick (d) lovable

37. euthenics — (a) doctrine of life after death (b) science of improving environment (c) theory of human origins (d) belief in "mercy-killings"

38. exorcise — (a) expel an evil spirit (b) impress (c) train thoroughly (d) torture

39. feckless — (a) light-hearted (b) shiftless (c) malodorous (d) stingy

40. floe — (a) mass of floating ice (b) Arctic hut (c) winter sport (d) white caviar

41. fruition — (a) parsimoniousness (b) realization (c) seed dispersal (d) temporary use

42. fustian — (a) patrician (b) moldy (c) pretentious (d) antique

43. hackles — (a) small bones (b) worn-out horses (c) bristles on dog's back (d) open carriages

44. harridan — (a) curved dagger (b) proud lady (c) vicious hag (d) long cape

45. hieratic — (a) superior (b) classified (c) priestly (d) uncertain

46. ineluctable   (a) unpalatable (b) inescapable (c) opaque (d) transparent

47. inexpugnable   (a) slow to anger (b) unconquerable (c) distasteful (d) inexcusable

48. interstices   (a) stitches (b) small openings (c) digressions (d) intestines

49. kinetic   pertaining to: (a) gas (b) motion (c) study of national groups (d) theory of heredity

50. lectern   (a) reference book (b) reading desk (c) storm lantern (d) literary conference

51. libidinous   (a) lustful (b) disagreeable (c) discolored (d) headstrong

52. mandrill   (a) narcotic herb (b) baboon (c) tropical fruit (d) ancient musical instrument

53. manumit   (a) copy by hand (b) set free (c) read palms (d) memorize

54. marmot   (a) tureen (b) tile (c) rodent (d) small monkey

55. minatory   (a) spiral (b) threatening (c) imitative (d) wandering

56. miscreant   (a) misunderstood person (b) victim (c) scoundrel (d) misfit

57. necromancy   (a) massacre (b) mortuary (c) black magic (d) higher mathematics

58. overweening   (a) crushing (b) arrogant (c) pampering (d) massive

59. pannier   (a) basket (b) rapier (c) small pan (d) brooch

60. pastiche   (a) thin wafer (b) small pill (c) diversion (d) imitative artistic composition

61. patina   (a) greenish film on metal (b) gloss (c) ancient pottery (d) Latin-American courtyard

62. plinth   (a) square stone base (b) crossbeam (c) kindling material (d) large tomb

63. polity   (a) rules of etiquette (b) tenure of office (c) basic structure of a government (d) diplomatic action

64. postprandial   (a) after midnight (b) after-dinner (c) dilatory (d) posthumous

65. primordial   (a) first-rate (b) strenuous (c) original (d) predestined

66. prognathous   (a) closely related (b) before birth (c) having a quarrelsome disposition (d) having projecting jaws

67. purblind   (a) conceited (b) dazzling (c) lacking vision (d) incomprehensible

68. refulgent — (a) brilliant (b) unstable (c) decaying (d) capacious

69. rime — (a) sediment (b) filth (c) foam (d) hoar-frost

70. salver — (a) salute (b) tray (c) ointment (d) rescuer

71. sapid — (a) flavorsome (b) wise (c) spirited (d) stupid

72. scurf — (a) menial attendant (b) rough water (c) coarse linen (d) dandruff

73. sententious — (a) quibbling (b) filled with maxims (c) emotional (d) imaginative

74. sentient — (a) conscious (b) harmonizing (c) judicious (d) voting

75. sibylline — (a) hissing (b) oracular (c) luxurious (d) poetic

76. simulacrum — (a) persuasive speech (b) candle-holder (c) shadowy likeness (d) coincidence

77. sirocco — (a) hot wind (b) leather binding (c) style of painting (d) contagious disease

78. sodality — (a) temperance (b) fellowship (c) saltiness (d) sogginess

79. stertorous — (a) loud-voiced (b) snoring (c) undecided (d) persistent

80. stricture — (a) theory (b) emergency (c) severe criticism (d) contention

81. stultify — (a) revile (b) make a fool of (c) confuse (d) hinder progress

82. supernal — (a) needless (b) heavenly (c) official (d) haughty

83. symbiotic — (a) living in close association (b) attacking bacteria (c) unreal (d) evolutionary

84. tatterdemalion — (a) maniac (b) ragamuffin (c) obstructionist (d) mythical monster

85. temerarious — (a) cowardly (b) watchful (c) rash (d) delicate

86. tenebrous — (a) overhanging (b) fragile (c) gloomy (d) obstinate

87. tocsin — (a) deadly poison (b) alarm bell (c) charm (d) decree

88. tonsure — (a) ecclesiastical robe (b) musical passage (c) shaving of the head (d) vibration

89. transmogrify — (a) change completely (b) haunt (c) pierce (d) terrify

90. traumatic — (a) dreamy (b) magic (c) caused by wound (d) turbulent

91. trencherman — (a) ditch digger (b) hearty eater (c) foot soldier (d) hospital attendant

92. troglodyte — (a) prehistoric animal (b) figure of speech (c) cave dweller (d) grotesque idol

93. trumpery   (a) deceptive maneuver (b) loud blast (c) easy victory (d) showy trash

94. tumid   (a) heated (b) puffed up (c) sullen (d) infected

95. turpitude   (a) beauty (b) depravity (c) glossiness (d) weariness

96. tutelary   (a) protective (b) submissive (c) official (d) ingenious

97. unwonted   (a) not habitual (b) unwilling (c) neglected (d) unpleasing

98. vertiginous   (a) avoidable (b) dizzy (c) upright (d) greenish

99. viscid   (a) deadly (b) corrupt (c) sticky (d) glowing

100. whilom   (a) temporary (b) quaint (c) pensive (d) former

VII. But Tough!

1. adumbrate   (a) be silent (b) foreshadow (c) curve (d) color

2. affiant   (a) affidavit signer (b) betrothed (c) relative (d) confidential agent

3. animadversion   (a) impromptu remark (b) disapproving comment (c) commendation (d) lengthy explanation

4. anneal   (a) patch (b) temper (c) forget (d) commence

5. anthropomorphic   (a) changeable (b) having human form (c) exceptional (d) geological

6. apologue   (a) afterthought (b) explanation (c) ancient legend (d) moral fable

7. aureole   (a) halo (b) gold cloth (c) bird (d) vestment

8. austral   (a) severe (b) mystical (c) eastern (d) southern

9. benisons   (a) blessings (b) antlers (c) chants (d) toasts

10. bezel   (a) theft (b) precious stone (c) edge of chisel (d) kind of nut

11. bibelot   (a) trinket (b) small book (c) idle chatter (d) article of infant's wear

12. bilboes   (a) fetters (b) southern vegetable (c) signposts (d) elbows

13. brummagem   (a) trash (b) senseless chatter (c) foul odor (d) vagabondage

14. buccal   (a) nasal (b) pertaining to mouth (c) piratical (d) shrewd

15. cabala — (a) committee (b) conspiracy (c) secret science (d) scholarly

16. caesura — (a) rippling sound (b) surgical operation (c) aria (d) rhythmic break

17. caitiff — (a) person of low character (b) species of leopard (c) judicial officer (d) defendant in a lawsuit

18. carious — (a) decayed (b) solicitous (c) covered with scars (d) blighted

19. caryatid — (a) kind of beetle (b) turtle shell (c) painful dental decay (d) sculptured female figure used as a support

20. catharsis — (a) in a Chinese manner (b) eternal damnation (c) inner stress (d) emotional relief

21. chaffer — (a) small bird (b) gossip (c) haggle (d) vex

22. clamant — (a) owner (b) secretive (c) urgent (d) gentle

23. coadjutor — (a) partner (b) arbitrator (c) assistant (d) extra juror

24. comity — (a) beauty (b) union (c) council (d) courtesy

25. comstockery — (a) blockhouse (b) overzealous censorship (c) large warehouse (d) trading in shares

26. concatenated — (a) resounding (b) indented (c) hollow (d) linked together

27. contemn — (a) despise (b) mar (c) convict (d) struggle with

28. contravene — (a) substitute (b) thwart (c) balance (d) juxtapose

29. contumacy — (a) slander (b) adeptness (c) defiance of authority (d) conceit

30. cosset — (a) article of attire (b) milk dish (c) wheedling speech (d) pet lamb

31. cozen — (a) convince (b) flatter (c) cheat (d) ridicule

32. denigrate — (a) deny (b) defame (c) ridicule (d) irritate

33. deracinate — (a) shunt off (b) pull up by the roots (c) tear to shreds (d) slow down

34. desuetude — (a) disuse (b) rich style of cooking (c) persuasive talk (d) bluntness

35. discomfited — (a) frustrated (b) uncomfortable (c) uncertain (d) reduced

36. emollient — (a) fragrant (b) soothing (c) milky (d) compensatory

37. erose — (a) centralized (b) sweet-smelling (c) having uneven margin (d) self-educated

38. escarpment — (a) threat (b) limbo (c) cliff (d) blight

39. escheat (a) confiscate (b) swindle (c) avoid (d) chew thoroughly

40. exordium (a) beginning of a speech (b) plea (c) essence (d) final appeal

41. fane (a) fabulous (b) temple (c) booth (d) willing

42. farrier (a) landlord of an inn (b) carriage maker (c) blacksmith (d) tanner

43. gravid (a) solemn (b) pregnant (c) bitter (d) formidable

44. guerdon (a) reward (b) shield (c) watchman (d) old watch

45. hortatory (a) unscientific (b) inciting (c) time-consuming (d) unpleasant

46. hummock (a) cassock (b) knoll (c) hassock (d) small bird

47. hustings (a) arched point (b) cornice (c) electioneering platform (d) ladder

48. imbrue (a) simmer (b) stain (c) persuade (d) prevent

49. immanent (a) inherent (b) decisive (c) impending (d) prominent

50. incarnadine (a) blemish (b) redden (c) flourish (d) enslave

51. incubus (a) oppressive burden (b) newborn child (c) growth (d) mystery

52. integument (a) mathematical term (b) outer covering (c) complete whole (d) discourse

53. jejune (a) yellow (b) barren (c) intestinal (d) youthful

54. joist (a) juncture (b) mortise (c) timber laid horizontally (d) tenon

55. lanyard (a) short rope (b) sail (c) anchor chain (d) lower deck

56. litotes (a) literary output (b) poetic stanza (c) two negatives making affirmative (d) exaggeration

57. lubricity (a) elasticity (b) stolidity (c) stickiness (d) lewdness

58. mordacious (a) surly (b) bold (c) caustic (d) deathly

59. morganatic related to: (a) marriage for wealth (b) marriage with a commoner (c) pompous ceremony (d) crossbreeding

60. nascent (a) disgusting (b) bubbling (c) moist (d) beginning to exist

61. niggling (a) prodding (b) teasing (c) petty (d) stingy

62. nirvana (a) pacifism (b) fantasy (c) exotic flower (d) inner calm

63. nonage — (a) senility (b) convent (c) immaturity (d) state of being old-fashioned

64. nugatory — (a) negative (b) trivial (c) solid (d) impressionable

65. oblation — (a) solemn offering (b) responsibility (c) cleansing (d) reduction

66. offertory — (a) musical chant (b) church aisle (c) ancient instrument (d) church collectio[n]

67. otiose — (a) indolent (b) humid (c) talkative (d) full of bounce

68. panache — (a) cake (b) remedy (c) plume (d) baske[t]

69. paralepsis — (a) study of butterflies (b) type of paralysis (c) elliptical figure (d) a passin[g] over with brief mention

70. pennate — (a) winged (b) long-tailed (c) tooth-edge[d] (d) pointed

71. percipience — (a) realism (b) steadfastness (c) keen perception (d) clarity

72. peristyle — (a) quill pen (b) nautical instrument (c) decoration (d) inner court

73. picaresque — relating to: (a) rogues (b) fish (c) bull-fights (d) spears

74. porphyry — (a) carved gold (b) reddish purple rock (c) velvet hanging (d) ointment

75. pother — (a) comforting agent (b) medicinal drink (c) disturbance (d) dull story

76. proem — (a) conclusion (b) preface (c) long poem (d) proclamation

77. prurient — (a) guiltless (b) prudish (c) lewd (d) impoverished

78. putative — (a) tentative (b) supposed (c) mighty (d) decaying

79. raptorial — (a) enamored (b) authoritative (c) selfish (d) preying upon

80. recrudescene — (a) rawness (b) revival (c) refinement (d) lack of manners

81. refection — (a) meditation (b) chronic disease (c) dessert (d) light meal

82. replevin — (a) constant complaint (b) horse ailment (c) recovery of property (d) second helping

83. reticulated — (a) drawn back (b) netted (c) sewed together (d) purchased

84. rood — (a) oath (b) crucifix (c) pennant (d) stuff

85. saltatory — (a) leaping (b) spicy (c) healthy (d) reassuring

86. screed — (a) long-drawn-out tirade (b) slogan (c) sharp retort (d) gentleman's agreement

87. sequestration   (a) horseback riding (b) distinction (c) reservoir (d) segregation

88. sirdar   (a) Arabian sword (b) Turkish smoking vessel (c) military commander (d) water boy

89. splenetic   (a) spiteful (b) damaging (c) gorgeous (d) effusive

90. sudorific   (a) sleep inducing (b) promoting perspiration (c) unpleasant (d) magnificent

91. sumptuary   (a) impressive (b) regulating expenditure (c) illegal (d) extravagant

92. tarn   (a) hedge (b) dry meadow (c) small mountain lake (d) heather

93. tautology   (a) superfluous repetition (b) hasty judgment (c) fine distinction (d) tension

94. thaumaturgist   (a) appraiser (b) heating expert (c) magician (d) translator

95. threnody   (a) symposium (b) funeral song (c) melodic line (d) ancient ballad

96. trope   (a) figure of speech (b) superabundance (c) exaggeration (d) insincerity

97. tumbril   (a) two-wheeled cart (b) musical instrument (c) juggler's trick (d) climbing vine

98. ursine   (a) tangential (b) degenerate (c) outlandish (d) bearlike

99. vermicular   (a) slangy (b) farinaceous (c) similar (d) worm-shaped

100. whorl   (a) globe (b) confusion (c) token (d) coil

VIII. 100 Words to Crack Your Wisdom Teeth On

1. acephalous   (a) without a ruler (b) formless (c) bitter (d) sterilized

2. adventitious   (a) exciting (b) incidental (c) deeply religious (d) opportune

3. afferent   (a) leading to a central point (b) removing (c) unaffected (d) timid

4. afflatus   (a) egoism (b) notoriety (c) inspiration (d) gastric ailment

5. ampersand   (a) the symbol "&" (b) material to grind glass (c) unit of electricity (d) figure of speech

6. ana   (a) collection of odd literary items (b) insect group (c) worthless bric-a-brac (d) foolish action

7. anodyne   (a) terminal of a battery (b) book of notes (c) knotted rope (d) soothing medicine

349

8. appetency — (a) capability (b) craving (c) rivalry (d) glamour

9. atrabilious — (a) melancholy (b) heinous (c) resentful (d) ungrateful

10. auscultation — act of (a) vibrating (b) listening (c) kissing (d) hiding

11. autochthonous — (a) pertaining to an extinct mammal (b) native (c) independent (d) self-starting

12. avuncular — (a) greedy (b) curved (c) like an uncle (d) relating to one's ancestor

13. baldric — (a) belt for sword (b) melody on a horn (c) coat of mail (d) part of a castle

14. barratry — (a) enclosure (b) emptiness (c) kind of fraud (d) legal opinion

15. batten — (a) grow fat (b) pound to a pulp (c) make into a paste (d) roast lightly

16. beldam — (a) prima donna (b) old woman (c) poisonous drug (d) cosmetic

17. buskin — (a) small vehicle (b) kiss (c) high shoe (d) type of leather

18. cachinnation — (a) loud laughter (b) evil scheme (c) hypocritical applause (d) confused medley

19. carapace — (a) animal shell (b) sea snail (c) medieval carriage (d) gaudy banner

20. casuistry — (a) expounding laws of chance (b) fatalism (c) unsubstantiated conclusion (d) specious reasoning

21. catafalque — (a) fatal error (b) complete upheaval (c) large waterfall (d) funeral scaffold

22. cenobite — (a) monk living in a community (b) empty tomb (c) beginner (d) individualist

23. cenotaph — (a) inscription on a statue (b) wax engraving (c) optical illusion (d) empty tomb

24. chiromancy — (a) care of the feet (b) period of trial (c) palmistry (d) beautiful handwriting

25. cicatrix — (a) female guardian (b) cricket (c) scar mark (d) sharp spur

26. collop — (a) small drinking cup (b) part of harness (c) fruit pudding (d) small piece of meat

27. colophon — (a) cabbagelike plant (b) inscription at end of book (c) sound-recording device (d) oriental headdress

28. concupiscence — (a) secret plotting (b) burning desire (c) brotherly love (d) recovery from illness

29. coruscate — (a) befuddle (b) sparkle (c) take away by force (d) roughen

30. crepitate   (a) crawl (b) become weak (c) make a crackling sound (d) be fearful

31. crepuscular   pertaining to: (a) twilight (b) feebleness (c) circulation of blood (d) drunkenness

32. dado   (a) school of painting (b) extinct bird (c) middle section of a pedestal (d) frantic caper

33. descant   (a) talk at length (b) fill a bottle (c) pour (d) filter

34. detrition   (a) sorrow (b) wearing away (c) prevention (d) sudden exit

35. diaeresis   (a) gastric disorder (b) ascent of a plane (c) two dots over a vowel (d) scattering of a people

36. dithyramb   (a) poisonous insect (b) gland (c) drug addict (d) passionate poem

37. doxology   (a) heresy (b) hymn of praise (c) study of propaganda (d) obstinate belief

38. empirical   (a) relating to a market (b) based upon experience (c) ruling despotically (d) expansionist

39. eolithic   pertaining to: (a) modern sculpture (b) mineral spring (c) earliest human culture (d) harp music

40. eructate   (a) get rid of (b) burp (c) plead against (d) falsify

41. eschatology   (a) study of obscene literature (b) doctrine relating to death (c) study of shell life (d) study of foreign lands

42. estivate   (a) pass the summer (b) procrastinate (c) have high regard for (d) cram full

43. euphuism   (a) excessive elegance of language (b) concise manner of speech (c) pleasant harmony of sound (d) constant attention to health

44. exegesis   (a) crucial moment (b) outward show (c) strict accuracy (d) critical explanation of a text

45. falchion   (a) bird of prey (b) sword (c) prop (d) coward

46. feral   (a) iron clad (b) festive (c) wild (d) portable

47. gasconade   (a) gallantry (b) company of musketeers (c) trumpet call (d) boastfulness

48. glaucous   (a) bluish-green (b) crimson (c) opalescent (d) mottled

49. gravamen — (a) serious disposition (b) sepulcher (c) essential part of an accusation (d) measurement of weight

50. hyperborean — (a) frigid (b) exaggerated (c) tedious (d) sensitive

51. hypothecate — (a) mortgage (b) conjecture (c) store away (d) reason

52. intaglio — (a) figure cut out in hard material (b) ancient coin (c) delicate tapestry (d) worthless imitation

53. irrefragable — (a) lost (b) unchangeable (c) unanswerable (d) unstable

54. lambent — (a) docile (b) clear (c) flickering (d) halting

55. mantic — (a) exuberant (b) prophetic (c) depressed (d) drugged

56. mastic — (a) kind of gum (b) disease of the ear (c) overlordship (d) extinct mammal

57. maunder — (a) talk foolishly (b) go astray (c) chew thoroughly (d) hesitate

58. moiety — (a) large portion (b) half (c) easy disposition (d) delicacy

59. murrain — (a) plague (b) swampy land (c) small mouse (d) walled city

60. neap — (a) ebb (b) back of neck (c) short hair (d) dance step

61. nubile — (a) dark-skinned (b) marriageable (c) lithe (d) lascivious

62. objurgation — (a) refusal (b) burden (c) rebuke (d) oath

63. obloquy — (a) conference (b) defamation (c) prejudice (d) forgetfulness

64. obsidian — (a) siege (b) fixed idea (c) glassy rock (d) obstruction

65. odalisque — (a) tiled floor (b) female slave (c) couch (d) style of painting

66. operose — (a) flowery (b) tuneful (c) laborious (d) surgical

67. oriflamme — (a) display of fireworks (b) battle standard (c) sparkling jewel (d) detonation

68. orison — (a) prayer (b) distant view (c) the east (d) early rising

69. palimpsest — (a) parchment with layers of writing (b) front of a Greek temple (c) fossil of prehistoric plant (d) words written backwards

70. palpate — (a) shock (b) quiver (c) examine by touch (d) conciliate

71. paradigm — (a) figure having equal sides (b) model (c) contradiction (d) pompous display

72. parturition — (a) division (b) childbirth (c) plunder (d) exodus

73. peculation — (a) trading in cattle (b) sinning (c) gambling (d) embezzlement

74. pelagic — (a) mountainous (b) oceanic (c) icy (d) prehistoric

75. pharisaical — (a) cruel (b) uncultured (c) self-righteous (d) prophetic

76. piebald — (a) mottled (b) tawny (c) with trimmed mane (d) chattering

77. plangent — (a) resounding deeply (b) affected with great joy (c) soft and mellow (d) precipitate

78. preciosity — (a) costliness (b) pedantic refinement (c) prodigy (d) advance knowledge

79. prevenience — (a) foresighted action (d) hindrance (c) origin (d) foregathering

80. prorogue — (a) act haughtily (b) end a session (c) summon (d) cross-examine

81. quotidian — (a) trite (b) occurring every day (c) apportioning (d) word for word

82. recreant — (a) life-giving (b) cowardly (c) repentant (d) faithful

83. redaction — (a) rehearsal (b) submission (c) editing (d) conquest

84. reprobate — (a) official in charge of wills (b) sinner (c) stickler for accuracy (d) deserter

85. sabulous — (a) sandy (b) furry (c) itching (d) splotched

86. scarify — (a) frighten (b) deform (c) make a scratch (d) flee

87. sciolism — (a) annotation (b) superficial knowledge (c) belief in supernatural (d) grammatical error

88. skittles — (a) trifles (b) ale (c) bowling game (d) pretzels

89. sleazy — (a) slippery (b) flimsy (c) asthmatic (d) disgusting

90. sternutation — (a) hardening (b) reversal (c) trepidation (d) sneezing

91. subliminal — (a) dejected (b) subconscious (c) highly colored (d) lofty in tone

92. supposititious — (a) undetermined (b) assumed (c) counterfeit (d) underrated

93. tergiversation — (a) dizziness (b) endless repetition (c) elusiveness (d) desertion of a cause

94. triturated — (a) three-pronged (b) pulverized (c) eliminated (d) fatigued

353

95. ululate (a) howl (b) plead with (c) sing nonsense syllables (d) mumble

96. vaticination (a) prophecy (b) brewing (c) neighborhood (d) inoculation

97. viable (a) temporary (b) easily transported (c) capable of living (d) rivaling

98. vitreous (a) malicious (b) sticky (c) lifelike (d) glassy

99. vulpine (a) crafty (b) wolfish (c) hoggish (d) ravenous

100. wattle (a) awkward creature (b) slow gait (c) form of fowl (d) featherless, fleshy flap

IX. Wow!

1. acronym (a) high peak (b) sharp point (c) word formed from initial letters (d) abusive name

2. adit (a) mine entrance (b) ledger balance (c) publicity release (d) calculating machine

3. adscititious (a) well-known (b) anonymous (c) pedantic (d) additional

4. aleatory (a) depending on chance (b) congratulatory (c) airtight (d) comforting

5. allolalia (a) dislike of food (b) close of a hymn (c) form of speech disorder (d) loud greeting

6. amaranthine (a) deathless (b) flowery (c) lovesick (d) pitch-covered

7. amerce (a) trade away (b) punish by fine (c) rinse (d) pound to bits

8. amphibology (a) double sense (b) ability to live on land and sea (c) perimeter (d) state of being double-jointed

9. anagogic (a) parallel (b) mystical (c) leading astray (d) relieving pain

10. analects (a) legal codes (b) word games (c) proverbs (d) miscellaneous passages

11. ancipital (a) doubtful (b) sudden (c) two-edged (d) tasteless

12. anfractuous (a) full of twists and turns (b) lacking polish (c) unmanageable (d) domineering

13. annular (a) ring-shaped (b) alimentary (c) arboreal (d) occurring yearly

14. ansate (a) gooselike (b) responsible (c) crooked (d) having a handle

15. anserine — (a) quick-tongued (b) knotted (c) surly (d) stupid

16. antinomy — (a) metallic element (b) rebellious spirit (c) opposition between principles (d) lack of reason

17. apocalyptic — pertaining to: (a) catastrophe (b) prophetic revelation (c) horsemanship (d) church architecture

18. apodictic — (a) judicial (b) inciting love (c) nomadic (d) clearly discernible

19. aposiopesis — (a) pacification (b) opposition (c) sentence left incomplete (d) foot ailment

20. appanage — (a) dependency (b) long plume (c) pain-killer (d) panoramic view

21. apteral — (a) eminently fitted (b) wingless (c) related to church altar (d) most likely

22. arcana — (a) record files (b) ethereal spirits (c) secrets (d) memoirs

23. asthenic — (a) weak (b) breathing heavily (c) cultured (d) baseless

24. asyndeton — (a) omission of conjunctions (b) poetic license (c) inclination to wrongdoing (d) flowery language

25. avatar — (a) ancestor (b) perfume (c) incarnation (d) magician

26. baleen — (a) bad skin (b) beautiful girl (c) evil look (d) whalebone

27. calescent — (a) growing warm (b) merging (c) beautifying (d) waning

28. camber — (a) curve upward (b) climb quickly (c) curdle milk (d) make an exchange

29. caudle — (a) birthmark (b) short tail (c) overfondness (d) warm drink for invalids

30. charismatic — (a) of many colors (b) rubbed with oil (c) possessing divine gift of prophecy (d) kind and gracious

31. chine — (a) cattle (b) succession of bell sounds (c) kiln (d) backbone

32. chitterling — (a) smattering (b) small child (c) part of small intestine (d) trifling expense

33. cockatrice — (a) fabulous serpent (b) deep wound (c) tropical bird (d) breed of dog

34. conation — (a) geometric problem (b) crowning of a ruler (c) treaty of alliance (d) striving

35. consortium — (a) financial combine (b) marriage (c) selection (d) fortune-telling

36. costive — (a) expensive (b) constipated (c) restless (d) forward

37. crapulous — (a) bloated (b) long-winded (c) depending on luck (d) ill from overdrinking

38. daedal — (a) lethal (b) two-faced (c) active (d) ingenious

39. deglutition — (a) separation (b) swallowing food (c) satiety (d) stickiness

40. delitescence — (a) growing old (b) inclination to argue (c) pretense of joy (d) hiding

41. demiurge — (a) half-baked wish (b) power creating a world (c) leader of the people (d) minor artisan

42. dimidiate — (a) slow (b) halved (c) very small (d) interfering

43. discalced — (a) ejected (b) whitewashed (c) without shoes (d) severed

44. dragoman — (a) cavalry officer (b) interpreter (c) oriental judge (d) mythological monster

45. ecdysis — (a) frenzy (b) partition (c) migration (d) molting

46. edacious — (a) devouring (b) bold (c) eatable (d) proud

47. embrocate — (a) embroider (b) entangle (c) rub with liniment (d) pour into a flask

48. epicene — (a) common to both sexes (b) luxurious (c) pertaining to the stage (d) resembling a narrative poem

49. esurient — (a) refractory (b) crafty (c) voracious (d) inaudible

50. etiolated — (a) fan-shaped (b) bleached (c) branching out (d) jubilant

51. etiology — (a) rules of poetic structure (b) theory of motion (c) study of temperature (d) inquiry into physical causes

52. farthingale — (a) small coin (b) framework for hoop skirt (c) horse's harness (d) small bird

53. feculent — (a) productive (b) foolish (c) covered with filth (d) falling apart

54. feracious — (a) predatory (b) fierce (c) overpowering (d) fertile

55. flagitious — (a) persistent (b) atrocious (c) jingoistic (d) emblematic

56. flocculent — (a) wooly (b) insipid (c) congregating (d) pretentious

57. friable — (a) cooked quickly (b) easily crumbled (c) of a genial nature (d) belonging to a religious order

58. fuliginous — (a) laudatory (b) gleaming (c) thundering (d) sooty

59. glabrous — (a) pertaining to the soil (b) resplendent (c) swordlike (d) smooth

60. googol — (a) sticky mass (b) figure 1 followed by 100 zeros (c) baby talk (d) theory of language origin

61. hebetude — (a) stupidity (b) beauty (c) sharpness (d) happiness

62. heuristic — (a) persuading pupil to find out by himself (b) related to investigation of holy works (c) pseudo-scientific (d) associated with rank of religious office

63. ictus — (a) small fish (b) cutting tool (c) stress (d) foot of verse

64. illative — (a) unrelated (b) inferential (c) demonstrative (d) overjoyed

65. imbricate — (a) overlap (b) accuse of conspiracy (c) become entangled in thorns (d) rain heavily

66. inspissated — (a) scattered (b) encouraged (c) sloping (d) thickened

67. intercalate — (a) measure a diet (b) warm up (c) keep records (d) insert a day in a calendar

68. laches — (a) contrivance to close a door (b) inexcusable delay (c) cowardice (d) skin disease

69. macaronic — (a) feeble-minded (b) jumbled (c) spicy (d) humorous

70. martingale — (a) forked strap (b) warbler (c) atmospheric disturbance (d) period costume

71. misprision — (a) illegal arrest (b) contempt (c) egregious error (d) official misconduct

72. nepenthe — (a) forgiveness (b) poverty (c) opiate (d) geometric curve

73. nimiety — (a) imitation (b) excess (c) undervaluation (d) good manners

74. nuncupative — (a) unsophisticated (b) not written (c) lacking desire (d) secluded

75. pandet — (a) ancient ruler (b) serious operation (c) complete digest (d) universal cure

76. paraclete — (a) advocate (b) sycophant (c) selfish person (d) eminent author

77. patchouli — (a) fish stew (b) mint perfume (c) parlor game (d) minced-meat cake

78. pejorative — (a) causing evil (b) ameliorative (c) depreciatory (d) magical

79. prolegomena — (a) mannered style of writing (b) hereditary estate (c) compilation of laws (d) preliminary remarks

80. provenance — (a) source (b) government (c) foresight (d) accommodation

81. quietist — (a) comforter (b) conservative (c) soft-spoken person (d) advocate of passive attitude

82. recidivism — (a) confirmed criminality (b) suicide (c) ancestor worship (d) revival

83. recusant — (a) dilatory (b) dissenting in religion (c) extremely shy (d) hard-hearted

84. rimose — (a) full of cracks (b) possessing poetic quality (c) covered with ice (d) having a circular surface

85. rugose — (a) shy (b) reddish (c) wrinkled (d) coldish

86. scabrous — (a) rough (b) inflamed (c) disease-ridden (d) totally bald

87. scatological — relating to: (a) study of obscene literature (b) distant planets (c) secret poisons (d) life after death

88. scutate — (a) chivalrous (b) evanescent (c) indistinguishable (d) shield-shaped

89. suppurate — (a) breathe with difficulty (b) crush (c) form pus (d) condemn

90. susurrate — (a) whisper (b) become infected (c) revive (d) affirm

91. swale — (a) bandage (b) marshy prairie (c) wide path (d) roll of a ship

92. sillabub — (a) sweet dish (b) course of study (c) type of argument (d) word formation

93. teleology — (a) doctrine of purpose in nature (b) study of sound (c) investigation of primitive life (d) belief in chance as the determiner of human affairs

94. tendentious — (a) obstinate (b) inclined to quarrel (c) strongly biased (d) solicitous

95. traduce — (a) slander (b) prosecute (c) cheat (d) betray

96. usufruct — (a) gradual wasting away (b) exorbitant interest (c) enjoyment of property belonging to another (d) scientific farm management

97. velleity — (a) elegance (b) specimen of parchment (c) drapery (d) slight wish

98. verbigerate — (a) cause a repeated echo (b) repeat senselessly (c) become evasive (d) revolve ceaselessly

99. verecund — a) springlike (b) bashful (c) truthful (d) awe-inspiring

100. vesicant — (a) causing burns (b) glossy (c) poisonous (d) relating to a mathematical term

Answers

$$\begin{array}{r} +\;2 \\ \underline{2} \\ 4 \end{array}$$

"Well, I did it . . . but don't ask me how." *

Answers

Chapter 1

(Pages 20-22)

1 : 5	5 : 2	9 : 5	13 : 2	17 : 3	21 : 3
2 : 3	6 : 1	10 : 1	14 : 2	18 : 2	22 : 5
3 : 4	7 : 1	11 : 4	15 : 4	19 : 5	23 : 4
4 : 1	8 : 5	12 : 5	16 : 5	20 : 4	24 : 5

25 : 4	31 : 4	37 : 5	43 : 3	49 : 3	55 : 4
26 : 4	32 : 2	38 : 1	44 : 4	50 : 3	56 : 4
27 : 5	33 : 1	39 : 1	45 : 4	51 : 2	
28 : 3	34 : 3	40 : 5	46 : 2	52 : 4	
29 : 1	35 : 1	41 : 2	47 : 3	53 : 1	
30 : 5	36 : 4	42 : 4	48 : 5	54 : 5	

Chapter 2

(Pages 23-29)

1. (a)	5. (c)	9. (b)	13. (d)	17. (d)
2. (b)	6. (c)	10. (a)	14. (b)	18. (c)
3. (d)	7. (a)	11. (c)	15. (b)	19. (d)
4. (a)	8. (d)	12. (c)	16. (b)	20. (a)

Answers to words in phrases

(Pages 35-39)

1. (b)	16. (c)	31. (c)	46. (b)	61. (c)
2. (c)	17. (c)	32. (c)	47. (a)	62. (d)
3. (b)	18. (b)	33. (b)	48. (a)	63. (b)
4. (c)	19. (c)	34. (c)	49. (b)	64. (c)
5. (c)	20. (b)	35. (d)	50. (a)	65. (d)
6. (b)	21. (d)	36. (a)	51. (c)	66. (b)
7. (a)	22. (d)	37. (d)	52. (c)	67. (b)
8. (b)	23. (c)	38. (a)	53. (d)	68. (c)
9. (d)	24. (a)	39. (c)	54. (c)	69. (d)
10. (a)	25. (a)	40. (b)	55. (a)	70. (a)
11. (b)	26. (d)	41. (a)	56. (c)	71. (b)
12. (a)	27. (b)	42. (d)	57. (b)	72. (b)
13. (c)	28. (c)	43. (a)	58. (b)	73. (d)
14. (a)	29. (b)	44. (b)	59. (b)	74. (b)
15. (d)	30. (b)	45. (b)	60. (c)	75. (a)

Chapter 3

(Page 46)

1. f	3. l	5. g	7. j	9. a
2. e	4. b	6. c	8. i	10. k

Chapter 4

(Pages 56-58)

I. 1. know
   2. foreknowledge; foretelling
   3. diagnosis
   4. gnomon
   5. gnomes
   6. gnomic

II. 1. homonyms
   2. antonyms
   3. anonymous
   4. patronymics
   5. synonyms
   6. paronomasia
   7. onomatopoeia
   8. pseudonym

III. 1,e 2,d 3,b 4,c 5,a 6,h 7,j 8,k 9,i 10,g

IV. A. 1. genesis 2. progeny 3. indigenous 4. engendered
   B. 1.d 2.e 3.a 4.b 5.c 6.f
V. A. 1.e 2.d 3.f 4.b 5.c 6.a
   B. 1. contemporary 2. temporize 3. tempo 4. extemporaneous
      5. temporal 6. temporary

Chapter 5

(Pages 66-68)

I.

1. (d)	7. (d)	13. (b)	19. (c)	25. (c)
2. (b)	8. (a)	14. (a)	20. (b)	26. (a)
3. (c)	9. (b)	15. (a)	21. (c)	27. (d)
4. (a)	10. (d)	16. (c)	22. (c)	28. (c)
5. (b)	11. (c)	17. (b)	23. (b)	29. (b)
6. (c)	12. (b)	18. (b)	24. (c)	30. (c)

II.

1. (d)	2. (b)	3. (c)	4. (c)	5. (b)

III.

1. (b)	4. (a)	7. (a)	10. (a)
2. (a)	5. (b)	8. (b)	11. (b)
3. (b)	6. (b)	9. (b)	12. (a)

Chapter 6

(Pages 74-76)

1. (b)	11. (c)	21. (c)	31. (a)	41. (d)
2. (b)	12. (d)	22. (d)	32. (c)	42. (d)
3. (c)	13. (a)	23. (d)	33. (a)	43. (c)
4. (a)	14. (d)	24. (b)	34. (b)	44. (b)
5. (d)	15. (b)	25. (a)	35. (d)	45. (c)
6. (c)	16. (b)	26. (c)	36. (b)	46. (d)
7. (b)	17. (c)	27. (c)	37. (a)	47. (c)
8. (c)	18. (d)	28. (a)	38. (c)	48. (a)
9. (a)	19. (a)	29. (a)	39. (b)	49. (a)
10. (b)	20. (b)	30. (b)	40. (d)	50. (d)

Chapter 7

(Pages 86-88)

I. Negative words: 1, 2, 5, 8, 9, 10, 12, 14, 15, 17, 19, 20

II.

1. malignant	6. hypothyroid
2. euphony	7. extrovert
3. diffident	8. benefactor
4. inhibit	9. postnatal
5. heterogeneous	10. protract

III.

1. suppress	6. correlate
2. allocate	7. assign
3. occult	8. accredit
4. impalpable	9. pellucid
5. irrational	10. diffusion

IV.
1. away; wandering away, deviation
2. to; addition to, growth
3. not; formless
4. before; happening before
5. around; come around, outwit
6. from; frighten off discourage
7. apart; distend, swell, enlarge, expand
8. from; running from the subject, rambling
9. faulty; lack of nourishment
10. not; stainless
11. not; not able to be appeased, merciless
12. not; powerless, weak
13. between; come between, interfere
14. within; within the walls
15. in way of; shut off
16. through; penetrate
17. many; many-colored
18. backward; go back, decline
19. apart, away; rebellion
20. together; putting together, combining into a unit

V. line 1: in, in; line 3: dis, un, un, im, in;
line 4: in, per (or re); line 5: in, dis;
line 6: in; line 7: non, un; line 8: in, as, in, a

Chapter 8

(Pages 97-98)

I. A. THREE B. THREE or FOUR. C. SEVEN. TWO. D. (c)
E. 1776. F. FIVE.

II. A. nonagenarian B. quadricentennial C. unanimously; unanimity
D. protozoa

III.

1. (d)	3. (d)	5. (c)	7. (a)	9. (b)
2. (b)	4. (c)	6. (c)	8. (a)	10. (d)

IV.

1. c	3. k	5. f	7. h	9. d	14. b
2. l	4. a	6. i	8. e	10. j	40. g

Chapter 9

(Pages 104-106)

I.

1. l	3. k	5. f	7. a	9. h
2. i	4. b	6. d	8. e	10. g

II. A.

1. f	3. g	5. e	7. c	9. h
2. d	4. b	6. a	8. i	10. j

B.

1. j	3. i	5. f	7. e	9. d
2. h	4. c	6. g	8. b	10. a

III.

1. e	3. g	5. a	7. d	9. j
2. h	4. f	6. b	8. c	10. i

IV.

1. d	3. a	5. i	7. h	9. f
2. e	4. j	6. g	8. b	10. c

Chapter 10
(Page 118)

I.

1. (c)	3. (c)	5. (d)	7. (e)	9. (d)
2. (a)	4. (e)	6. (b)	8. (a)	10. (b)

II.

1. (f)	3. (e)	5. (h)	7. (k)	9. (c)
2. (g)	4. (a)	6. (b)	8. (l)	10. (d)

Chapter 11
(Pages 126-130)

I. Review of preliminary test in Chapter 1. Answers on page 361.

II.

1. (b)	21. (c)	41. (a)	61. (d)	81. (b)
2. (a)	22. (c)	42. (a)	62. (d)	82. (a)
3. (b)	23. (a)	43. (c)	63. (b)	83. (b)
4. (b)	24. (d)	44. (c)	64. (c)	84. (d)
5. (c)	25. (a)	45. (d)	65. (a)	85. (d)
6. (a)	26. (c)	46. (a)	66. (d)	86. (b)
7. (b)	27. (b)	47. (b)	67. (d)	87. (b)
8. (d)	28. (c)	48. (d)	68. (a)	88. (b)
9. (d)	29. (b)	49. (c)	69. (b)	89. (c)
10. (d)	30. (b)	50. (c)	70. (c)	90. (d)
11. (d)	31. (d)	51. (a)	71. (c)	91. (b)
12. (a)	32. (d)	52. (a)	72. (d)	92. (c)
13. (b)	33. (a)	53. (a)	73. (c)	93. (b)
14. (c)	34. (b)	54. (a)	74. (a)	94. (b)
15. (a)	35. (d)	55. (d)	75. (a)	95. (c)
16. (c)	36. (a)	56. (c)	76. (b)	96. (b)
17. (d)	37. (b)	57. (b)	77. (d)	97. (a)
18. (c)	38. (a)	58. (d)	78. (c)	98. (b)
19. (b)	39. (c)	59. (b)	79. (a)	99. (c)
20. (c)	40. (c)	60. (c)	80. (a)	100. (d)

Chapter 13
(Pages 154-156)

I.

1. b	3. b	5. a	7. b	9. b
2. a	4. a	6. b	8. a	10. b

II.

1. inter-species	11. unexceptionable
2. imply	12. flaunt
3. enthusiastic	13. fortunate
4. venal	14. exotic
5. militated	15. uninterested
6. depreciated	16. participation
7. besides	17. discomfort
8. complementary	18. precipitate
9. enormousness	19. flout
10. unequivocally	20. laid

Chapter 14
(Pages 166-170)

1. (b)	12. (a)	23. (b)	34. (a)	45. (b)
2. (a)	13. (a)	24. (a)	35. (b)	46. (a)
3. (a)	14. (a)	25. (b)	36. (a)	47. (a)
4. (a)	15. (b)	26. (b)	37. (a)	48. (b)
5. (b)	16. (a)	27. (a)	38. (a)	49. (b)
6. (a)	17. (a)	28. (b)	39. (b)	50. (b)
7. (a)	18. (a)	29. (a)	40. (b)	51. (a)
8. (a)	19. (b)	30. (a)	41. (b)	52. (c)
9. (b)	20. (b)	31. (b)	42. (c)	53. (b)
10. (c)	21. (a)	32. (a)	43. (a)	54. (b)
11. (b)	22. (a)	33. (b)	44. (b)	55. (a)

Chapter 15
(Pages 179-180)

A

1. e	5. i	9. o	13. a	17. i
2. a	6. a	10. a	14. o	18. o
3. o	7. a	11. i	15. a	19. e
4. a	8. a	12. i	16. o	20. a

B

1. chiseling	16. deferring
2. counseling	17. differing
3. extolling	18. occurrence
4. marvelous	19. occurring
5. modeling	20. offering
6. paralleling	21. proffered
7. patrolling	22. referee
8. shriveled	23. referral
9. unequaled	24. acquittal
10. unpatrolled	25. acquitting
11. beckoning	26. allotment
12. balooning	27. allotting
13. happening	28. ballotting
14. pardoning	29. benefiting
15. trepanning	30. profitable

Chapter 16
(Pages 186-191)

I.

1. (c)	5. (c)	9. (b)	13. (a)	17. (c)
2. (b)	6. (d)	10. (a)	14. (d)	18. (b)
3. (a)	7. (b)	11. (c)	15. (b)	19. (d)
4. (b)	8. (c)	12. (b)	16. (b)	20. (b)

II.

1. (a)	6. (b)	11. (b)	16. (c)	21. (c)
2. (b)	7. (c)	12. (d)	17. (a)	22. (b)
3. (d)	8. (c)	13. (c)	18. (d)	23. (d)
4. (a)	9. (d)	14. (b)	19. (c)	24. (b)
5. (b)	10. (a)	15. (a)	20. (d)	25. (b)

III.

1. i	4. k	7. a	10. i
2. g	5. h	8. d	11. j
3. b	6. c	9. f	12. e

Chapter 17
(Pages 206-207)

I.

1. h	3. f	5. g	7. i	9. a
2. d	4. b	6. j	8. e	10. c

II.

1. (d)	3. (c)	5. (b)	7. (d)	9. (a)
2. (a)	4. (d)	6. (a)	8. (b)	10. (c)

Chapter 18
(Page 215)

1. incensed	7. volatile
2. pretext	8. effrontery
3. recant	9. divulge
4. impose	10. punctual
5. exaggerate	11. perplexed
6. comprehend	12. circumvent

ANSWERS

Chapter 19
(Pages 226-227)

I.

1. f	3. e	5. g	7. 1	9. b
2. d	4. c	6. o	8. a	10. h

II.

1. e	3. g	5. h	7. a	9. c
2. j	4. d	6. i	8. b	10. f

Chapter 20
(Pages 244-246)

I.

1. extricate
2. obliterate
3. allusions
4. prodigy
5. ineligible
6. influence
7. alligator
8. informatory
9. (a) comprehend or apprehend
   (b) vernacular
   (c) arrangement
   (d) epigrams
10. (a) superficial
   (b) geography
   (c) contiguous
   (d) orthography

II.

1. d	2. c	3. a	4. b	5. e

III.

1. e	2. c	3. d	4. b	5. a

Chapter 21
(Pages 264-268)

I.

1. (c)	2. (b)	3. (a)	4. (b)	5. (a)

II.

1. (f)	3. (g)	5. (j)	7. (i)	9. (d)
2. (e)	4. (a)	6. (h)	8. (b)	10. (c)

III.

1. (c)	2. (b)	3. (c)	4. (a)	5. (b)

IV. A.

1. e	3. f	5. i	7. b	9. a
2. j	4. h	6. c	8. d	10. g

IV. B.

1. g	3. h	5. c	7. d	9. j
2. e	4. i	6. b	8. a	10. f

V. A.

1. f	3. k	5. h	7. j	9. a
2. i	4. c	6. e	8. g	10. d

V. B.

1. f	3. i	5. h	7. c	9. g
2. e	4. a	6. j	8. d	10. b

Chapter 22
(Pages 289-290)

I.

1. (a)	3. (b)	5. (d)	7. (d)	9. (c)
2. (c)	4. (d)	6. (a)	8. (c)	10. (d)

II.

1. f	3. e	5. i	7. c	9. b
2. h	4. j	6. a	8. d	10. g

III.

1. f	3. a	5. b	7. d	9. c
2. h	4. g	6. j	8. 1	10. e

IV.

1. f	3. j	5. i	7. a	9. e
2. d	4. h	6. b	8. c	10. g

Chapter 23
(Pages 294-319)

I.   1. i   3. k   5. o   7. d   9. c
     2. m   4. f   6. j   8. e   10. a

II. 1. B   3. E   5. C   7. D   9. B
     2. C   4. A   6. B   8. E   10. D

III. 1. (c) and (d)   6. (b) and (c)
     2. (b) and (d)   7. (a) and (d)
     3. (c) and (d)   8. (b) and (d)
     4. (b) and (d)   9. (a) and (c)
     5. (a) and (c)   10. (a) and (b)

IV. 1. (b) and (d)   6. (c) and (e)
     2. (a) and (e)   7. (a) and (d)
     3. (b) and (e)   8. (b) and (d)
     4. (c) and (d)   9. (a) and (d)
     5. (a) and (e)   10. (b) and (d)

V.   1. (b)   2. (c)   5. (d)   7. (a)   9. (b)
     2. (a)   4. (c)   6. (a)   8. (d)   10. (a)

VI. 1. (d)   3. (a)   5. (c)   7. (c)   9. (d)
     2. (c)   4. (b)   6. (d)   8. (b)   10. (c)

VII. 1. (c)   3. (a)   6. (d)   9. (a)   12. (e)
     2. (a)   4. (b)   7. (b)   10. (c)   13. (b)
     3. (b)   5. (a)   8. (c)   11. (d)   14. (e)
                                                     15. (b)

VIII. A. 1. (a)   3. (c)   5. (c)   7. (b)   9. (d)
         2. (d)   4. (a)   6. (e)   8. (c)   10. (c)

VIII. B. 1. (c)   5. (a)   9. (e)   13. (a)   17. (a)
         2. (d)   6. (b)   10. (b)   14. (d)   18. (d)
         3. (b)   7. (d)   11. (d)   15. (b)   19. (b)
         4. (e)   8. (d)   12. (c)   16. (b)   20. (c)

IX. A. 1. (b)   7. (d)   13. (d)   19. (e)   25. (a)
       2. (c)   8. (b)   14. (d)   20. (c)   26. (d)
       3. (a)   9. (b)   15. (b)   21. (a)   27. (c)
       4. (e)   10. (e)   16. (c)   22. (b)   28. (b)
       5. (a)   11. (a)   17. (e)   23. (c)   29. (e)
       6. (b)   12. (d)   18. (b)   24. (e)   30. (b)

IX. B. 1. (c)   4. (a)   7. (e)   10. (c)   13. (e)
       2. (a)   5. (c)   8. (e)   11. (b)   14. (a)
       3. (b)   6. (b)   9. (d)   12. (d)   15. (e)

X.   1. (j)   3. (f)   5. (c)   7. (a)   9. (l)
     2. (b)   4. (g)   6. (e)   8. (d)   10. (e)

ANSWERS

XI.

1. admonitory
2. apostolic
3. arboreal
4. Aristotelian
5. auctorial
6. axial
7. Cantabrigian
8. comatose
9. coniferous
10. contextual
11. deltoid
12. derisive
13. Cartesian
14. dubious
15. encomiastic
16. inimical
17. enigmatic
18. epistolary
19. equinoctial
20. eulogistic
21. exemplary
22. exegetical
23. forensic
24. fragmentary
25. geodetic
26. gubernatorial
27. homiletic
28. Jovian
29. labyrinthine
30. libidinous
31. leonine
32. litigious
33. minatory
34. monetary
35. nitrogenous
36. oracular
37. orgiastic
38. Oxonian
39. periphrastic
40. recessive
41. revelatory
42. sectarian
43. septic
44. Shavian
45. solstitial
46. therapeutic
47. Thomist
48. titular
49. usurious
50. viceregal

XII.

1. adsolution
2. absorption
3. anonymity
4. banality
5. compulsion
6. constraint
7. contention
8. contingency
9. decrepitude
10. deification
11. disbursement
12. discernment
13. liquefaction
14. manumission
15. osmosis
16. periodicity
17. prodigality
18. pungency
19. pusillanimity
20. rickets
21. rarefaction
22. rescission
23. resentment
24. retrogression
25. scansion
26. scurvy
27. senility
28. spatula
29. temerity
30. virulence

XIII.

1. S amanuenses
2. S attorneys general
   attorney generals
3. P automaton
4. S axes
5. P bacillus
6. P candelabrum
7. S chateaux
8. S courts-martial
9. S crises
10. P criterion
11. P datum
12. S errata
13. P fungus
14. S genera
15. S handfuls
16. S larvae
17. S phenomena
18. S or P species
19. P stigma
20. S theses

XIV.

1. M abbess
2. F sire
3. F buck
4. M duck
5. M countess
6. M equestrienne
7. F executrix
8. F colt
9. F gander
10. M hind, doe
11. F bull
12. F marquis
13. M peahen
14. M ewe
15. F boar
16. M testatrix
17. F tragedienne
18. M traitress
19. F fox
20. F wizard

XV.

1. (b)
2. (d)
3. (b)
4. (e)
5. (d)
6. (e)
7. (d)
8. (d)
9. (a)
10. (e)
11. (e)
12. (a)
13. (a)
14. (b)
15. (c)
16. (e)
17. (e)
18. (b)
19. (a)
20. (c)

XVI.

1. (d)
2. (a)
3. (a)
4. (b)
5. (c)
6. (b)
7. (b)
8. (c)
9. (d)
10. (a)
11. (d)
12. (b)
13. (c)
14. (d)
15. (d)
16. (d)
17. (c)
18. (a)
19. (c)
20. (a)

369

Chapter 24

(Pages 322-358)

I.

1. (b)	21. (d)	41. (c)	61. (b)	81. (b)
2. (c)	22. (d)	42. (a)	62. (b)	82. (a)
3. (b)	23. (b)	43. (d)	63. (d)	83. (d)
4. (b)	24. (c)	44. (d)	64. (d)	84. (c)
5. (a)	25. (c)	45. (b)	65. (b)	85. (c)
6. (a)	26. (d)	46. (b)	66. (c)	86. (b)
7. (b)	27. (c)	47. (d)	67. (d)	87. (c)
8. (a)	28. (a)	48. (a)	68. (a)	88. (c)
9. (c)	29. (d)	49. (c)	69. (b)	89. (b)
10. (a)	30. (c)	50. (d)	70. (c)	90. (d)
11. (b)	31. (c)	51. (d)	71. (a)	91. (c)
12. (c)	32. (b)	52. (b)	72. (c)	92. (c)
13. (b)	33. (d)	53. (d)	73. (b)	93. (d)
14. (d)	34. (c)	54. (d)	74. (d)	94. (b)
15. (d)	35. (a)	55. (a)	75. (d)	95. (a)
16. (b)	36. (d)	56. (b)	76. (a)	96. (d)
17. (a)	37. (a)	57. (a)	77. (a)	97. (d)
18. (d)	38. (a)	58. (c)	78. (d)	98. (a)
19. (c)	39. (d)	59. (b)	79. (b)	99. (c)
20. (a)	40. (b)	60. (a)	80. (c)	100. (d)

II.

1. (c)	11. (d)	21. (c)	31. (d)	41. (c)
2. (d)	12. (a)	22. (b)	32. (a)	42. (b)
3. (a)	13. (c)	23. (a)	33. (b)	43. (b)
4. (b)	14. (d)	24. (b)	34. (a)	44. (d)
5. (a)	15. (a)	25. (b)	35. (a)	45. (d)
6. (c)	16. (b)	26. (c)	36. (d)	46. (b)
7. (d)	17. (a)	27. (c)	37. (d)	47. (d)
8. (b)	18. (c)	28. (c)	38. (a)	48. (c)
9. (a)	19. (a)	29. (d)	39. (c)	49. (b)
10. (b)	20. (d)	30. (b)	40. (b)	50. (d)

III.

1. (b)	21. (a)	41. (c)	61. (b)	81. (c)
2. (a)	22. (c)	42. (a)	62. (d)	82. (d)
3. (c)	23. (b)	43. (a)	63. (c)	83. (a)
4. (a)	24. (a)	44. (b)	64. (b)	84. (c)
5. (c)	25. (a)	45. (d)	65. (a)	85. (b)
6. (a)	26. (b)	46. (d)	66. (b)	86. (a)
7. (d)	27. (c)	47. (a)	67. (b)	87. (b)
8. (a)	28. (b)	48. (d)	68. (c)	88. (c)
9. (b)	29. (d)	49. (c)	69. (b)	89. (b)
10. (a)	30. (a)	50. (c)	70. (a)	90. (b)
11. (a)	31. (a)	51. (b)	71. (b)	91. (b)
12. (b)	32. (b)	52. (a)	72. (b)	92. (c)
13. (b)	33. (a)	53. (c)	73. (c)	93. (a)
14. (c)	34. (b)	54. (c)	74. (a)	94. (d)
15. (b)	35. (a)	55. (c)	75. (b)	95. (d)
16. (d)	36. (d)	56. (a)	76. (a)	96. (b)
17. (a)	37. (a)	57. (d)	77. (a)	97. (c)
18. (b)	38. (c)	58. (c)	78. (b)	98. (b)
19. (d)	39. (b)	59. (b)	79. (b)	99. (b)
20. (b)	40. (a)	60. (b)	80. (a)	100. (a)

ANSWERS

IV.

1. (c)	21. (c)	41. (c)	61. (a)	81. (a)
2. (b)	22. (d)	42. (a)	62. (d)	82. (b)
3. (c)	23. (a)	43. (b)	63. (b)	83. (b)
4. (b)	24. (d)	44. (d)	64. (b)	84. (a)
5. (a)	25. (a)	45. (a)	65. (d)	85. (b)
6. (c)	26. (b)	46. (a)	66. (c)	86. (b)
7. (c)	27. (c)	47. (b)	67. (c)	87. (b)
8. (b)	28. (c)	48. (c)	68. (b)	88. (d)
9. (c)	29. (b)	49. (b)	69. (a)	89. (a)
10. (d)	30. (c)	50. (a)	70. (a)	90. (b)
11. (c)	31. (a)	51. (b)	71. (d)	91. (a)
12. (c)	32. (d)	52. (d)	72. (b)	92. (b)
13. (b)	33. (c)	53. (b)	73. (a)	93. (d)
14. (a)	34. (a)	54. (d)	74. (c)	94. (a)
15. (c)	35. (a)	55. (c)	75. (a)	95. (c)
16. (c)	36. (a)	56. (a)	76. (b)	96. (c)
17. (a)	37. (c)	57. (d)	77. (c)	97. (b)
18. (a)	38. (c)	58. (c)	78. (c)	98. (d)
19. (d)	39. (d)	59. (c)	79. (a)	99. (b)
20. (b)	40. (b)	60. (b)	80. (d)	100. (d)

V.

1. (b)	21. (c)	41. (a)	61. (b)	81. (d)
2. (b)	22. (a)	42. (c)	62. (c)	82. (c)
3. (b)	23. (a)	43. (b)	63. (d)	83. (b)
4. (c)	24. (b)	44. (d)	64. (a)	84. (d)
5. (d)	25. (c)	45. (a)	65. (c)	85. (b)
6. (c)	26. (d)	46. (c)	66. (c)	86. (c)
7. (b)	27. (c)	47. (a)	67. (b)	87. (a)
8. (c)	28. (d)	48. (b)	68. (c)	88. (b)
9. (d)	29. (b)	49. (a)	69. (c)	89. (c)
10. (b)	30. (b)	50. (d)	70. (c)	90. (b)
11. (d)	31. (a)	51. (c)	71. (b)	91. (b)
12. (b)	32. (d)	52. (c)	72. (c)	92. (b)
13. (c)	33. (b)	53. (a)	73. (c)	93. (d)
14. (d)	34. (b)	54. (b)	74. (a)	94. (b)
15. (a)	35. (d)	55. (b)	75. (c)	95. (c)
16. (d)	36. (b)	56. (b)	76. (b)	96. (b)
17. (c)	37. (c)	57. (c)	77. (a)	97. (b)
18. (c)	38. (c)	58. (c)	78. (c)	98. (a)
19. (c)	39. (c)	59. (d)	79. (b)	99. (b)
20. (a)	40. (d)	60. (b)	80. (d)	100. (d)

VI.

1. (d)	21. (b)	41. (b)	61. (a)	81. (b)
2. (b)	22. (a)	42. (c)	62. (a)	82. (b)
3. (d)	23. (a)	43. (c)	63. (c)	83. (a)
4. (a)	24. (b)	44. (c)	64. (b)	84. (b)
5. (c)	25. (b)	45. (c)	65. (c)	85. (c)
6. (b)	26. (d)	46. (b)	66. (d)	86. (b)
7. (a)	27. (c)	47. (b)	67. (c)	87. (b)
8. (a)	28. (c)	48. (b)	68. (a)	88. (c)
9. (d)	29. (a)	49. (b)	69. (d)	89. (a)
10. (c)	30. (a)	50. (b)	70. (b)	90. (c)
11. (d)	31. (b)	51. (a)	71. (a)	91. (b)
12. (c)	32. (a)	52. (b)	72. (d)	92. (c)
13. (b)	33. (c)	53. (b)	73. (b)	93. (d)
14. (b)	34. (d)	54. (c)	74. (a)	94. (b)
15. (b)	35. (a)	55. (b)	75. (b)	95. (b)
16. (c)	36. (a)	56. (c)	76. (c)	96. (a)
17. (a)	37. (b)	57. (c)	77. (a)	97. (a)
18. (d)	38. (a)	58. (b)	78. (b)	98. (b)
19. (c)	39. (b)	59. (a)	79. (b)	99. (c)
20. (a)	40. (a)	60. (d)	80. (c)	100. (d)

VII.

1. (b)	21. (c)	41. (b)	61. (c)	81. (d)
2. (a)	22. (c)	42. (c)	62. (d)	82. (c)
3. (b)	23. (c)	43. (b)	63. (c)	83. (b)
4. (b)	24. (d)	44. (a)	64. (b)	84. (b)
5. (b)	25. (d)	45. (b)	65. (a)	85. (a)
6. (d)	26. (d)	46. (b)	66. (d)	86. (a)
7. (a)	27. (a)	47. (c)	67. (a)	87. (d)
8. (d)	28. (b)	48. (b)	68. (c)	88. (c)
9. (a)	29. (c)	49. (a)	69. (d)	89. (a)
10. (c)	30. (d)	50. (b)	70. (a)	90. (b)
11. (a)	31. (c)	51. (a)	71. (c)	91. (b)
12. (a)	32. (b)	52. (b)	72. (d)	92. (c)
13. (a)	33. (b)	53. (b)	73. (a)	93. (a)
14. (b)	34. (a)	54. (c)	74. (b)	94. (c)
15. (c)	35. (a)	55. (a)	75. (c)	95. (c)
16. (d)	36. (b)	56. (c)	76. (b)	96. (a)
17. (a)	37. (c)	57. (d)	77. (c)	97. (a)
18. (a)	38. (c)	58. (c)	78. (b)	98. (d)
19. (d)	39. (a)	59. (b)	79. (d)	99. (d)
20. (d)	40. (a)	60. (d)	80. (b)	100. (d)

VIII.

1. (a)	21. (d)	41. (b)	61. (b)	81. (b)
2. (b)	22. (a)	42. (a)	62. (c)	82. (b)
3. (a)	23. (d)	43. (a)	63. (b)	83. (c)
4. (c)	24. (c)	44. (d)	64. (c)	84. (b)
5. (a)	25. (c)	45. (b)	65. (b)	85. (a)
6. (a)	26. (d)	46. (c)	66. (c)	86. (c)
7. (d)	27. (b)	47. (d)	67. (b)	87. (b)
8. (b)	28. (b)	48. (a)	68. (a)	88. (c)
9. (a)	29. (b)	49. (c)	69. (a)	89. (b)
10. (b)	30. (c)	50. (a)	70. (c)	90. (d)
11. (b)	31. (a)	51. (a)	71. (b)	91. (b)
12. (c)	32. (c)	52. (a)	72. (b)	92. (c)
13. (a)	33. (a)	53. (c)	73. (d)	93. (d)
14. (c)	34. (b)	54. (c)	74. (b)	94. (b)
15. (a)	35. (c)	55. (b)	75. (c)	95. (a)
16. (d)	36. (d)	56. (a)	76. (a)	96. (a)
17. (c)	37. (b)	57. (a)	77. (b)	97. (c)
18. (a)	38. (b)	58. (b)	78. (b)	98. (d)
19. (a)	39. (c)	59. (a)	79. (a)	99. (a)
20. (d)	40. (b)	60. (a)	80. (b)	100. (d)

IX.

1. (c)	21. (b)	41. (b)	61. (a)	81. (d)
2. (a)	22. (c)	42. (b)	62. (a)	82. (a)
3. (d)	23. (a)	43. (c)	63. (c)	83. (b)
4. (a)	24. (a)	44. (b)	64. (b)	84. (a)
5. (c)	25. (c)	45. (d)	65. (a)	85. (c)
6. (a)	26. (d)	46. (a)	66. (d)	86. (a)
7. (b)	27. (a)	47. (c)	67. (d)	87. (a)
8. (a)	28. (a)	48. (a)	68. (b)	88. (d)
9. (b)	29. (d)	49. (c)	69. (b)	89. (c)
10. (d)	30. (c)	50. (b)	70. (a)	90. (a)
11. (c)	31. (d)	51. (d)	71. (d)	91. (b)
12. (a)	32. (c)	52. (b)	72. (c)	92. (a)
13. (a)	33. (a)	53. (c)	73. (b)	93. (a)
14. (d)	34. (d)	54. (d)	74. (b)	94. (c)
15. (d)	35. (a)	55. (b)	75. (c)	95. (a)
16. (c)	36. (b)	56. (a)	76. (a)	96. (c)
17. (b)	37. (d)	57. (b)	77. (b)	97. (d)
18. (a)	38. (d)	58. (d)	78. (c)	98. (b)
19. (c)	39. (b)	59. (d)	79. (d)	99. (b)
20. (a)	40. (d)	60. (b)	80. (a)	100. (a)

Index

Only words that receive more than passing mention in the text are listed here. Words used in exercises and tests can be found (generally in alphabetical order) at ends of chapters and in the body of chapters 24 and 25. Lists of foreign words and phrases used in English appear in chapters 21 and 22.

Special subjects are listed in small capitals in this index.

THE AUTHORS

Maxwell Nurnberg, like his co-author, an expert in the science of words and names, has written many books and articles on the subject, including a series regularly featured in *Good Housekeeping,* as well as a radio series called WHAT'S THE GOOD WORD? Now an assistant professor at New York University, Division of General Education, Mr. Nurnberg is also Chairman of the Department of English at Abraham Lincoln High School, Brooklyn, N. Y. Among his many other books are SENTENCE SENSE, WHAT'S THE GOOD WORD? (on which the radio series was based), and A NEW WAY TO BETTER ENGLISH.

Dr. Morris Rosenblum has contributed articles on literature, the classics, and the study of words to many popular periodicals and scholarly magazines. Among other works, he edited STORIES FROM MANY LANDS and authored an award-winning study and translation of the Latin poet Luxorius. Dr. Rosenblum is a lecturer in classics, comparative literature, and education at Brooklyn College and Queens College, New York.